FREEDOM TO PRACTISE
VOLUME II

DEVELOPING PERSON-CENTRED

APPROACHES TO SUPERVISION

Dedication

We dedicate this book to Pete Sanders and Maggie Taylor-Sanders. Their continuing work in the fields of person-centred and critical psychology creates and maintains an intellectual space which supports the freedom to think and to practise.

FREEDOM TO PRACTISE
VOLUME II

DEVELOPING PERSON-CENTRED

APPROACHES TO SUPERVISION

EDITED BY
KEITH TUDOR
AND
MIKE WORRALL

PCCS Books
Monmouth

First published in 2007, PCCS Books, Ross-on-Wye

PCCS Books Ltd
Wyastone Business Park
Wyastone Leys
Monmouth
NP25 3SR
UK
Tel +44 (0)1600 891509
contact@pccs-books.co.uk
www.pccs-books.co.uk

Text: this collection © Keith Tudor and Mike Worrall, 2007
the chapters © individual authors, 2007

Cover photograph © Pete Sanders, 2007

All rights reserved.
No part of this publication may be reproduced, stored
in a retrieval system, transmitted or utilised in any
form by any means, electronic, mechanical,
photocopying or recording or otherwise without
permission in writing from the publishers.

**Freedom to Practise, Volume II:
Developing person-centred approaches to supervision**

British Library Cataloguing in Publication Data.
A catalogue record for this book is available from the British Library.

ISBN 978 1 898059 97 4

Cover design by Old Dog Graphics
Cover photograph taken on the Gower Peninsular, South Wales
Printed in the UK by Severn, Gloucester

CONTENTS

Introduction		1
Keith Tudor and Mike Worrall		

Part One—Process

Chapter 1	Choosing a Supervisor	11
	Carolin Friederike Herwig	
Chapter 2	Supervision as Maieutic Process:	16
	The birthing of insight	
	Louise Embleton Tudor and Mike Worrall	
Chapter 3	Responsibilities in Supervision	26
	Keith Tudor	
Chapter 4	Using Appreciative Inquiry in Person-Centred	37
	Supervision	
	Julie Barnes	

Part Two—Traditions

Chapter 5	Person-Centred Expressive Supervision	59
	Jenny Bell	
Chapter 6	Student-Centered Supervision for Pre-Therapy	72
	Garry Prouty and Dion Van Werde	

Part Three—Form

Chapter 7	Group Supervision *Keith Tudor*	85
Chapter 8	E-mail Supervision *Colin Lago and Jeannie Wright*	102

Part Four—Debates, Developments and Domains

Chapter 9	Supervision and Training of 'Rogers-1' and 'Rogers-2' Therapists: Basic concepts and methods *Marvin Frankel and Lisbeth Sommerbeck*	121
Chapter 10	Hoops, Hurdles and Thresholds: Supervising therapists through training and qualification *Geraldine Thomson*	139
Chapter 11	Supervising a Therapist Through a Complaint *Wendy Traynor*	154
Chapter 12	Supervision as Continuing Personal Development *Keith Tudor and Mike Worrall*	169
Chapter 13	Supervision in the Dock? Supervision and the Law *Peter Jenkins*	176
Chapter 14	Supervision of Short-term Therapy *Keith Tudor*	195
Chapter 15	Person-Centred Supervision Across Theoretical Orientations *Mike Worrall*	205

Part Five—Training

Chapter 16	Training Supervisors *Keith Tudor and Mike Worrall*	211

About the Editors and Contributors	221
Author Index	225
Subject Index	228

INTRODUCTION

KEITH TUDOR AND MIKE WORRALL

We are delighted to introduce this book which represents the fruits of a professional and personal friendship over fifteen years and the culmination of a writing and editing partnership over thirteen of those years. Our own experience as therapists and supervisees, as supervisors of therapists and supervisors and as trainers of supervisors, led us to write and edit the first book published on person-centred supervision: *Freedom to Practise: Person-Centred Perspectives on Supervision* (Tudor and Worrall, 2004a). In that book we outline our perspectives on person-centred philosophy and theory as they relate to the practice of supervision, and consider generic models of supervision from a person-centred perspective, including the process models of Casement (1985, 1990) and of Hawkins and Shohet, whose *Supervision in the Helping Professions* is now in its third edition (2006). The rest of our previous book comprises chapters on different aspects of supervision.

In that volume we advanced what we see as an important distinction between 'client-centred supervision', in which the focus of the supervision is on the therapist's clients, and 'person-centred supervision' in which the focus is on the person of the therapist. The former is the more traditional model of supervision, common across most theoretical orientations; the latter raises important issues of trust in the therapist of whatever level of experience, and the extent to which supervision and personal therapy are distinct activities. That the relationship between practitioner/supervisee and supervisor is one based on trust is of crucial importance, especially in the light of research which suggests that supervisees 'non-disclose' more than they disclose in supervision (see Ladany, 2007). Most therapists in the UK are required to have ongoing supervision as part of their training and, post-qualification, their continuing professional development, and membership, registration or accreditation of their professional bodies. If this is justified at all, it is on the basis of what is often referred to as 'the protection of clients' and the promotion of 'good practice'. However, there is little if any research which demonstrates the efficacy of supervision with regard to its impact on clients at one remove, let alone their protection (see Wheeler and Richards, 2007). Furthermore, supervision is not a universal requirement. There are a number of countries in the world in which professional bodies do not require therapists to be in supervision, and we know of no evidence to suggest that clients of therapists in these countries are any the less protected or safe. We think that these arguments challenge the basic assumption that supervision is *necessary* or sufficient, and effective or protective. They also support our preference and advocacy for *person-centred* supervision: if the practitioner does have to have supervision, at least he or she should be the focus of it. These perspectives and issues are developed throughout this volume, especially in our own contributions in Chapters 3, 12, 15 and 16.

In the three years since the publication of that first book the field of supervision has developed, and the need to emphasise practitioners' freedom remains undiminished. We have, therefore, retained the title of the first volume. In the context of increasing moves towards the statutory regulation of psychotherapists and counsellors, professional registration and accreditation, a general defensiveness in the field of psychotherapy and counselling, and often unchallenged assumptions about the responsibilities of supervisors, the practice of freedom is as necessary as ever. The cover of the first volume reflected this theme with a view taken on Kinder Scout, the site in 1932 of a mass trespass of working-class fell-walkers whose direct action secured certain access rights for walkers and the 'freedom to roam'. Whilst such freedom is not confined, we did claim this land for Yorkshire when, as several readers have pointed out, it is in fact in Derbyshire.

In that first book four specific chapters contributed to discussions about the process of supervision: describing supervision from the perspective of a supervisee; the use of Interpersonal Process Recall in person-centred supervision; subtle energy in supervision; and supervision as heuristic research inquiry. Four chapters in Part I of this current volume focus on process. Chapter 1 considers the issues involved in choosing a supervisor. Writing from her own experience of the process of having and choosing different supervisors, Carolin Friederike Herwig identifies a number of necessary qualities in a supervisor. It is appropriate that this is the first chapter as, for most of us, the task of choosing a supervisor comes before the task of beginning to work with our first client. In Chapter 2 Louise Embleton Tudor and Mike Worrall reflect on supervision as analogous to the birth process, and on the role of the supervisor as analogous to that of the midwife. Drawing on personal experiences, and from some of the literature on birth, birthing and midwifery, they draw precise parallels between these and processes in supervision. In Chapter 3 Keith Tudor explores responsibilities in supervision, often the cause of much anxiety on the part of the supervisor. The chapter identifies what are usually viewed as the supervisor's responsibilities, and reframes them as the subject of discussion, negotiation and agreement between supervisor and practitioner in a relationship marked by mutuality, if not symmetry. Keith thanks the British Association of Psychoanalytic and Psychodynamic Supervision (BAPPS) for access to its *Code of Ethics & Practice* (BAPPS, 2003). In Chapter 4 Julie Barnes discusses Appreciative Inquiry (AI), an approach to strengths-based change, which invites reflection on achievements rather than on problems. She discusses the similarities and differences between AI and person-centred approaches to inquiry, and describes how she uses AI to complement and supplement her practice as a person-centred supervisor.

Differences—from emphasis, through shades of opinion, to splits—are as much a part of the history of psychotherapy as they are of life. Ever since the termination of the Wisconsin project, distinct factions have been discernable within the person-centred approach (see Lietaer, 1990). In 2000 Warner published an article addressing the issue of the many tribes in the one person-centred nation and argued that it is possible to distinguish between practitioners on the basis of their interventiveness. Inspired by the analogy of 'tribes' Sanders (2004) edited a book identifying and introducing what he saw as the 'schools' of therapy related to the person-centred approach, comprising classical, focusing, experiential, existential, and integrative. However, by Sanders' own admission, the book is parochial in that it is only a gathering of those 'tribes' represented by training opportunities available in the UK. It doesn't account for expressive therapy or Pre-Therapy. In Part 2 of this volume we are delighted to include two chapters which represent the first writing on the subject of supervision from these two traditions. In Chapter 5 Jenny Bell describes person-centred expressive approaches in supervision, introducing this with reference to person-centred expressive therapy, and illustrating it (see plates at the beginning of the chapter) with four examples of expressive supervision with supervisees who had different experiences of working expressively. The chapter concludes with some expressive interpretations of theoretical models of supervision. In Chapter 6 Garry Prouty, the founder of Pre-Therapy, and Dion Van Werde, a leading exponent of its practice in Europe, write about supervision of Pre-Therapy. Prouty introduces Pre-Therapy and describes his own formative experiences of supervision with Eugene Gendlin. Van Werde then discusses some of his own learnings from his practice of and discussions about Pre-Therapy.

Part 3 comprises two chapters on the form of supervision. Despite the fact that a lot of supervision is conducted or facilitated in groups, the 'default setting' or assumption in the literature is, with few exceptions, individual supervision. In Chapter 7 Keith Tudor explores the nature of 'group' and the form of group supervision; discusses the purpose, form, possibilities and practicalities of group supervision; and concludes with some thoughts on the facilitation of group supervision. Alongside, and facilitated by developments in new technology, there has been a significant development of online counselling. In Chapter 8 Colin Lago and Jeannie Wright trace this development and consider the implications for e-mail supervision. They bring this to life by including excerpts from their own e-mail correspondence, which informed their writing of this chapter.

In the previous volume we outlined a model of domains of influence (see Figure I.1), which we find useful in locating different aspects of supervision viewed in a wider context.

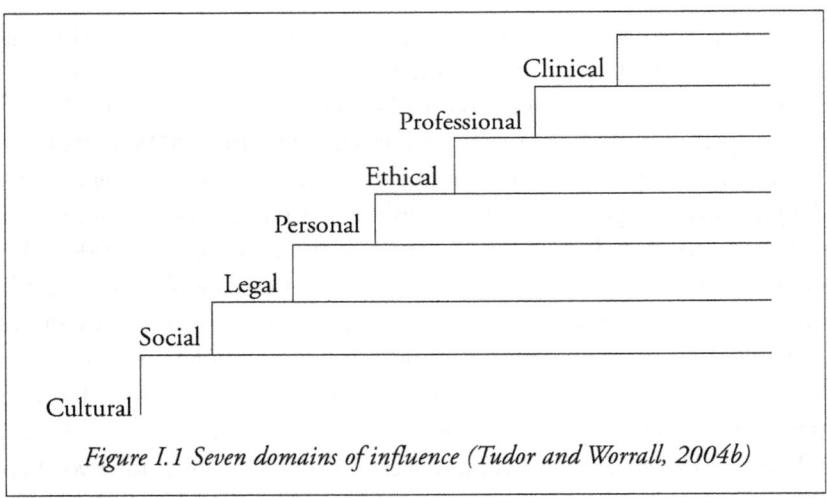

Figure I.1 Seven domains of influence (Tudor and Worrall, 2004b)

The chapters in Part 4 represent these seven identified domains. In the first volume we reviewed the relevance of the person-centred theory of therapy (Rogers, 1957, 1959) to supervision. In these formulations, Rogers hypothesises that it is the communication to the client (1957) and the client's experience and perception (1959) of unconditional positive regard and empathic understanding that initiates and sustains therapeutic growth. Over half a century Rogers' conditions have been the subject of much research and debate. Marvin Frankel and Lisbeth Sommerbeck have been involved in this debate and, in a close re-reading of Rogers, have identified a radical change in Rogers' description of therapy in *Client-Centered Therapy* (1951), which they refer to as 'Rogers-1', compared with his later descriptions ('Rogers-2'). In Chapter 9 they distinguish between these two understandings and offer a robust critique of 'Rogers-2' and the clinical practice that follows from that development. They identify and comment on the implications for the education or training of therapists, and for their supervision, arguing that all 'person-centred' therapists should know the difference between the two 'schools of thought'. This chapter aims to help supervisors sharpen the clinical practice of their supervisees, especially with regard to the 'core conditions' of therapy. Chapter 10 considers the supervision of therapists through training and qualification (the professional domain). Geraldine Thomson draws on Rogers' concept of the organism whence she derives her profound trust in the human organism and the therapist in training. She also draws on Rogers' ideas about learning and creativity to advance her argument. Thomson's approach to the supervision of therapists in training is 'broadening', as distinct from 'narrowing', terms which describe different supervisory processes which are the subject of recent research by Gazzola and Theriault (2007). One of the features of life in a service industry is that customers can complain. They are, after all, always right—even when they're wrong! (see Embleton Tudor and Tudor, 1996). We may, from a human rights perspective, welcome the freedom to complain. Given the nature of therapy, however, a complaint can be a painful process for both parties; especially in so far as it symbolises the breakdown of a relationship intended originally to be helpful. Also, with regard to counsellors and psychotherapists who are members of the British Association for Counselling and Psychotherapy, there has been the additional problem that their professional association also receives their clients' complaints, upon which, in the experience of a number of members, the therapist is regarded as guilty until proved guilty. The medical profession distinguishes the role of professional association (and defence) from the role of receiving and examining public complaints. This distinction has informed the establishment by the United Kingdom Council for Psychotherapy of a new Independent Complaints Organisation (www.independentcomplaints.org.uk). Whatever professional structures may or may not be in place (professional domain), therapists who are the subject of a complaint need support. In Chapter 11 Wendy Traynor discusses the experience of complaint and the issues involved in supervising a therapist through a complaint: a chapter which represents the ethical domain in our schema. She describes a number of psychological responses to a complaint, and the importance of the supervisor's role in offering containment to the respondent/supervisee through an undoubtedly difficult process. Traynor acknowledges the difficulty at times of maintaining a person-centred perspective in the context of legalistic thinking. In Chapter 12, in the personal domain, Keith Tudor and Mike Worrall explore supervision as continuing personal development. We question assumptions about the separation between supervision and personal therapy and look at some of the benefits that might accrue to a more comprehensive view of what's possible in supervision. One of our concerns in this field is the assumptions that are made about the responsibilities of supervisors. We spend much of our time as supervisors and as trainers deconstructing such assumptions (see Chapters 3 and 16). We are delighted to include in this volume a chapter by Peter Jenkins on supervision and the law (Chapter 13), representing the legal domain. In his publications, Jenkins has done much to clarify the legal aspects and implications of therapy and we are grateful to him for the opportunity to publish this chapter, adapted from his keynote presentation to the Annual Conference of the British Association for Supervision Practice and Research in 2005. We live in a society which, by and large, values and favours the short-term, and this is now a feature of therapeutic life and practice. In Chapter 14 Keith Tudor discusses the supervision of short-term work, and frames this as a discussion within the social domain. He identifies concerns with regard to structure and limits, contact and relationship, and expectations and responsibilities, all of which commonly present challenges for therapist and supervisor. With regard to the supervision of short-term work, he focuses on the question of supervisors' experience, the frequency of supervision, and the integrity of the person-centred approach in this context. Keith is appreciative of a number of discussions with colleagues on this subject and especially wishes to thank Jane Monach for her input to this chapter. It is a requirement of training and of professional accreditation/registration, at least in the UK, that practitioners have a theoretical orientation and thus this has become a part of the culture of therapy. In the previous volume, we included a chapter on supervision across theoretical orientations (Hitchings, 2004). In Chapter 15 Mike Worrall builds on Hitchings' work and looks at the person-centred supervision of practitioners from other orientations and disciplines.

In 2000 Temenos launched its first person-centred supervision course, which we designed and jointly facilitated (see www.temenos.ac.uk for current details). Since then we have co-facilitated ten courses and continue to offer one or two courses each year. To date over 200 practitioners have participated in these courses. We conclude this collaboration with a final chapter based on our experience of training supervisors. We discuss the importance of a congruence, or fit, between the practitioner's philosophy, practice and theory, and how this is reflected in the training of supervisors and the practice of supervision.

When we were discussing this book with someone who had trained with us, she said that she would appreciate a book which would help her 'to stay grounded in this world of evidence, regulation and pressure from powerful organisations'. One of the concepts of positive mental health we draw on is that it comprises individual resilience and supportive environments (Joubert and Raeburn, 1998). We hope that in some way this book and its companion volume support practitioners' individual resilience in their work as supervisors and, through their ideas, challenges and references, provide something of a supportive professional and intellectual environment.

References

British Association of Psychoanalytic and Psychodynamic Supervision. (2003) *Code of Ethics & Practice*. Redhill: BAPPS

Casement, P. (1985) *On Learning from the Patient*. London: Tavistock

Casement, P. (1990) *Further Learning from the Patient: The Analytic Space and Process*. London: Routledge

Embleton Tudor, L. and Tudor, K. (1996) Is the client always right?—A person-centred perspective. *Cahoots*, 55, pp. 33, 43

Gazzola, N. and Theriault, A. (2007) Super- (and not-so-super-) vision of counsellors-in-training: Supervisee perspectives on broadening and narrowing processes. *British Journal of Guidance & Counselling*, 35(2), 189–204

Hawkins, P. and Shohet, R. (2006) *Supervision in the Helping Professions* (3rd edn.). Buckingham: Open University Press

Hitchings, P. (2004) On supervision across theoretical orientations. In K. Tudor and M. Worrall (Eds.) *Freedom to Practise: Person-Centred Approaches to Supervision* (pp. 203–24). Ross-on-Wye: PCCS Books

Joubert, N. and Raeburn, J. (1998) Mental health promotion: People, power and passion. *International Journal of Mental Health Promotion*, 1, 15–22

Ladany, N. (2007) *Supervision Secrets: Fibbing, Fighting, and Fornicating*. Paper presented at the Conference of the Society for Psychotherapy Research UK, Ravenscar

Lietaer, G. (1990). The client-centered approach after the Wisconsin project: A personal view on its evolution. In G. Lietaer, J. Rombauts and R. Van Balen (Eds.) *Client-Centered and Experiential Psychotherapy in the Nineties* (pp. 19–45). Leuven: Leuven University Press

Rogers, C.R. (1951) *Client-Centered Therapy*. London: Constable

Rogers, C.R. (1957) The necessary and sufficient conditions of therapeutic personality change. *Journal of Consulting Psychology*, 21, 95–103

Rogers, C.R. (1959) A theory of therapy, personality and interpersonal relationships, as developed in the client-centred framework. In S. Koch (Ed.) *Psychology: A Study of a Science. Vol. 3: Formulations of the Person and the Social Context* (pp. 184–256). New York: McGraw-Hill

Sanders, P. (Ed.) (2004) *The Tribes of the Person-Centred Nation*. Ross-on-Wye: PCCS Books

Tudor, K. and Worrall, M. (Eds.) (2004a) *Freedom to Practise: Person-Centred Approaches to Supervision*. Ross-on-Wye: PCCS Books

Tudor, K. and Worrall, M. (2004b) Issues, questions, dilemmas and domains in supervision. In K. Tudor and M. Worrall (Eds.) *Freedom to Practise: Person-Centred Approaches to Supervision* (pp. 79–96). Ross-on-Wye: PCCS Books

Warner, M.S. (2000) Person-centered psychotherapy: One nation, many tribes. *The Person-Centered Journal*, 7(1), 28–39

Wheeler, S. and Richards, K. (2007) *Supervision Systematic Scoping Review*. Paper presented at the Conference of the Society for Psychotherapy Research UK, Ravenscar

Part One

Process

Chapter One

Choosing a Supervisor

Carolin Friederike Herwig

Worrall (2001) points out that supervision is, in the UK, and under most ethical codes and frameworks, mandatory. Therapists who want to abide by their professional codes have little or no choice about whether to be in supervision, and he argues that we lose something significant when we deny ourselves the opportunity to experience freely for ourselves our emerging need for supervisory support or consultation. Feltham (2002, p. 26) agrees: 'the requirement that we all must engage in something identified as supervision denies professional self-determination.' If we have little choice about *whether* to be in supervision, most of us can at least exercise some degree of choice about our supervisor. I know that many placements, and some training organisations, insist either that practitioners see particular supervisors, or that they choose their supervisor from a list of approved or accredited supervisors. In such circumstances, the practitioner's choice is to some extent circumscribed. I believe that this is unfortunate, and that practitioners, whether qualified or in training, should have as much freedom and support as possible to find a supervisor with whom they can work well. Most qualified practitioners in independent practice have freedom to choose for themselves. This brief and personally written chapter is about the significance and implications of that choice.

When I began to look for a supervisor, I felt excited at the prospect of finding and working with someone who would accept, support and challenge me. I wanted to be able to turn to someone with questions about my practice, about my experiences with my clients, about professional dilemmas and ethical considerations, and about the law. I wanted to be able to talk to a colleague about my work, about my experience of my work, and about myself in my work, without the fear of being judged, shamed or evaluated.

I'm aware that when I began looking, my locus of evaluation was external and located with the un-met supervisor, whom I saw as inevitably more senior and more experienced. Rather than finding this limiting, or experiencing myself as subject to what Feltham (2002) calls a 'surveillance culture', I expected it to free me in my work. I was just beginning my practice as a therapist and I envisaged myself being able to explore my work, safe in the knowledge that the supervisor I had yet to find would attend to my clients' interests as well as my own.

Rogers (Hackney and Goodyear,1984, p. 283) said of supervision that its 'major goal' was 'to help the therapist to grow in self-confidence and to grow in understanding of himself or herself, and to grow in understanding the therapeutic process.' Mearns and Thorne (2000, p. 29) agree: 'In person-centred supervision the principle focus is the *therapist* and not the client. The view is taken that nothing can meaningfully be done to understand the client because he is not present in the supervision room.' This focus has always been important to me. Nevertheless, the first supervisor I met told me that her priority when supervising was to pay attention not to me but to my clients. I welcomed this. I felt confident, but not experienced, and I was looking for someone whose priority was my client. I felt that I could talk with her and decided that I would like to work with her.

I worked with this supervisor for some time and, over time, grew increasingly frustrated and disappointed. I felt she lacked concentration and I shared with her less and less about my work with clients. I felt uncomfortable not sharing *with* her my experience *of* her, and knew also that I was not doing in supervision the work I wanted to be doing. I saw at the time that I had a part in maintaining an unsatisfactory status quo. I tried to say how I was experiencing our relationship but felt unheard, and therefore discouraged, from saying what my experience genuinely was, and I did not continue to communicate my frustration beyond a few attempts. I held this supervisor (and hold her still) in high regard, but at the same time I knew that I wasn't getting what I needed for my personal and professional growth.

I met with several other supervisors and became increasingly clear about what I was looking for in a supervisor. I wanted someone who:

- was committed to personal and professional integrity;
- would collaborate with me towards finding and establishing the best possible way of working together;
- was confident, congruent and challenging;

- would anticipate situations that might occur;
- was to some extent familiar with the law in so far as it impinged upon the practice of therapy;
- worked ethically;
- was also clear and articulate about ethical considerations; and
- enjoyed her/his work and had energy and passion for it.

For myself, I needed to feel that I could be congruent, or fully myself. I enjoy being able to be myself and when I feel that I can't, I know that I tend to disappear. I feel invisible and I say less. I did not want to *start* my relationship with a supervisor by having to explore my own disappearance. I knew then that I needed someone who would start from a position of trusting me and believing in my integrity. This, I hoped, would offer me the opportunity to explore my work with my clients in depth, in detail and without reserve.

I became clear over time that I was also looking for mutual trust and a mutual and reciprocal willingness to be open to one another. For that to be possible I had to experience some degree of authentic contact, or at least the possibility of such contact. This was especially important to me because I recognised that I was entrusting not only myself and my work to my supervisor, but to some extent my clients and their stories too. They had risked sharing themselves with me, and I wanted a supervisor who would appreciate that risk as fully and as sensitively as I aspired to myself.

There were several times in my original supervision relationship when I knew that I was not experiencing the above conditions, but I wanted to get on with my practice and I considered that, on balance, I would rather work without those conditions than not work. This was despite the fact that I felt uncomfortable in those initial sessions, and uncomfortable to such an extent that I did not even want to discuss how uncomfortable I felt.

I began to look for another supervisor. Some of my experiences along the way helped me to clarify and articulate for myself what I thought about professional standards and ethical practice. I rang one supervisor to ask if she had any spaces for supervisees and whether she would consider working with me. She told me that she could not supervise me as she was already supervising my own therapist. Her response showed me that she had been able to identify me from what my therapist had said to her in supervision. I felt that my confidentiality had been breached and my relationship with my therapist was subsequently changed, although we continued to work together.

I did, eventually, find someone I wanted to work with; someone I enjoy working with, and someone I experience as embodying the philosophy of the person-centred approach in his relationship with me. He engages with my fears and insecurities as well as with my joys and successes. He sees and trusts my ability as a counsellor and believes in my integrity, and because the above are based on his knowledge of my work and of me, I can explore with him who I am and who I want to be in my relationships with my clients. And because I *experience* his belief in my integrity, and feel seen and trusted, I feel free to tell him about the situations that do not feel 'right'; moments where I am uncomfortable and question myself about what I've done and about what I might have done differently. My experience of his acceptance leaves me free and able to challenge myself and to learn from my own experiences. If one of the functions of supervision is, at some level, to safeguard the clients with whom I work, then I believe that this is the best safeguard my clients can have.

My emerging sense of the significance of finding a supervisor who would be right for me was confirmed when I heard the following from a colleague. One of my colleague's clients had threatened to sue her. My colleague felt confident that her contact and conduct with this client had been appropriate, but it transpired that she did *not* feel confident about her work with her supervisor. She regretted not having taken action when she had known that her work with this supervisor was not satisfactory for her. She had stayed with her supervisor despite knowing that she needed more than she was getting in supervision, and despite feeling sure she would not find what she needed in this relationship. She had had difficulties finding a supervisor in the past, and having supervision, even if that supervision was inadequate, meant that at least she could practise. Despite her misgivings, she had continued to work with her supervisor.

This incident confirmed for me that I need supervision that is more than merely good enough. I need, and my clients deserve, supervision that covers the work that I, and we, need to do. I want to work with a supervisor with whom I feel in contact; from whom I experience empathic understanding and unconditional acceptance; and to whom I feel free to communicate my own experiencing, congruently and robustly. I want also to feel challenged within those conditions rather than outside of them. In other words, I want my supervisor to challenge me, when necessary, from a consistent and enduring level of care for me, manifested in empathic understanding and unconditional acceptance. I want him also to be confident enough not to stop my responses to his challenge. Given these conditions, I know that I will feel free to explore my work in depth and detail, however uncomfortable that might be. If I were not to be in such a relationship, and if I should find myself in a situation similar to the one my colleague described, then I would be unable to say that I had done my best by my client. I would, from where I am now, at least consider deciding not to work with clients until I had found a supervisor with whom I could work well, and who could hold and support me in the work I was doing with my clients.

REFERENCES

Feltham C. (2002) A surveillance culture. *CPJ*, *13*(1), 26–7

Hackney, H. and Goodyear, R. (1984) Carl Rogers's client-centered approach to supervision. In R.F. Levant and J.M. Shlien (Eds.) *Client-Centered Therapy and the Person-Centered Approach: New Directions in Theory, Research, and Practice* (pp. 278–96). New York: Praeger

Mearns, D. and Thorne, B. (2000) *Person-Centred Therapy Today: New Frontiers in Theory and Practice*. London: Sage

Worrall, M. (2001) Supervision and empathic understanding. In S. Haugh and T. Merry (Eds.) *Rogers' Therapeutic Conditions: Evolution, Theory and Practice. Volume 2: Empathy* (pp. 206–17). Ross-on-Wye: PCCS Books

Chapter Two

Supervision as Maieutic Process: The Birthing of Insight

Louise Embleton Tudor and Mike Worrall

Introduction

We see supervision as a practice that is both allied to and discrete from the practice of psychotherapy. They are both relational spaces within which a person can reflect upon her own experiences, and examine the sense, meaning and significance of those experiences in the presence of an attentive other. We resist, however, the temptation to take what we think we know about psychotherapy and simply import that uncritically into what we think about supervision. We don't, for instance, assume that the six conditions that Rogers suggests are necessary and sufficient for effective therapy are either necessary or sufficient for the practice of supervision. The context is different, and the needs and demands of a supervisee may differ from the needs and demands of a client. We do, though, want to develop ways of thinking about supervision, and therefore also ways of practising supervision, that are congruent with the values of the approach and distinctively person-centred.

In new areas of thought and practice, metaphors and analogies can help both to clarify the field and to generate an appropriate, specific and descriptive vocabulary. In Rogers' terms, an appropriate metaphor helps us symbolise our experience, or shape it in words. Langer (1942/1957, p. 63) describes a symbol as 'an instrument of thought', and it's in that sense that we see symbols as important here. They help us, in the first instance, to think about our experiences. Once we have the words, or symbols, we can then share what we think, and when we can do that we can begin to dialogue with others. We hope that this chapter will begin a dialogue within which we can all talk about our own experiences of supervision and develop our thinking in the light of those experiences.

Metaphors and analogies have limited accuracy and therefore limited usefulness. They are, says Keen (1983, p. 32), both 'revelatory and inaccurate'. Finding their limits is a necessary part of the process of using them as we've described. So, although we're using a particular image here to stand for and shed light on the process of supervision and on the role of a supervisor, we don't expect the analogy to fit exactly. We may learn as much from where it doesn't fit as from where it does.

Definition and history

Maieusis is the process of helping a person to give birth, and especially to give birth to thoughts, ideas and meanings. If we see supervision as a process of maieusis, or midwifery, then we can see a supervisor as midwife.

The metaphor comes originally from Socrates (470–399 BCE), who called himself a midwife to men's thoughts. Some sources suggest also that Socrates was himself the son of a midwife. The Socratic method of questioning was originally a co-operative search for truth and understanding. That might serve as a working definition of supervision: a co-operative search for truth and understanding. Bohart and Greenberg (1997, p. 6) describe empathy as 'a process of co-constructing symbols for experience'. We would say the same of supervision: that it is a space and a process, characterised by empathic understanding, within which supervisor and supervisee together develop and co-construct an increasingly subtle, supple and accurate language with which a supervisee can narrate and examine his experiences with his clients.

The idea of therapist as midwife is not new. Rogers (1951, p. x) talks about 'the privilege of being a midwife to a new personality', about standing by 'with awe at the emergence of a self, a person', and about 'a birth process in which I have had an important and facilitating part'. Continuing the theme some years later, he describes psychotherapy (1963, p. 4) as 'a psychological amniotic fluid' which allows 'forward movement of a constructive sort'. Just as we may see a therapist as midwife to therapeutic processes, so we may see a supervisor as midwife to supervisory processes.

Taft (1933, p. 3), an early and significant influence on Rogers, describes the role of the therapist more precisely:

> The word 'therapy' has no verb in English, for which I am grateful; it cannot do anything to anybody, hence can better represent a process going on, observed perhaps, understood perhaps, assisted perhaps, but

not applied. The Greek noun from which therapy is derived means 'a servant', the verb means 'to wait'.

Taft is writing about therapy, and we've said already that we don't want to import ideas about therapy uncritically into our thinking about supervision. However, the notions of observing, understanding, assisting, serving and waiting are important elements in what we think about supervision. Collectively, they imply humility and patience, both of which we think are important qualities in a supervisor.

MAIEUSIS

By way of beginning to unpack the analogy we want to say a little about midwifery.

From the Middle English, mid-wife means literally the person who is 'mid' or 'with' the 'wife' or 'woman' giving birth. Clearly, there are different kinds of midwife and different kinds of supervisor. Some are more respectful than others, some more active, directive and interventive. There are also radical midwives who are concerned about the increasing medicalisation of and intervention in maternity care, and who provide a more sympathetic, personalised, woman-centred practice. They will often protect the woman giving birth from unnecessary medical intervention. There are 'radical' therapists and supervisors who are also concerned about the medicalisation of distress (see Sanders, 2006). We're not wanting to prescribe how midwives or supervisors should be. We're simply wanting to look at how practitioners work, to learn from practice in one field, and to use what we learn to inform and enhance practice in another.

There is much written and verbal evidence of women who have suffered interventive and, therefore, painful or emotionally distressing births resulting in difficulties caring physically for or bonding with their infants. Similarly, a therapist whose relationship with a client has been disturbed by a supervisor's directive interventions is likely to find her ability to trust her own knowing and sensing of herself and of her client compromised.

One of the first champions of natural childbirth, Dick-Read, a contemporary of Rogers, writes in 1959 of factors disposing women in labour to higher levels of pain. Among them he cites the insult to the mind and senses of cheerful conversation or of consolation. At the same time he rebukes obstetricians who allow women to become depressed and disappointed, and recognises (p. 50) that: 'There is no greater loneliness in the life of a human being than being alone with one's suffering.' He suggests that attendants at a birth need to show the utmost sensitivity to the predicament of the woman giving birth. We are equally concerned that the cheerfulness, consolation or sympathy of a supervisor can be an insult to the mind and senses of the supervisee/therapist who, rather, needs sensitivity and empathy in order to make the fullest use of her experience.

We asked around a little to find out what people's best experiences of midwives were. A friend who had had two significantly good experiences of giving birth said that her midwife:

- did 'as little as possible';
- was 'a really strong presence';
- was 'absolutely present and yet not at all in the way'; and
- inspired her with the confidence that she could give birth in her own way.

She said also that she trusted her midwife:

- to be attentive;
- to be available;
- to be respectful of and responsive to what she needed;
- to let the process happen as naturally as possible; and
- to act, quickly and calmly, if anything seemed to be going awry.

These all seem to us to catch something of what supervision can be like, at its best.

Analogy

We're interested to see what happens if we look at the process of supervision and the role of the supervisor in the light of the process of birth and the role of the midwife. So we want to draw some loose parallels:

- A woman comes bearing a child. A supervisee comes bearing something: a question, a concern, a dilemma, a struggle of some sort. The word 'bearing' here means both 'carrying' and 'tolerating': 'bearing gifts' and 'bearing up under the strain'. Supervision and birth are both processes. For some women, awareness of the first stage of birth, the onset of labour, is gradual, like the burgeoning awareness of a supervisee engaged in an attempt to focus, to name, or to more fully sense the matter. In the first stage of labour, a gentle, relaxed, dissociated state is best maintained to allow the uterus to get on with its natural autonomic function of dilating. At the end of this stage there can be a temporary increase in pain, usually lasting about six to eight contractions. At this point, a woman is likely to recognise that the process is taking a long time, that it hurts and that she's not even in the second stage yet. Many women experience this as a point of despair and benefit from encouragement and reassurance in the form of a reminder that what is happening is natural and that the pain will pass as she enters the second stage.

- When the matter has been identified and is the focus of a considerable expenditure of energy, we can see a correspondence with the second stage of labour, in which the baby travels down the birth canal and enters the world. As the second stage is established, according to Gaskin (2003, pp. 141–2), the woman becomes completely 'engrossed in her task and concentrates on the all-important occupation of the moment … normally, in the absence of any dominating fear she is devoid of any consciousness of herself and employs all her energies to the fulfilment of the immediate purpose'. There is the possibility of restful sleep between contractions at this point; a lowering of mental activity; release of conscious control; and a total focus on the baby's journey. This is comparable to accessing all the systems of the brain in supervision: going deeper, allowing the cortex of the brain to rest so that material sensed in the limbic systems of the brain-body (to do with information about relating, and about impressions at the edge of our awareness) may emerge.

- The third stage of labour, the delivery of the placenta, the face-to-face encounter between the new mother and her baby, is analogous to the part of the supervisory process in which meaning and realisation are further explored and become integrated. There may be intense feelings also at this point.

- Ideally, and in most cases, pregnancy ends with the birth of a child. We see the end of the process of supervision as the emergence of clarified and articulated meaning, with all that that then allows in terms of a supervisee deciding what to do or not do next. We see this emergence of meaning as central. The person-centred approach has affinities with existential thinking, one of the central tenets of which is that as human beings we make our own meaning: that's just one of the things we seek naturally to do. Rogers echoes this when he describes the organism as naturally truth-seeking. From this perspective we can trust that our supervisees are already interested in making meaning for themselves of what they experience as they work. Our work as supervisors is simply to allow this meaning to emerge, and to recognise that it may not necessarily be the meaning that would emerge for us.

- Just as it's the woman and not the midwife who gives birth to the child, so it's the supervisee and not the supervisor whose meaning matters. The midwife is in attendance, as is the supervisor, and serves the process of birth, as does the supervisor. As we see it, therefore, supervision that is consonant with the values of the person-centred approach is primarily supervisee-centred. That is to say it begins with what matters to the supervisee, is guided by his needs, and is tailored to what he finds useful and helpful. In this it resembles Bowen's philosophy-oriented rather than form-oriented supervision (Villas-Boas Bowen, 1986). This line of thought also allows us to see that a supervisor can be *person*-centred, and attend primarily to the person of the supervisee, or *client*-centred, and attend primarily to the clients of the supervisee, through the supervisee's account of them. We take the view that *person*-centred supervision, as we describe it here, is more consistent with the values of the broader person-centred approach. A person-centred supervisor, attending to the person of the supervisee, manifests an active trust in her supervisee's integrity and competence. A supervisor who takes a more *client*-centred approach to supervision is suggesting a lack of trust in her supervisee, and presuming to know more or better than her supervisee about what's happening in the therapeutic relationship. Such a supervisor may also have ideas about her supervisee's clients, and about how her supervisee should respond. This perspective informs much of the debate about the responsibilities of supervisors (see Chapter 3).

- The process of giving birth, at its best and most of the time, is a natural process. It isn't necessarily easy or pain-free, and there are often complications. We're in the area of new life and potential death, and the risks of any complications that do occur are high. Medical, chemical or surgical interventions are often helpful or even necessary. It is, though, a natural process, and one that can often be trusted to run its own course at its own pace and in its own way. Giving birth is part of the natural order of things. As the process of giving birth is a natural and trustworthy one, so the process of giving birth to articulated meaning in supervision is also natural, and trustworthy. However, as Dick-Read, 1942/2004, p. 210) puts it: 'Nothing disturbs the course of natural labour more than fear.' Writing about the mother he continues (p. 136): 'if her neuromuscular systems are deranged by fear–tension influences, she does not experience the phenomenon of a normal labour'. Corticothalamic systems produce abnormal conditions of body and mind which inhibit the natural processes (ibid., p. 136): 'Fear promotes the desire to escape, mental turmoil, tension and disturbed neuromuscular harmony with the sympathetic nervous system impulses overriding the pelvic autonomic.' One of us had a supervisee who liked rather formally to read from her meticulous and detailed written case histories of her clients. This supervisee felt 'stuck' with every one of her clients and had felt some trepidation about 'admitting' this to her new supervisor. It transpired that her previous experience of supervision had been one in which she'd felt 'put on the spot', ashamed and humiliated by her lack of knowledge and skill. Her fear of a repetition of this experience meant that she arrived so full of adrenaline that she had very limited access to her 'gut feelings', and her capacity to remember and think clearly was also compromised. She was relieved and delighted by insight, her own and that of her clients, and crucially, the relationship between them, which she developed once she was sure that she had no need to fear her supervisor or the experience of supervision. At times, adrenaline can have a positive effect, as in the case of a woman warned that if her cervix wasn't dilated within twenty minutes, her baby would need a Caesarian birth. She managed to dilate the necessary five centimeters in the required time and her baby was born safely without intervention (see Gaskin, 2003). We also have experience of a well-judged challenge from a supervisor facilitating and hastening a process with benefit to the client–therapist relationship.

- Having mentioned adrenaline, the 'brakes' on labour and the process of supervision, it is important to mention its opposite, the 'accelerator', oxytocin. This is the hormone which causes the uterus to contract, helping the baby at the beginning of its journey and which is later present in greater quantities, when it facilitates the mother and baby falling in love with each other. Research demonstrates that through the quality of her gaze and her handling of her infant, a mother psychobiologically regulates her baby (Schore, 1994). In an ordinarily good enough situation, as the mother's level of oxytocin rises on sight and touch of her baby, so does the baby's in response to her delight. There is a positive feedback loop in which each party experiences increasing levels of pleasure, each affecting and being affected by the other. A similar psychobiological regulation happens in effective therapy and, we think, in effective supervision. In those moments of shared understanding, when realisation connects with gut feeling, when the supervisee knows that his perception or his predicament has been appreciated by the supervisor, when the supervisor knows that she has been received, psychobiological states are being regulated.

- Neither the birth process nor the process of supervision need to be painful. Whilst it appears to be the experience of a small minority of women, certainly in the West, some women report experiences (in Gaskin, 2003,

p. 158) such as 'waves of pleasure rippling through the body' as the baby emerges from the birth canal. Possibly in supervision, as in birth, the greater the degree of trust in the natural process, all other factors being equal, the greater the satisfaction that may be experienced, and the less the degree of pain.

- In the best circumstances, the difficulties that come with the process of giving birth are to do with the process of giving birth: they're part of the territory. The difficulties a supervisee brings to supervision are to do with what it is to be a therapist and we don't need to see them as evidence of a supervisee's or a client's pathology. They accompany the work, and they're not necessarily cause for undue, excessive or over-hasty concern.

- A woman giving birth may be more experienced at giving birth than her midwife. This doesn't render her midwife redundant. She needs a midwife because she's going to give birth and not because she's not experienced. This line of thought allows us to challenge the received wisdom in therapeutic circles that a supervisor needs to be more experienced than a supervisee. Our experience of training therapists to become supervisors is that the hierarchy of experience doesn't necessarily need to be in a supervisor's favour. We've seen less experienced therapists offer exquisite supervision to more senior and experienced colleagues. What seems to matter is not the relative levels of experience, but one person's need for and willingness to accept help, and another's willingness to serve. This allows for supervision to become more easily a creative and co-created relationship between colleagues.

Implications for practice

Putting all of this together we can say that the role of the midwife or supervisor is:

- to attend the 'birth';
- to recognise that the process on which she's attending is a natural one; to sense when it is most facilitative to listen, to respond or to initiate; to be available, supportive and sensitive so that the supervisee does not feel alone in her labour and in her suffering if it is painful. She also needs to feel secure and safe enough to bring forth anything, whatever its shape or implications;
- to be a potent influence when necessary, giving of her knowledge and experience as appropriate, so that the supervisee has the opportunity to

develop in her work. Offered judiciously, the effectiveness of the client–therapist relationship is enhanced and ultimately, if necessary, the client is protected; and

- to know what an emergency looks like and be willing to take appropriate action to minimise risk or harm to the client, and to support the supervisee to work within her competence.

This demands a number of qualities of a supervisor:

- Humility: this recognises that the supervisee is the one giving birth. We note in this context that Angyal (1965/1973, p. 260, whose early work influenced Rogers, refers to the healthy organisation of the person as a 'humility system'.
- Patience: birth is a natural process, and natural processes take time. They shouldn't be, and maybe can't be hurried.
- Availability: you may not know when you'll be needed. In our experience, most therapists value a supervisor's offer to be available in a crisis or emergency and few abuse, misuse, or overuse the offer.
- Attention: even when everything seems to be running smoothly, and perhaps *especially* when everything seems to be running smoothly. This requires deep attunement to the supervisee, to both his physical and his emotional state, to the implicit as well as to the explicit. It requires highly developed observation skills; for example, to notice a fleeting facial expression. It also demands that the supervisor be willing to use her own body in order to receive non-verbally expressed information about the therapist's inner states or about the relationship between therapist and client.
- Generosity: you may have information or analogous experiences to share.
- Readiness to act: there may be times when you and your supervisee agree a need for you to do something.

This maieutic process may happen many times in the course of a single supervision session, or gradually over a longer period. Insights and new ideas seem not to follow a consistent pattern of conception, gestation or birth. This in itself demands of a maieutic supervisor not only the qualities we've described above but the sensitivity to recognise which of them a supervisee may need at any moment, the flexibility to offer them when they're needed, and the endurance to hold them ready until that moment arrives.

REFERENCES

Angyal, A. (1973) *Neurosis and Treatment: A Holistic Theory*. New York: John Wiley and Sons. (Original work published 1965)

Bohart, A.C. and Greenberg, L.S. (1997) Empathy and psychotherapy: An introductory overview. In A.C. Bohart and L.S. Greenberg (Eds.) *Empathy Reconsidered: New Directions in Psychotherapy* (pp. 3–31). Washington, DC: American Psychological Association

Dick-Read, G. (2004) *Childbirth Without Fear: The Principles and Practice of Natural Childbirth*. London: Pinter and Martin. (Original work published 1942)

Gaskin, I.M. (2003) *Ina May's Guide to Childbirth*. New York: Bantam Books

Keen, S. (1983) *The Passionate Life: Stages of Loving*. London: Gateway Books

Langer, S.K. (1957) *Philosophy in a New Key* (3rd edn.). Cambridge, MA: Harvard University Press. (Original work published 1942)

Rogers, C.R. (1951) *Client-Centered Therapy*. London: Constable

Rogers, C.R. (1963) The actualizing tendency in relation to 'motives' and to consciousness. In M.R. Jones (Ed.) *Nebraska Symposium on Motivation. Volume XI* (pp. 1–24). Lincoln, NE: University of Nebraska Press

Sanders, P. (2006) Why person-centred therapists must reject the medicalisation of distress. *Self and Society*, 34(3), 32–39

Schore, A.N. (1994) *Affect Regulation and the Origin of the Self: The Neurobiology of Emotional Development*. Hillsdale, NJ: Lawrence Erlbaum Associates

Taft, J. (1933) *The Dynamics of Therapy in a Controlled Relationship*. New York: Macmillan

Villas-Boas Bowen, M. (1986) Personality differences and person-centered supervision. *Person-Centered Review*, 1(3), 291–309

Chapter Three

Responsibilities in Supervision

Keith Tudor

One of the principal and recurring issues about which supervisors appear especially concerned is that of their responsibilities as supervisors. This subject provokes particular anxiety and fantasies, especially with regard to legal liability. On training courses we facilitate,[1] it is often the first theme which emerges; it is the subject on which we and the group may spend the most time and it is the aspect of supervision we most deconstruct (see Chapter 16). In the absence of clarity or certainty, practitioners and organisations appear to create fantasies about the range and scope of their responsibilities, such as: having a 'duty of care' (e.g. Lockett, 2001; Wheeler, 2001), ensuring and monitoring good practice, safeguarding clients' rights (e.g. Lockett, 2001) and protecting the client. Also, 'responsibility' is often confused with accountability and associated with finding fault and blaming. On closer reading, most of these responsibilities, many of which are confirmed and elaborated in the literature on supervision, are assumed ones. In my private/independent practice as a supervisor, I often spend some time, especially in the early days of a new supervisory relationship, in effect, helping the practitioner to deconstruct previously introjected beliefs, as distinct from integrated views, about supervision. As someone who takes the human organism as the starting point for enquiry and who values freedom of thought and practice (see Rogers, 1969) and fluidity (see Rogers, 1958/1967), I also encourage diversity and divergent thinking (in contrast to convergent thinking).

---

1. When I use 'we' I am referring to my work with Mike Worrall.

As a contribution to these processes of deconstruction, diversity and divergence, this chapter places the question of the supervisor's responsibility in some context. It addresses and questions what are traditionally viewed as the supervisor's responsibilities, and relocates them within a mutual and co-created supervisory relationship.

Context

There are, in my view, a number of factors which contribute to supervisors' anxieties and fantasies:

- The profession's defensive and overprotective attitude towards the general public and, especially, towards clients.
- The increasing moves towards statutory regulation of psychotherapy and counselling, which encourages a more legalistic than therapeutic frame of reference about rights and responsibilities.
- A hierarchical view of education, training and professional organisation in which perceived truths and certainties are handed down as what's 'right'.
- An overemphasis in the literature on the supervisor's responsibilities and tasks.
- An unquestioning and compliant attitude on the part of many therapists with regard to practice, theory, training, and the organisation and development of the profession.

A number of therapists and writers have challenged and continue to challenge these trends, including Mowbray (1995) who takes on the case against psychotherapy registration; House and Totton (1997) who argue for autonomy and pluralism in the profession; and Parker (1999) and House (2003) who represent an intellectual tradition which deconstructs profession-centred therapy. In the same tradition, we have been, and are, concerned to open up practical and intellectual space in which practitioners enjoy the freedom to learn and to practise, and to reflect on and to think about their practice. A necessary part of this process is to explore what it means to be a supervisor, and to question what are or what are said to be a supervisor's responsibilities. Jenkins' work with regard to the law and professional codes and frameworks is a major contribution towards clarifying the responsibilities of practitioners and supervisors. In 2001 he published a chapter based on codes of ethics drawn up by the then British Association for Counselling (BAC, 1996/1998). His chapter in this volume with regard to the *Ethical Framework for Good Practice in Counselling and Psychotherapy*, produced by the British Association for Counselling and Psychotherapy (BACP, 2002), stands as part of this process of clarification and deconstruction. I also refer to the BACP's *Ethical Framework* here as the majority of person-centred practitioners in the UK are members of BACP and its *Ethical Framework* is widely viewed as the 'industry standard'. Other practitioners, who are members of Member Organisations of the United Kingdom Council for Psychotherapy (UKCP) or of other national bodies and associations, will need to consider their relevant codes and frameworks of ethics and professional practice for guidance with regard to responsibilities in supervision. The other document I refer to here is the *Code of Ethics and Practice* of the British Association of Psychoanalytic and Psychodynamic Supervision (BAPPS, 2003). This is the only organisational member of UKCP comprised solely of supervisors.

In his present chapter Jenkins makes three salient points on the subject of the supervisor's responsibility:

1. That responsibilities are defined by law, policy or context—and, therefore, are not simply abstract or given.
2. That, in terms of the *Ethical Framework*, supervisors have certain *ethical* responsibilities—and these are distinct from any *legal* responsibilities.
3. That, with regard to work with clients, there is an emphasis on responsibilities of the supervisee/therapist—not of the supervisor.

In my view these points are immediately reassuring. They also imply that supervisors can and should clarify their responsibilities with regard to their context (workplace, employer, policies, etc.); with regard to the codes and/or frameworks to which they subscribe (see below); and directly with their supervisees. Such clarification enhances the view and the experience of supervision as a mutual relationship between colleagues. It also helps to deconstruct a hierarchical perspective of supervision, and of the role and responsibilities of the supervisor.

Responsibilities and requirements

BACP's *Ethical Framework* is widely viewed as being more thoughtful and less rigid than the organisation's previous codes of ethics and practice for counsellors, for supervisors and for trainers. The *Framework* is certainly more concerned with values, principles and personal moral qualities than were the previous codes—although, strangely enough, these qualities do not include love, an omission which Spence (2006) points out. Quoting Fromm (1957) who views love as an active concern for life and growth, and the basis of acts of giving and a generally productive orientation, Spence (p. 2) argues that 'love understood in this way implies ethical values ... [which] is of particular relevance in supervision where there is increasing emphasis on the legal and ethical responsibilities of supervisors'. Also, on closer inspection, with twelve references to practitioners' responsibility or to being responsible, over twenty references to requirements or what is required of practitioners, and three references to what practitioners must or 'must not' do, the *Framework* is, in effect, as prescriptive as its predecessors. The BAPPS *Code* has fifteen references to 'issues of responsibility'. Webb (2001, p. 190) goes further and questions the term 'responsibility': 'We cannot, as a profession, even agree on what constitutes responsibility—clinical or otherwise—or even whether it is an appropriate concept to maintain.' Here, I present and make explicit what are considered, by BACP and BAPPS, to be the practitioner's responsibilities and apply them to supervision. I do so from the point of view that supervision is a process and that 'responsibility' is subject to negotiation between supervisor and supervisee.

- 'Practitioners are responsible for clarifying who holds the responsibility for the work with the client.' (BACP, Clause 25, p. 6)
  This clause is a key one. It is the first in the section of the *Framework* on supervising and managing and, in my view, it should be first since it clarifies all other responsibilities. It supports the approach taken in this present work of both practitioner and supervisor sharing responsibility for any discussion about responsibilities and, implicitly, it allows for different approaches to and models of supervision. In effect, this clause promotes, even demands, explicit discussions (rather than implicit assumptions) about clinical responsibility. As King (2001, p. 8) observes: 'The term "clinical responsibility" is often used, but there is a lack of clarity about the nature of responsibility it implies.' Indeed, BAC's (1996) own *Code of Ethics and Practice for Supervisors of Counsellors* only mentioned the term once and that in a clause (B.1.2) which acknowledged that clinical responsibility remains with the counsellor, and the term does not appear in the BACP's *Ethical Framework*. BAPPS' (2003) *Code of Ethics and Practice* does refer to clinical responsibility but also acknowledges (Clause B3 ii) that 'this remains with the supervisee'. Whilst the supervisor *may have some* responsibility or duty of care to the supervisee this is dependent on the organisational context of the practitioner, the supervisor and the supervision. In his chapter, Jenkins makes it clear that this 'duty' is used too widely and (it is worth repeating) that 'the client is too remote (in a legal sense) from the activity of supervision to be considered as being owed a direct duty of care by the supervisor'. This contrasts with some writers who emphasise and, in my view, overemphasise the duties and responsibilities of supervisors (see Wheeler and King, 2001). Other writers,

such as Lockett (2001), go even further. Echoing the language of human rights, she makes the unsubstantiated assertion (p. 153) that: 'One of the major responsibilities of any supervisor is to safeguard the rights of the client.'

Significantly, BAPPS' *Code* emphasises the supervisee's responsibilities. In two clauses about the management of work, it refers to the fact that members, i.e. supervisors (B1 xii), 'should monitor regularly how their supervisees engage in self-assessment and self-evaluation of their work', and (B1 xiii) 'must ensure that their supervisees acknowledge their individual responsibility for ongoing professional development'.

One of the areas in which supervisors are viewed as having a lot of responsibility, and an area which causes much concern for supervisors, is that of 'ensuring' that supervisees have 'appropriate' clients. This is often described in terms of competence, theoretical orientation, efficacy of 'treatment', setting, and the psychopathology of the client (see, for example, Wheeler, 2001). In traditional terms such responsibility is predominantly 'ensured' through assessment by a more experienced therapist. This, in turn, raises a number of issues as to the purpose and nature of assessment, the role, attitudes and skills of the person making the assessment, and (a point which is often overlooked) the diversity of views about assessment. In the context of voluntary agencies offering counselling services, I have often heard of more experienced, psychodynamic colleagues conducting assessments as a result of which they decide whether a client is 'suitable' for 'supportive' person-centred counselling. I have never heard of a more experienced person-centred therapist deciding whether or not a client is suitable to work with a psychodynamic colleague, for example, on the basis that such a colleague might be prone to interpretation or not sufficiently empathic. Such assessments and assessment procedures are highly suspect: they are often based on a lack of in-depth knowledge of other approaches, let alone 'evidence-based' practice; they are generally more concerned about the assumption that assessments protect clients and, in any case, they do not obviate another process of assessment involving the second therapist. Sometimes supervisors themselves take on this gatekeeping function of assessment and referral, a process which adds a further complexity to subsequent supervision. Two of Carroll's (1996) seven tasks of supervision involve monitoring (the administrative aspects of supervision, and professional/ethical issues). Another perspective is for the supervisor to support the therapist in assessing the client, in the initial meeting and throughout the therapy, offering more supervision if necessary (see Mearns, 1997).

- An 'ethical responsibility to strive to mitigate any harm caused to a client'. (BACP Ethical principle of non-maleficence, p. 3)

- 'Supervisors and managers have a responsibility to maintain and enhance good practice by practitioners, to protect clients from poor practice.' (Clause 27, p. 6)
- 'Practitioners have a responsibility to protect clients when they have good reason for believing that other practitioners are placing them at risk of harm.' (Clause 39, p. 7)

    I consider these clauses together. The first describes one aspect of the principle of non-maleficence. Whilst this principle may appear uncontroversial, in practice it is used to support the notion that supervisors can somehow protect the client. In my view, too much is made of the power of the supervisor to protect clients and to keep them safe against harmful, unsafe practitioners and poor practice. As Webb (2001, p. 190) puts it: 'No longer, it seems, can we delude ourselves into thinking that supervision can adequately ensure the safety of clients or the ethical standards of the work of counsellors.' The overweening concern to protect especially adult clients also smacks of a patronising and infantilising approach. Furthermore, the image of the long arm of the supervisor (as in the law), determining or dictating practice from a distance, only makes for defensive, avoidant and paranoid supervisees—and narcissistic or paranoid supervisors! Instead, if supervision is a forum in which the concepts of harm, safety and protection can be discussed, and this ethical responsibility shared, then the therapist is more likely to be open about their practice, including their potential for being harmful. Person-centred approaches tend to emphasise a trust in people (client and therapist); to acknowledge the importance of personal power (Rogers, 1978), which includes supporting the client's ability to discuss their response to both therapy and therapist; and to promote collaborative power (Natiello, 1990) between client and therapist. Of course, if things do go wrong or clients are 'at risk', we need to respond, but, in my view, this needs to be more of a collective, organisational response than an individual one. Such risk assessment on the part of the therapist and the supervisor may relate to questions of child protection (see Douglas and Tudor, 2007) or the protection of vulnerable adults (see Department of Health, 2006). In either circumstance, it is important that both parties are as clear as possible about their respective responsibilities and roles.

- 'Practitioners have a personal responsibility to challenge, where appropriate, the incompetence or malpractice of others.' (Ethical principle of non-maleficence, p. 3)

    Whilst the sentiment of this clause is clear, it is strangely worded. Given the context, it is strange that BACP frames this in terms of a *personal* as distinct from a *professional* responsibility. The only sense I make of this is that BACP intends this to mean a person's *individual* responsibility rather than an individual's *personal* responsibility. It also presumes some common understanding of competence, incompetence, good practice and malpractice—all of which could and perhaps should be the subject of some discussion in supervision.

- 'There is an ethical responsibility to use supervision for appropriate personal and professional support and development.' (Ethical principle of self-respect, p. 3)
- 'Practitioners have a responsibility to monitor and maintain their fitness to practise.' (Clause 32, p. 7)

The first clause clearly defines supervision as a place for personal support and development, and echoes the restorative and formative modes of Proctor's (1988) functional model of supervision. It may also be read as supporting the practitioner's therapeutic use of supervision and even its use as a place for personal therapy. These functions clearly overlap and may at times be blurred. Carroll (1996) sees one of the tasks of supervision as being 'to counsel', and sometimes practitioners ask supervisors to fulfil this function and role. In the context of a course where students were not required to be in personal therapy, one supervisor felt a certain concern and pressure to offer 'personal development/therapy' to a student on placement. This raises issues of boundaries; multi-handed contracts between students, course, placement provider and supervisor; and, in this instance, students' personal responsibility for their own development. There is a similar overlap between supervision and teaching. One of Carroll's (1996) identified tasks for supervisors is 'to teach' and, again, supervisors of students/trainees often feel some responsibility to supplement their supervisees' training needs. (For further discussion of this, see Chapter 16.) Importantly, these clauses also name this use of supervision as the practitioner's ethical responsibility. For further discussion of supervision as personal development see Chapter 12.

- 'Practitioners should take into account their responsibilities and their client's rights under data-protection legislation and any other legal requirements.' (Clause 5, p. 5)

This reminds practitioners of the fact that there is always a legal context to our work and describes one specific aspect of this. It also frames responsibilities in terms of 'rights', perhaps hinting at human rights' legislation. In a rare article on this, Keys (1999) discusses how key concepts of the United Nations' (1948) *Universal Declaration of Human Rights* underpin the counselling work she does. Drawing on Keys' example, it may be useful to think about applying a similar analysis to supervision in terms of: freedom of speech and belief (Preamble to the *Declaration*); dignity and worth (Preamble); recognition (Article 6); fair and public hearing (Article 10); peaceful assembly and association, including that 'No one may be compelled to belong to an association' (Article 20); dignity and free development of personality (Article 22); and duties to the community (Article 29). In the context of a *Declaration* framed principally in the language of rights, this last Article outlines the citizen's responsibilities. One of the clauses in BACP's (2002) *Framework* echoes this when it states that: 'All members of this Association share a responsibility to take part in its professional conduct procedures'.

- 'The practitioner is responsible for learning about and taking account of the different protocols, conventions and customs that can pertain to different working contexts and cultures.' (Clause 48, p. 8)
This clause acknowledges context, culture and, by implication, diversity. With regard to supervision, it implies that any and every model of or approach to supervision should be sensitive to context or field.

- 'Practitioners are responsible for clarifying the terms on which their services are being offered in advance of the client incurring any financial obligation or other reasonably foreseeable costs or liabilities.' (Clause 51, p. 8)
This point is similar to one made in the previous *Code of Ethics and Practice for Counsellors* (BAC, 1998) which (Section B.2.2.11) stated that: 'counsellors are responsible for communicating the terms on which counselling is being offered ... [and that] the communication of these terms and any negotiation over these terms should be concluded before the client incurs any financial liability.' This requires the practitioner (therapist or supervisor) to offer an initial free session, or at least some free time on the telephone, to clients or supervisees enquiring about their services (see Tudor, 1998).

Alongside these responsibilities, the *Framework* contains over twenty references to requirements. Those of particular relevance to supervisors are:

- Consideration of any legal requirements and obligations (see Chapter 12).
- A commitment to fairness which, according to BACP (Ethical principle of justice, p. 3) 'requires the ability to appreciate differences between people and to be committed to equality of opportunity' and to avoid discrimination.

- The maintenance of good practice and care, which requires competence.
- Consideration of the implications of dual relationships.
- Regular and formal ongoing supervision/consultative support, in accordance with professional requirements.
- Keeping up to date with latest knowledge—which we identify as a condition of supervision (see Tudor and Worrall, 2004).
- Respecting confidentiality.
- Being responsive to requests from supervisees for information about the way they work.
- To be honest, straightforward and accountable in all financial matters.

Finally, the *Framework* contains three references to what the practitioner must or rather 'must not' do, all of which could apply to supervisors and supervision:

- In the context of keeping trust: 'Practitioners must not abuse their client's trust in order to gain sexual, emotional, financial or any other kind of personal advantage.' (Clause 18, p. 6)
- In the context of research: 'The research methods used should comply with the standards of good practice in counselling and psychotherapy and must not adversely affect clients.' (Clause 31, p. 7)
- In the context of working in teams: 'Practitioners must not undermine a colleague's relationships with clients by making unjustified or unsustainable comments.' (Clause 46, p. 8)

RESPONSIBILITY, ACCOUNTABILITY AND INFLUENCE

Supervision is a space in which supervisee or supervisees meet with a supervisor. At best it is a co-created space and a collaborative relationship marked, at least from person-centred perspectives, by trust, contact, honesty, acceptance, understanding and being received. In this context, any responsibilities defined by both parties (supervisee/s and supervisor), or by the context of the therapist's practice, can be discussed, negotiated and agreed. If the supervisor believes that the practitioner tends to actualise and, therefore, is interested in supporting his or her personal power as a practitioner, then the supervisor will facilitate the practitioner's thinking rather than take responsibility for, or away from, the practitioner's work.

In this chapter I have argued for clarity about responsibilities in supervision. However, no amount of clarity or contracting can inoculate us against the chaos and complexity of life or the situations and dilemmas which clients, in effect, and supervisees directly, present to supervisors. I have also sought to deconstruct many of the responsibilities that supervisors think they have or should have. In this sense, we may say that supervisors are responsible for providing good quality supervision but that they are not responsible for their supervisees or for their work. Of course, in a managerial sense and context the practitioner may be accountable to both a supervisor *and* a manager—as, indeed, the supervisor may also be accountable to the organisation for which the supervisee works. For some this distinction is useful. However, if we take the point (made earlier) that supervisors have certain *ethical* responsibilities, as distinct from any *legal* responsibilities, then this places us within the field of morals and moral philosophy. Moreover, if we think about others and ourselves as having a homonomous trend alongside an autonomous one (see Angyal, 1941), we may consider that, as supervisors and as people, we have a broader responsibility to those we influence. After all, as Lewis, Amini and Lannon (2000, p. 142) put it: 'All of us, when we engage in relatedness, fall under the gravitational influence of another's emotional world, at the same time that we are bending his emotional world with ours.'

REFERENCES

Angyal, A. (1941) *Foundations for a Science of Personality.* New York: Commonwealth Fund

British Association for Counselling. (1996) *Codes of Ethics and Practice for Supervisors of Counsellors.* Rugby: BAC

British Association for Counselling. (1998) *Codes of Ethics and Practice for Counsellors.* Rugby: BAC

British Association for Counselling and Psychotherapy. (2002) *Ethical Framework for Good Practice in Counselling and Psychotherapy.* Rugby: BACP

British Association of Psychoanalytic and Psychodynamic Supervision. (2003) *Code of Ethics and Practice.* Redhill: BAPPS

Carroll, M. (1996) *Counselling Supervision: Theory, Skills and Practice.* London: Cassell

Department of Health. (2006) *Protection of Vulnerable Adults Scheme in England and Wales for Adult Placement Schemes, Domiciliary Care Agencies and Care Homes: A Practical Guide.* London: DoH

Douglas, M. and Tudor, K. (2007, in press) Child protection. In K. Tudor (Ed.) *The Adult is Parent to the Child: Transactional Analysis with Children and Young People.* Lyme Regis: Russell House

Fromm, E. (1957) *The Art of Loving.* London: Allen and Unwin

House, R. (2003) *Therapy Beyond Modernity: Deconstructing and Transcending Profession-Centred Therapy.* London: Karnac

House, R. and Totton, N. (Eds.) (1997) *Implausible Professions: Arguments for Pluralism and Autonomy in Psychotherapy and Counselling.* Ross-on-Wye: PCCS Books

Jenkins, P. (2001) Supervisory responsibility and the law. In S. Wheeler and D. King (Eds.) *Supervising Counsellors: Issues of Responsibility* (pp. 22–40). London: Sage

Jenkins, P. (2007) Supervisors in the dock?: Supervision and the law. In K. Tudor and M. Worrall (Eds.) *Freedom to Practise, Volume II: Developing Person-Centred Approaches to Supervision* (pp. 176–94). Ross-on-Wye: PCCS Books

Keys, S. (1999) The person-centred counsellor as an agent of human rights. *Person-Centred Practice, 7*(1), 41–47

King, D. (2001) Clinical responsibility and the supervision of counsellors. In S. Wheeler and D. King (Eds.) *Supervising Counsellors: Issues of Responsibility* (pp. 7–21). London: Sage

Lewis, T., Amini, F. and Lannon, R. (2000) *A General Theory of Love.* New York: Vintage

Lockett, M. (2001) The responsibilities of group supervisors. In S. Wheeler and D. King (Eds.) *Supervising Counsellors: Issues of Responsibility* (pp. 153–67). London: Sage

Mearns, D. (1997) *Person-Centred Counselling Training.* London: Sage

Mowbray, R. (1995) *The Case Against Psychotherapy Registration: A Conservation Issue for the Human Potential Movement.* London: Transmarginal Press

Natiello, P. (1990) The person-centered approach, collaborative power, and cultural transformation. *Person-Centered Review, 5*(3), 268–86

Parker, I. (1999) *Deconstructing Psychotherapy.* London: Sage

Proctor, B. (1988) Supervision: A co-operative exercise in accountability. In M. Marken and M. Payne (Eds.) *Enabling and Ensuring.* Leicester: Leicester National Youth Bureau/Council for Education and Training in Youth and Community Work

Rogers, C.R. (1967) A process conception of psychotherapy. In *On Becoming a Person* (pp. 125–59). London: Constable. (Original work published in 1958)

Rogers, C.R. (1969) *Freedom to Learn.* Columbus, OH: Charles E. Merrill

Rogers, C.R. (1978) *Carl Rogers on Personal Power.* London: Constable

Spence, S. (2006, August) The amateur supervisor: Supervision as an offer of love. *Person-Centred Quarterly,* pp. 1–6

Tudor, K. (1998) Value for money? Issues of fees in counselling and psychotherapy. *British Journal of Guidance and Counselling, 25*(4), 447–53.

Tudor, K. and Worrall, M. (2004) Person-centred philosophy and theory in the practice of supervision. In K. Tudor and M. Worrall (Eds.) *Freedom to Practise: Person-Centred Approaches to Supervision* (pp. 11–30). Ross-on-Wye: PCCS Books

United Nations. (1948) *Universal Declaration of Human Rights.* New York: UN

Webb, A. (2001) Expecting the impossible? What responsibility do counsellors expect their supervisors to take? In S. Wheeler and D. King (Eds.) *Supervising Counsellors: Issues of Responsibility* (pp. 179–92). London: Sage

Wheeler, S. (2001) Supervision of counsellors working independently in private practice: What responsibility does the supervisor have for the counsellor and their work? In S. Wheeler and D. King (Eds.) *Supervising Counsellors: Issues of Responsibility* (pp. 110–29). London: Sage

Wheeler, S. and King, D. (Eds.) (2001) *Supervising Counsellors: Issues of Responsibility* London: Sage

CHAPTER FOUR

USING APPRECIATIVE INQUIRY IN PERSON-CENTRED SUPERVISION

JULIE BARNES

If you believe in the individual, then the words that flow will reflect that. If you are focusing on the positive, then the words will flow from that source as well. If you are looking to shift attention from what is not working to what is working and what can work, then words will flow that support such forward movement. (Torres, 2001, p. 20)

You can still 'solve problems', you are simply using a different technique. Even better news, this technique promises to be faster, more direct and creates a great deal more joy, aliveness and motivation along the way. (Torres, 2001, p. 21)

INTRODUCTION

- What is working well? What are you proud of? How can you create more of that?
- What problems are you having? What went wrong? How can you avoid that in future?

These are all legitimate questions, but do you notice a difference between them? How do you respond to them? If the initial questions we ask are fateful in setting the direction, tone, energy and context for our conversations, which questions are more likely to encourage us to discuss our counselling practice with enthusiasm and honesty?

Questions which invite us to reflect on our achievements rather than our problems are central to an approach to strengths-based change called Appreciative Inquiry (AI). With roots in organisational development and action research, it is variously viewed as a methodology for achieving change and a philosophy for life based on a clear set of principles. Its basic premise is 'to find out what works and figure out ways to do more of it' (New and Rich-New, 2003 p. 1). It offers a powerful and creative way for individuals, groups and organisations to learn from their successful experiences and to build on these in developing their future practice.

As a person-centred counsellor, Appreciative Inquiry facilitator and newly qualified supervisor, I am interested in the potential to learn from our successes, rather than our mistakes, by using 'appreciative' questions and this innovative approach. Are the principles, methods and questions of Appreciative Inquiry helpful in person-centred supervision? If so, how and when can we integrate them effectively into supervision practice? This chapter explores these questions using personal and professional examples from my supervision practice. They are questions I have discussed with colleagues in different contexts and their contributions have influenced my thinking, practice and writing.

WHAT IS APPRECIATIVE INQUIRY?

Definitions

> **Appreciate** (1) Valuing; the act of recognising the best in people or in the world around us; affirming past and present strengths, successes, and potentials; perceiving those things that give life (health, vitality, excellence) to living systems. (2) increasing in value. Synonyms: valuing, prizing, esteeming and honouring.
>
> **Inquire** (1) Exploration and discovery. (2) asking questions; being open to seeing new potentials and possibilities. Synonyms: discovery, search, systematic exploration, study.
>
> *Box 4.1 Appreciative Inquiry—definitions (from Cooperrider and Whitney, 2001)*

Appreciative Inquiry is a strengths-based, co-operative approach to creating change for individuals and organisations. It engages people with what already works well in their experience and helps them to build on this for the future. Participants are invited to recall the times when they or their situation was at its best and to identify the circumstances or conditions which created this. Working with others, they turn their stories and understandings into a shared vision and plan for the future.

Appreciative Inquiry seeks to discover and connect to those things that 'give life' to people, organisations and human systems when they are most alive, effective and healthy. It is founded on the assumption that inquiry into, and conversation about, strengths, successes, values, hopes and dreams triggers life-affirming change, and that 'human systems grow in the direction of what they persistently ask questions about' (Cooperrider and Whitney, 1999, p. 248).

Core Assumptions and Principles of Appreciative Inquiry

As the practice of AI has evolved, so have its core assumptions about the world and its underlying principles. For example, it assumes that:

- in every human situation something is working;
- reality is created in the moment and that there are multiple realities;
- what we focus on becomes our reality;
- the language we use shapes our reality;
- the act of asking questions influences the outcomes in some way;
- people have more confidence going into the unknown future when they carry forward parts of the known past; and
- if we carry parts of the past into the future, they should be those parts that represent what is best about the past.

These assumptions provide the theoretical base for Appreciative Inquiry and are implicit in its success. In developing AI theory and practice, social construction and the power of image-positive action are two of five key underlying principles (see Box 4.2).

Using Appreciative Inquiry

AI is used in different ways to suit the circumstances and interests of those involved in the inquiry. It has been used with multinational businesses, involving hundreds of people across the world; with non-governmental organisations in developing countries; in local communities and schools; with small groups and teams; and with individuals for coaching and personal development. The Appreciative Inquiry Commons website (www.appreciativeinquiry.case.edu) lists case studies and stories

> **Social construction**—Words create worlds. The language we use to describe ourselves and our experiences shapes our view of the world. Words determine what we know and how we know it.
> **Simultaneous**—Inquiry is intervention and creates change. The seeds of change are planted in the first questions we ask and the stories we are inspired to tell.
>
> **Poetic**—The world is an open book and the story is being co-authored continually by us all. All material is useful for learning and we can choose what we study. Telling our stories is a powerful source of learning.
> **Anticipatory**—Images inspire action. We move in the direction of our images of the future.
>
> **Positive**—Positive questions lead to positive change. Momentum is generated through questions that amplify and connect us to our positive core. Research and AI experience show a tendency for humans to turn toward positive images that give them energy and fulfilment.
>
> Box 4.2 Principles of Appreciative Inquiry (adapted from Cooperrider and Whitney, 1999)

of its application in various situations, many reporting startlingly successful outcomes.

For example, the Women's Empowerment Project (WEP) in Nepal used an AI-based empowerment literacy, savings, and village banking curriculum with 125,000 women in 6,500 economic groups. The project recorded a remarkable fourfold increase in the number of women with their own small businesses and an eightfold increase in their sales. The major factor, in the judgement of field staff explaining this phenomenon, was the sharing of success stories among women. Today, over a year after funding and direct support for these economic groups has ceased, the women themselves have created between 800 and 1,000 new economic groups with perhaps 20,000 women, largely using the sharing of success stories as their chosen method (Odell, 2005).

While commercial organisations measure success in financial terms, other groups and organisations seek it for people and relationships. AI projects consistently report positive and sustained outcomes, including greater harmony and collaborative working; more connection between people through developing relationships; increased motivation and enthusiasm; greater personal empowerment and responsibility. For some, AI enhances self-esteem and self-expression: 'Appreciative Inquiry helped me to express myself, and helped me learn to communicate in a better way. It helped me become more of who I've always been' (Renee Chavez, in Whitney and Trosten-Bloom, 2003, p. 234). These authors observe that once people have experienced this powerful expression, they are 'permanently transformed'.

How Appreciative Inquiry works

Whatever the situation, AI loosely follows five distinct stages within the following framework. The collaborative work always begins with reflection on, or conversation about, appreciative questions. The following model outlines the cycle (see Figure 4.1).

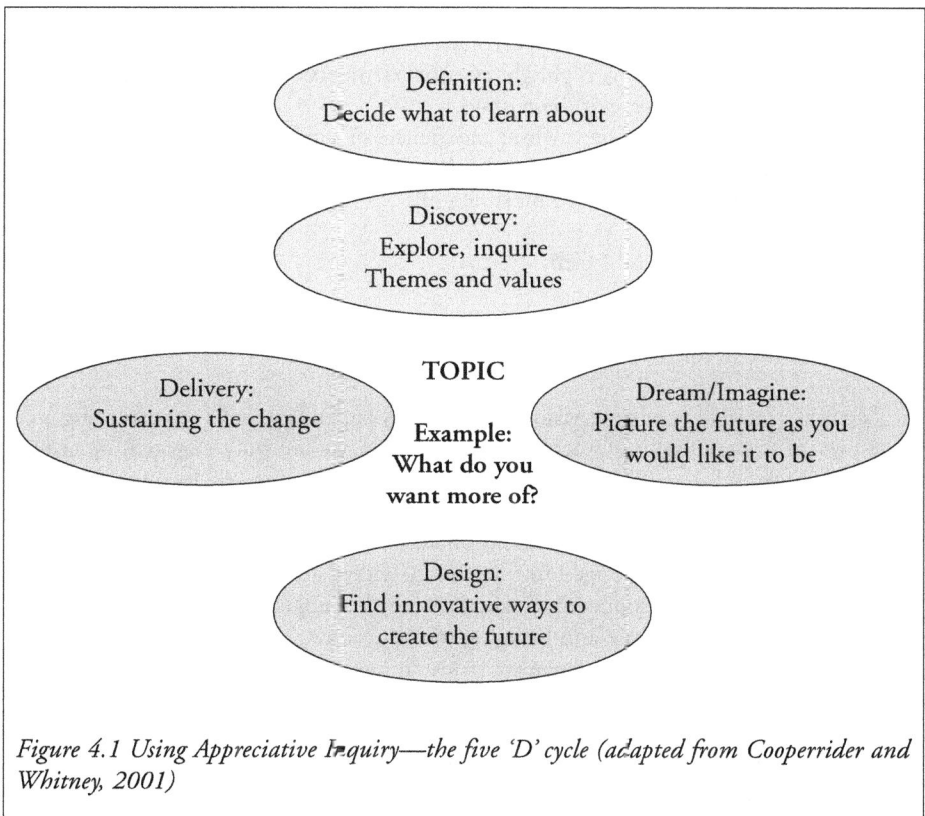

Figure 4.1 Using Appreciative Inquiry—the five 'D' cycle (adapted from Cooperrider and Whitney, 2001)

The following example demonstrates how these stages can be used to develop thinking and practice. In Box 4.3 I have used AI to explore and create my new supervision practice. While AI works best when shared with others, it is also effective for individual reflection.

This example illustrates the overall AI model and the activities involved at each stage of the five 'D' cycle. The approach helps me to think creatively about myself as a supervisor and to develop my practice from my own best experiences and beliefs about excellent supervision. The experience itself is stimulating and joyful and the outcome is grounded in my own experience and capabilities. It leaves me with powerful images and symbols with which to reconnect the feelings, hopes and energy for the future I have imagined and have now created.

Definition—Deciding what to learn and inquire about
Identify the inquiry focus or topic, ensuring that this is something you want more of.
Becoming the best supervisor I can be.

Discovery—Exploring, inquiring
Engage in reflection or conversation using specifically crafted appreciative questions to recall times when you have experienced the inquiry topic at its best. Through reflection and story-telling, highlight essential elements of these experiences which represent the positive core of these times.
Doing this alone I reflect on my best experiences of supervision in the past—what makes them so memorable and what I value about them:
When have I found supervision most helpful?
What was happening?
What did I do? What did I feel?
What was my supervisor doing?
What do I value most about this experience?
What do I wish for myself as a supervisor?

My best experiences of supervision are when my supervisor and I are exploring an aspect of my counselling practice together; when we are fully engaged, open to possibilities and making sense of what we are both reflecting and learning. We are mutually involved in this inquiry and both making full use of our respective skills, knowledge and experience in an atmosphere of constructive goodwill and trust. I feel supported and encouraged to think more widely about possibilities, knowing that I am being held supportively and will not be judged. My supervisor works alongside me, trusting me and bringing into the conversation ideas, theories and information which may challenge me to see things in a different way.

Dream/imagine—Picturing the possibilities
Work together to share and envision ideas for the future and use creative methods (pictures, collage, poems, skits, songs) to communicate how the future would look if it contained all the essential elements of this positive core. This is chance to give full rein to our imagination and to 'dream' about being the best that we can be.
For me, the image of a Tibetan singing-bowl symbolises being held supportively; creating a rich, open space in which to learn and develop alongside my supervisor. What we create together sounds like the hum of the bowl—it is solid, beautiful, and resonates deeply and harmoniously. Drawing this and later buying my own Tibetan bowl, helps me to fix in my mind both the image and what it symbolises. Staying with the image and the sounds of the bowl helps me to imagine how I will feel when I offer this to my supervisees. It enables me to feel deeply what this might be like for me and for them. I can swiftly recall the positive core of excellent supervision and what I would like to create as a supervisor: a supportive and challenging environment.

> **Design—Finding innovative ways to make it happen**
> Translate the symbols and dreams into verbal statements about the future which are punchy, focused, stretching and written in the present tense. Continue reflection and conversation about what needs to be done to make this actually happen. Now the imagined ideal becomes rooted in reality. What structures, people and relationships are important in making this future a reality? How might they need to change?
> For example, I will offer a stimulating and supportive environment, encouraging supervisees to be the best that they can be and helping them to build on their strengths. I think about how to provide that kind of support to others. What will it look like and how will I know?
> How do I present myself as a supervisor? Which words do I use to communicate my approach and my position in relation to ethical and professional boundaries? What might supervisees be expecting and what kinds of conversations might we have in order to establish how we will work together?
> I produce a leaflet to summarise my beliefs about and approach to supervision, possibly using some of the images and statements generated through this inquiry.
>
> **Delivery—Sustaining the change**
> *Invite people to identify and commit to taking specific actions in order to create what they have envisioned and planned. Sometimes called 'destiny', this phase is regarded as inevitable—people will start to create what they have invested in so meaningfully—and the changes need to be nurtured and supported.*
>
> I invite supervisees to say what they are looking for in supervision and together we create a mutual agreement about how we will work together.
>
> I hold an appreciative attitude to my supervisees and to what they bring; seek the positive core of any given situation; find ways to build on strengths and on what is working well. I use appreciative questions to focus our discussion on supervisees' strengths and help them to build on these.
>
> *Box 4.3 Developing my supervision practice with Appreciative Inquiry*

While it works in individual reflection, AI is essentially a collaborative model used most effectively with others. Through the sharing of stories and collaborative working it helps participants create something new, which is firmly rooted in their own previous experiences, and then to build on what they already know. The process is deeply personal: as participants recall the feelings and facts that give the topic life or energy, the envisioning and planning stages turn this experience into something tangible for the future. Overall, this is an energising experience based on hopeful and inspiring conversations. It combines words, feelings and pictures very powerfully and leads to a lasting investment in the outcome.

So what has all this to do with supervision?

If supervision is about learning and improving our counselling practice, then we have choices about how we do this and how we provide it as supervisors. As well as having great experiences in supervision, for me there have been times when it has felt like a confessional where I bring my mistakes, concerns and blunders to be picked over and examined. When I focus on my problems and the things that didn't go well, I can easily feel like a failure and be defeated by recurring themes in my practice. Colleagues have reported feeling judged or criticised by their supervisors, and described how difficult they found it to learn in these circumstances.

Annis Hammond (1998) notes that 'we are very good at talking about what doesn't work. By paying attention to problems, we emphasize and amplify them' (p. 6). According to Cooperrider and Whitney (2001), 'problem solving approaches to change are painfully slow ... rarely result in new vision [and] are notorious for generating defensiveness' (p. 23). AI brings a new perspective in which I can learn from my successes as well as my mistakes. In reflecting on both, I can draw on my own knowledge and experience in a way that increases rather than decreases my confidence and empowers me to be more, not less, creative. In having a good experience while doing so, I am more likely to go back to my practice with renewed enthusiasm and motivation.

In reflecting on how to make use of this approach in person-centred supervision, I started by exploring some of the similarities and differences between AI and person-centred theory.

Supervision as collaborative inquiry

The approaches share common principles including the intention to develop mutual, collaborative relationships for shared inquiry; addressing universal human needs for connection and relationship; providing facilitative conditions for learning, growth and change; and a shared concern with personal and collective empowerment and responsibility (Barnes, 2006).

Merry (1999, p. 140) makes a useful connection in his description of person-centred supervision as 'collaborative inquiry' in which:

> two people (the supervisor and the counsellor) collaborate or cooperate in an effort to understand what is going on within the counselling relationship and within the counsellor. This moves the emphasis away from 'doing things right or wrong' (which seems to be the case in some approaches to supervision) to 'how is the counsellor being and how is

that way of being contributing to the development of a counselling relationship based on the core conditions?'

In such a relationship, both people are self-directed and contribute equally to the process. All forms and sources of knowledge are regarded as legitimate, each has a valid perspective to bring and joint evaluations are made. 'The supervisor can be perceived as a "co-worker" able to offer expertise, knowledge and experience in the pursuit of deeper understanding rather than as a judge or police officer' (ibid., p. 141).

Merry concludes that the supervisor may ask more questions than might be the case in more traditional models, aimed at fulfilling his/her main concerns 'to clarify and understand how this counsellor is experiencing his relationships with his clients, and what sense or meaning he is making from those experiences' (ibid., p. 146). In this way, person-centred supervision:

> provides opportunities for supervisees to experience a relationship that is free of threat, and is supportive and understanding so that they can explore non-defensively what the counselling process means to them and how they experience themselves in relationship with their clients. (Ibid., p. 140)

Anderson (2001), in a draft paper published on her website (www.harleneanderson.org), compares her particular form of collaborative therapy with that of Carl Rogers. She concludes that, among many similarities, her challenge has been to ask 'how can therapists create the kinds of conversations and relationship with their clients that allow both parties to access their creativities and develop possibilities where none seemed to exist before? (p. 4). She considers her approach to be more 'active' than Rogers', engaging in 'a dialogical conversation' where people 'talk with rather than to each other' (p. 5). Engaging in a shared inquiry:

> The therapist tentatively offers her voice, including questions, comments, thoughts and suggestions as simply food for thought and dialogue. Tentatively does not refer to being timid or hesitant. It refers to the notion that the therapist's intent is to invite and facilitate collaborative relationship and dialogical conversations, not to impose, directly or indirectly, notions about what a client should be talking about, how they should be talking or how they should be living. (p. 7)

Anderson's (2000, p. 7) aim is to 'promote dialogue in which possibilities can emerge' and, applying this to supervision, she reports that supervisees find this collaborative, non-hierarchical model of supervision to be 'refreshing' compared to models in which they feel 'intimidated and judged' (1997, p. 4).

WORKING WITH THE DIFFERENCES BETWEEN AI AND THE PERSON-CENTRED APPROACH

Where AI and person-centred theory differ most clearly is in relation to the AI focus on the positive and in its application as a structured, if flexible, method. These two areas have proved the most challenging in integrating the two approaches in my practice.

Focusing on the positive

Rogers encourages us to value and accept all aspects of our feelings and experience rather than labelling them as positive or negative. Accepting our clients, supervisees and ourselves in all their and our triumphs and messiness is fundamental in providing a non-judgemental relationship in which we can learn and grow.

It is a clear AI principle to start from the positive core of how we feel when things are going well, to seek what gives life and energy to human systems, and to use this energy to motivate and inspire participants to move forward. It deliberately 'involves the art and practice of asking unconditional positive questions that strengthen a system's or person's capacity to heighten positive potential' (Cooperrider and Whitney, 1999, p. 248).

However, this is not to deny or ignore problems or what might be considered negative feelings or experiences, but to find ways of approaching them differently. As Thomas H. White, the President of GTE Telephone Operations said vividly in 1996 about AI: 'I'm not advocating mindless happy talk. We can't ignore problems, we just need to approach them from the other side.' (reported in Cooperrider and Whitney, 2005, p. 5). Kelm (2006, p. 7) indicates that:

> it is not the negative feelings themselves that we attempt to change in thinking appreciatively, it is the way we make sense of them and attach to them. We learn to find and appreciate the inherent learning and guidance they provide, and move on.

In working with both approaches, I aim to accept unconditionally the experience and feelings of supervisees, *and* to encourage them to work towards those experiences which give them life and energy. This is not about ignoring problems or mistakes, but taking from them what can be learned and finding ways to move towards desirable options. It may involve refocusing dilemmas and issues to identify what we want more of in any situation. Even the articulation of problems and mistakes can be understood in terms of the shortfall they represent—if we think there is a problem, we must have a notion of what it would be like if it were different. Refocusing the conversation can be extremely powerful in helping supervisees to visualise and move towards the practice they desire, rather than reducing or eliminating a specific aspect of their practice. As I integrate this into my practice, I appreciate all of our experiences and aim to take the best forward into the future.

A place for structure?

The other dilemma is when to offer this and how to do it in a way which respects a supervisee's own process. Is such a methodical approach compatible with working alongside an individual, however flexibly it is applied? I am wary of 'techniques', notwithstanding Rogers' (1957/1990, p. 233) view that a technique 'may serve as a technical channel by which the essential conditions of therapy are fulfilled'. I have found different ways of working with this, following my usual practice of offering possibilities and letting them go if they are not useful in the moment. Within supervision, I have done this in different ways. Occasionally, for example, I ask appreciative questions; bring an 'appreciative focus' to our conversation, and follow the AI methodology as described in the example of working with Sarah, which follows.

Asking appreciative questions

Appreciative questions 'encourage people to share peak experiences, values, hopes and dreams and elicit stories, experiences and aspirations that generate connections'. The act of asking and answering positive questions 'generates constructive thinking and action and offers direction to further dialogue and planning' (Miller et al., 2004 p. 14).

Introducing an appreciative question to a conversation in supervision can be powerful. This might involve asking the supervisee to say what she felt had gone well, what she was most proud of or what stood out for her in a particular piece of practice. Working with these 'highlights' or peak experiences creates a new perspective. It might also be useful to question what the supervisee most values and appreciates about her client or their relationship; and about what she herself has done. Again, this can shift thinking. Finally, asking a supervisee what she would like more of, what she would like to happen, and how the situation would look if everything were as she wished it to be, is a powerful way to harness future direction.

Questions like these are powerful and empowering ways to demonstrate that:

- supervisees are their own experts; who
- can learn from their past successes;
- can generate knowledge by sharing; and
- can use those successes to co-create future action or intentions.

As a supervisor, using questions like these:

- demonstrates that you value and appreciate both the supervisee and his experience;
- demonstrates trust in the supervisee;
- enables supervisees to talk about difficult things in a positive way;
- contributes to the mutual partnership of co-creating and learning; and
- initiates an exciting conversation.

There may be times when asking such questions will be inappropriate and insensitive; particularly where they cut across an experience or unhelpfully interrupt someone's thinking or feelings. Yet, at times where the supervisee is stuck, and even in the most serious situations, I believe there is room for this perspective. Anderson (2001, p. 8) comments that what is critical is the expression in 'intention, manner, timing and tentativeness. It is not a matter of whether there are thoughts or content that a therapist should or should not speak about, rather it is how, when and why they do it.'

Bringing an appreciative focus

This may be another aspect of what Rogers called 'prizing' the client. I think of it as something additional: holding an 'appreciative focus'. An appreciative focus does not mean that we ignore or deny the configurations of our selves or our feelings that are less acceptable to us. It means that we can appreciate them and allow them to have a voice—providing a space in which to let our anger, hurt or sadness be seen and heard. In searching for what gives life to a person, situation or organisation, everything matters and contributes to the inquiry.

As my AI practice has developed, 'being appreciative' has become as much a part of my way of being as have the principles of the person-centred approach. It is a way of living in which I look for the best in situations, appreciate my whole experience—even the hard bits—and focus on what I want to create, rather than wish to reduce. As a supervisor, I appreciate the people I am working with and the experiences that they bring. The conversations we have, the questions we ask and the words we use really matter in creating the changes we want to see.

In my experience, these principles are true for individuals, groups and whole organisations. Alongside my person-centred values, they add a new dimension, energy, and life force to conversations, whether that is for therapeutic discovery or for personal, social or professional development. Certainly, they don't seem to take anything away from the recipient, or from my professional integrity as a supervisor.

Applying the AI methodology

The AI stages (the '5D' cycle) described earlier in this chapter are used flexibly in different inquiries. While the whole process may be too formal or extended for individual supervision, it has some potential for use by groups or in team meetings. Supervision groups, in particular, may enjoy the collaborative emphasis and find it a stimulating and challenging way of working.

Using AI in supervision—a case example

During a meeting of my supervision group, we used AI in a discussion led by a colleague who was having difficulties at work. We used the generic AI questions to frame a one-to-one conversation, followed by a discussion in which everyone in the group participated. This is a facilitated group which works collaboratively to discuss and explore a wide range of professional issues and topics.

Here is the story of what happened set in the AI framework to illustrate the process. I have given my colleague another name for this account. She gave me permission to write about our work together and her comments on the experience are included below.

Immediate observations
Sarah's immediate feedback was that she felt able to speak of this difficult situation, even though she had almost decided not to because it was so depressing and her energy for it was low. Having a differently framed conversation helped her to talk about the situation in a way that she hadn't expected (i.e. positively) and increased her awareness of what was important to her amid the turmoil she was describing and feeling. She said she enjoyed our discussion and didn't feel unheard, cut across, directed or led by it.

I learnt that the focus of the first question is really important; if the story about best experience is too far from the current experience it can feel like too huge a gap to bridge. On the other hand it still generated positive energy and seemed to have had positive outcomes for Sarah.

AI CYCLE	KEY ELEMENTS	SARAH'S STORY
Define/ Focus	*Where are you now? What do you want more of?*	Sarah is a counsellor working in a public sector counselling service. A year ago, the team was functioning well. There was an open, supportive environment, in which ideas were listened to and taken up by the team manager. Since then, a new manager had been appointed and the atmosphere in the team had changed. Sarah described a new culture of fear and mistrust among the team members. They are not supporting each other in the same way, decisions are taken without discussion and it feels like a less safe environment for her. Some responsibilities have been taken away from her with no consultation or explanation and Sarah feels slighted and demoralised. She wanted to talk about her situation in the supervision group but was feeling depressed about it and had almost decided that she would rather not discuss it at all. However, she agreed to experiment using Appreciative Inquiry. This began as a one-to-one conversation and then became a group discussion. The whole session lasted for approximately forty-five minutes.
Discover/ Explore	*Best times, value, wishes— seek the positive core of the inquiry topic*	Three appreciative questions: *Tell me a story about your best experience when the team was functioning so well last year.* Response: The team was open, sharing and positive. It was a safe environment with trusting colleagues. Sarah described how she had taken her baby to the office to meet her colleagues—people with whom she had worked during her pregnancy. She felt safe and comfortable with them, fed her baby there and enjoyed passing her around to colleagues. *What is it you value about your work as a counsellor?* Response: Working and being alongside the clients in their development, helping them to grow, working with good colleagues that I trust in an equal way.

AI cycle	Key elements	Sarah's story
		If you had three wishes for this team now, what would they be? Response: 1. The new manager would be replaced by someone who is much more open. 2. There would be no backbiting and there would be a return to openness and a supportive environment. 3. I would look forward to going to work again. *Discussion about positive core* The whole group then joined in a discussion about the positive core from our conversation. We identified the following themes and elements of the team at its best to understand more of what Sarah values about her work: • Collaboration • Openness • Sharing • Trust between colleagues • Ideas welcomed and discussed • Shared authority
Dream/ Imagine	*Wishes/dream for ideal future*	In the final part of the conversation Sarah had described her wishes for the team and what it would be like if things could be the way she wanted. Even in that short time, our conversation had highlighted how good her team had been a year ago and the ways in which it had changed. In some respects this served to emphasise her despair about the situation. Perhaps we could have focused the first question more specifically on what was still positive about the team.
Design/ Plan/ Create	*What's possible and who cares? Where are you now? What (small) steps can you take? Statement of intentions*	Through further discussion, we explored Sarah's sense of the loss of the team she had once loved and her current feelings of powerlessness to change the situation. In focusing on her emotional response to current events it became apparent that this was not a situation she felt willing to continue with. However, she was unwilling to challenge the team manager openly because of a previous negative experience of 'whistle-blowing' in the team.

AI cycle	Key elements	Sarah's story
		At the end of the discussion Sarah had not decided what to do but had nevertheless appreciated the conversation and the chance to clarify some of the issues and their impact for her. In debriefing the experience, she said that she had enjoyed having a 'differently framed' conversation and the opportunity to explore her feelings in a positive way.
Deliver/ Action	*Take action*	There was a three-week gap between group meetings. When we reconvened, Sarah told us that she had appreciated the previous session and updated us on what had happened since.
Review/ Define	*Where are you now? What was the best of what happened? What do you want more of?*	Between the sessions, Sarah had: • asked the Service Director why responsibilities had been reallocated. She was amazed to be told that he was very impressed by her work and regarded her as one of the most competent members of the team. She had expected to be admonished and was astonished at this positive feedback. The reasons for redirecting the work were quite unconnected with competence. • identified who in the team she felt comfortable with and made a point of spending more time with them. • asked for, and been given, funding to undertake some further training during the coming year. This was arranged quickly; she had already started the course and was feeling very excited about it. • While things at work continued to be difficult, Sarah was feeling more positive about herself and the situation. She said she had taken back her own power in the situation. The manager's feedback had restored her confidence and the training was increasing her opportunities of working differently or leaving the team if necessary. • She was feeling more positive and in control of the situation.

Box 4.4 Using AI in Supervision—a case example

Reflections

Reflecting on this experience with the supervision group helped me to clarify the similarities and differences between AI and a person-centred approach to supervision, and to consider further the potential contribution of AI. In a more traditionally person-centred supervision discussion I might not have asked direct questions, or I might have asked no questions at all. I would have stayed more closely in Sarah's present experience and we would probably have spent longer processing her loss and feelings of despair at the situation. I would have stayed alongside her rather than directing the conversation.

By using AI, the discussion was genuinely positive and upbeat when she talked about the team as it had been. In turn, this highlighted the dissonance between then and now and sharpened her sense of loss. We stayed with her feelings about this and reflected together on how this was affecting her both emotionally and physically.

Our conversation highlighted the extent to which things had changed; Sarah's sense of loss and powerlessness, and the seeming impossibility of recapturing her enthusiasm and energy for the service. I felt at a loss too and welcomed the rest of the group facilitating further discussion. By focusing on the impact for her personally, the group helped her to acknowledge the loss of the good times with the team, to highlight the things she valued now and her discomfort around the team manager. She recognised that her present unwillingness to make major changes left her feeling 'diminished inside' and 'not acting in line with my good self'. By focusing on the personal Sarah stayed in touch with her own experience and her trusted intuition.

With more time we might have considered some of the questions in more depth and would have spent more time on the dream stage, which might have helped her to think more about what she wanted in the future. Nevertheless, we seemed to have achieved enough to help Sarah to initiate the conversations at work, to take further action and finally reap its rewards. This fits with the AI principles: seeds are sown with the first question and change is inevitable from the start of the conversation. What mattered was that we had the conversation at all.

Where I felt that the two approaches came together was in the way that we conducted this conversation. Rogers believed that individual growth and change will be achieved if the therapist can create and hold specific conditions, centring on empathy, congruence and unconditional positive regard, or acceptance for all aspects of that person. I was holding these conditions in the way that we talked, and the appreciative nature of the conversation added a further dimension—releasing Sarah's positive energy to have the conversation and to reflect constructively on her situation.

This was confirmed by subsequent feedback from Sarah about our work together:

> The session with you was a positive experience and at no point felt intrusive—quite the contrary, it gave me energy/impetus at a time when I was feeling overwhelmed by the situation. The questions you posed were certainly pertinent; however, ultimately, I felt it was how you presented yourself, with warmth and genuineness, rather than the questions per se that enabled me to move forward.

CONCLUSION

As a person-centred counsellor and supervisor with a passion for Appreciative Inquiry, it has been fascinating to explore ways of bringing these two approaches together in counselling supervision. Wary of extraneous techniques, I have been cautious in introducing AI with counselling clients. Supervision offers greater scope for using this approach, when there is a clearer, mutual agenda for reflecting and learning. So, for example, a supervision group or team might choose to work through all five AI stages to explore a topic or support a particular change. However, simply asking appreciative questions of supervisees can reinvigorate a tired or difficult conversation and, in a supportive environment, can free the supervisee to explore with more creativity, enthusiasm and energy.

Whitney (2003, p. 20) describes six reasons why AI is so powerful:

- it builds relationships, enabling people to be known in relationship rather than in a role;
- it creates an opportunity for people to be heard;
- it generates opportunities for people to dream and to share their dreams;
- it creates an environment in which people are able to choose how they contribute;
- it gives people both discretion and support to act; and
- it encourages and enables people to be positive.

In supervision, the approach also:

- diminishes the role of the supervisor as expert;
- creates a collaborative, shared inquiry;
- releases positive energy and motivation;

- reduces judgement and creates mutual respect; and
- is useful one-to-one and in groups.

Improving our practice by building on what we know works well is a powerful and joyful experience, and an approach from which I have found it impossible to turn back. The more I work appreciatively, the less tolerant I become of deficit-based conversations and traditional attempts to solve problems and fill gaps. Working appreciatively adds a new dimension to my practice, building on what I offer of congruence, empathic understanding and unconditional positive regard, and helping me to value everything that supervisees bring. When I can tap into my own energy and take my learning into future planning and action, I find myself building on solid ground, trusting my instincts and working with greater enthusiasm and confidence. When people do it together, through thoughtful conversations and creative planning, they generate a shared momentum for positive change.

REFERENCES

Anderson, H. (1997) *Conversations, Language and Possibilities: A Postmodern Approach to Therapy*. New York: Basic Books

Anderson, H. (2000) Supervision as a collaborative learning community. *American Association for Marriage and Family Therapy Supervision Bulletin*, 7–10

Anderson, H. (2001) Postmodern collaborative and person-centered therapies: What would Carl Rogers say? www.harleneanderson.org, last accessed 20 July 2007

Annis Hammond, S. (1998) *The Thin Book of Appreciative Inquiry* (2nd edn.). Bend, OR: Thin Book Publishing Co.

Barnes, J. (2006, February) A passionate presence: Appreciating person centred connections. *AI Practitioner*, pp. 29–30

Cooperrider, D.L., Sorensen, P.F., Jr., Yaeger, T.F. and Whitney, D. (Eds.) (2001) *Appreciative Inquiry: An Emerging Direction for Organization Development*. Champaign, IL: Stipes Publishing

Cooperrider, D.L. and Whitney, D. (1999) Appreciative Inquiry: A positive revolution in change. In P. Holman and T. Devane (Eds.) *The Change Handbook* (pp. 245–263). Washington, DC: Berrett-Koehler Publishers Inc.

Cooperrider, D.L. and Whitney D. (2001) A positive revolution in change: Appreciative Inquiry. In D.L. Cooperrider, P.F. Sorensen Jr., T.F. Yaeger and D. Whitney (Eds.) *Appreciative Inquiry: An Emerging Direction for Organization Development* (pp. 5–29). Champaign, IL: Stipes Publishing

Cooperrider, D.L. and Whitney, D. (2005) *Appreciative Inquiry: A Positive Revolution in Change*. San Francisco: Berrett-Koehler Publishers

Kelm, J. (2006, February) Walking the talk: The principles of AI in daily living. *AI Practitioner*, pp. 5–8

Merry, T. (1995) *Invitation to Person-Centred Psychology*. London: Whurr

Merry, T. (1999) *Learning and Being in Person-Centred Counselling*. Ross-on-Wye: PCCS Books

Miller, C.J., Aguilar, C.R., Maslowski, L., McDaniel, D. and Mantel, M.J. (2004) *The Nonprofits' Guide to the Power of Appreciative Inquiry*. Community Development Institute, Denver, Colorado

New, B. and Rich-New, K. (2003) *Looking for the Good Stuff*. Cape Canaveral, FL: Clarity Works

Odell, M. (2005, October 8). *Impacts Before Interventions*. Paper available at www.appreciativeinquiry.cwru/edu, last accessed 8 October 2005

Rogers, C.R. (1990) The necessary and sufficient conditions of therapeutic personality change. In H. Kirschenbaum and V.L. Henderson (Eds.) *The Carl Rogers Reader* (pp. 219–35). London: Constable. (Original work published 1957)

Torres, C.B. (2001) *The Appreciative Facilitator: A Handbook for Facilitators and Teachers*. Maryville, TN: Mobile Team Challenge

Whitney, D. and Trosten-Bloom, A. (2003) *The Power of Appreciative Inquiry, A Practical Guide to Positive Change*. Washington, DC: Berrett-Koehler Publishers Inc.

Part Two

Traditions

Chapter Five

Person-Centred Expressive Supervision

Jenny Bell

In this chapter I illustrate the practice of using expressive therapy in supervision. By way of introduction, I briefly describe what person-centred expressive therapy is. I then discuss how this can be applied in supervision and its especial value in helping when a supervisee feels stuck. In my experience and practice, this approach to supervision is very helpful in the exploration of all aspects of the process of the therapy and the therapeutic relationship, often helping to bring out feelings and connections which are just below the threshold of awareness. Finally, I discuss its application in understanding theoretical models of supervision.

What is person-centred expressive therapy?

This is an approach developed by Natalie Rogers and described fully in her book *The Creative Connection* (N. Rogers, 1993). The whole philosophy and process of person-centred therapy as described by Carl Rogers is unchanged. The uniqueness of the expressive aspect is simply that as therapists—or supervisors—we are not restricted to speech and words but can use other modes of expression such as sculpting, drawing, painting, noise and movement as well.

The person-centred expressive therapist does not need to 'structure' anything. The client knows at the start that they can use any medium to express themselves and that paper, paint and pastels, etc. are to hand if they want them. They are not restricted to using only verbal modes of expression. What Natalie discovered when working in this way was that if we move from one non-verbal mode to another non-verbal mode, our self-awareness seems to deepen significantly. We seem able to access deeper layers of consciousness and then bring them into verbal awareness and expression. She called this process 'the creative connection'.

This can occur naturally in anyone, so you don't have to think about yourself as 'creative' in order to work in this way. It is unfortunate that the Western education system has given so many of us the message that only a few of us are creative. The crushing put-downs of our early attempts at representational art have left many of us believing that we can't draw or that we're not creative. This is not true, of course. Betty Edwards' (1989) seminal work *Drawing on the Right Side of the Brain* is invaluable in showing us how we can all draw. However, this is another issue, as expressive therapy is not about trying to make art. It is simply about using paint and other materials as media of expression. In order to get away from the 'good/bad' judgements about art, it helps to use doodles, blobs of colour, random shaping-clay, arrangements of found objects (pebbles, leaves, petals, bits of paper). Because this is not 'art' and there is no 'right' or 'wrong' way of using these materials, it is easier to focus on both the *process* and the *content* of expression.

What emerges through the *process* of working with non-verbal media is often most important therapeutically. I notice, for instance, that I felt calm while slowly drawing the smooth green lines, and that I was more upset and tearful, stabbing at the paper, when I did the little purple dots. As person-centred therapists *we do not interpret* the images, colours or sounds the client produces any more than we would interpret their words for them. The focus remains on what it means for them.

As a therapist, I sometimes work purely verbally and at other times I work expressively. When working verbally with clients, I find they sometimes use metaphor to express poetically and richly the process they are experiencing. For example, I once had a male client who cried out: 'I want pearls in my cornflakes!' This was a cry from his heart to do with wanting some magic and specialness in his life. He was depressed by the greyness and convention of his life as it was then. On another occasion a client who was used to expressive therapy took some clay and created a small boat which she then filled completely with brightly coloured fallen petals. She explored this, seeing the grey boat as the 'dull little person' she felt she normally was, and the petals as the magic she wanted to bring into her life. Both clients were dealing with similar themes. One worked verbally, and one non-verbally. Neither piece of therapy was better than the other. They were different, and each client went on and worked very productively using the mode of expression most helpful to them.

Person-Centred Expressive Approaches in Supervision

If a supervisee is working using expressive therapy with their clients then it makes a lot of sense to use the same mode in supervision. In this case both supervisor and supervisee will be trained in this approach and will have a shared means of expression. However, it is an approach that can be used with supervisees who may be working in a traditional verbal mode but who are open to using other ways of expressing themselves. It will be important to discuss how the supervisee likes to work and the impact it may have on the supervisory relationship.

One counsellor recounted to me how his supervisor had, every single week at the start of their session, brought out a tray of miniatures (small models of animals, figurines, pebbles, shells, toys. etc.). The supervisor then asked the supervisee: 'Pick one that makes you think of your client and then discuss what this connection means for you in terms of the therapeutic relationship.' The supervisee endured this for some time before being able, one week, to blurt out that he really didn't like doing this and that it got in the way rather than helping him explore his work with his clients. The supervisor was surprised as she had assumed that it would make the supervision more interesting; nevertheless she listened and responded by putting the tray away, and things improved enormously. This is an example of how anything, whether a routine set of questions or a routine requirement to use miniatures can block the supervision process.

Thus, using person-centred expressive approaches in supervision needs to be done as *responsively* as it would be done in therapy. Offering an expressive medium to a supervisee is usually a response to whatever the supervisee is bringing at that moment in that particular supervision session. When I am the supervisee, I sometimes work non-verbally and sometimes verbally. I don't expect to always want to be expressive, but I do find it particularly helpful if I'm feeling stuck or if I want to explore process rather than content—and since the relationship is at the heart of the therapy and the supervision, then exploring process is central, whether it's the client/therapist relationship, the therapist/supervisor relationship, or the fantasy relationship between supervisor and client (see Hawkins and Shohet, 2000). Therapists who want to work mainly with the *content* of their client work may find this approach less useful.

Tudor and Worrall (2004) discuss Rogers' (1958/1967) seven elements of process. They explore how each of these descriptions of process in psychotherapy map directly onto the process of supervision. The first element is 'a loosening of feelings'. They quote Patterson (1968/2000) as arguing that 'the greatest problem in counsellor education … is getting counselling students to reduce the cognitive factor and attend to the affective aspects of the client, his problems and the relationship' (p. 79). Tudor and Worrall (2004) continue:

> If this is so, then anything to enhance the loosening of a practitioner's feelings in relation to his clients will be helpful. We each have experience of working with therapists who have come to supervision describing themselves as 'stuck' in their work with particular clients. In many cases, resolution has come when the therapist has felt safe enough to acknowledge what he feels, about his client, about himself, about their relationship, or about the situation ... Our experience suggests that the act of acknowledging and articulating feelings in supervision is in itself helpful, whether or not a therapist ever then shares those feelings with his client. (p. 24)

My experience is that using expressive means of exploring my work with clients enables me to contact with immediacy my feelings, which are often just below the threshold of awareness. I can then articulate them. It is then much easier to explore the process of the therapy.

Here I report four examples of expressive therapy with different supervisees with different experiences of working expressively. In order to protect confidentiality, I have disguised the identities of supervisor and supervisee and client. All four examples use drawings, as these are more easily incorporated into a one-hour supervision and are more easily shared in print. Other non-verbal means of expression, such as using clay, sound, sculpture are possible.

Expressive supervision with 'John'—Dealing with anger in the therapist/client process

John wanted to explore in supervision the process of his first session with Alicia. He reported:

> I'd just had a great lunch and was feeling cheerful, open and calm—in a good place. As soon as I met this client my first thought was, 'Wow, this is a person of very low spirit and little energy. I must pay very close and quiet attention to be alongside her.'

He gently drew her as a small dot and himself as a big blue dot. He then talked about the client sharing her history of depression (tentative beige bits) and empathy for her (soft blue lines from him to her).

Describing the session with the client, John reported a significant shift having taken place halfway into the session, after the following exchange:

Alicia: *Now there are aspects of my life that I'm not happy with and need to explore.*
John: *Would you like to name them?*

Alicia: *Yes. The main thing is that I've been in a relationship for six years and now it's going sour. My partner has always been there for me and has helped me through my depression. Now he has been diagnosed with chronic anxiety and he says it's pay back time and I've got to look after him. He wants me to be there for him but I feel I'm fading away ... I feel guilty and a little bit angry.*

In supervision, John went on to say that he was then aware of a huge shift in his feelings. He took the pastels and drew vigorously and with considerable force. He drew a solid bottle green line around Alicia (feeling that this other person has closed her off). He said he was suddenly feeling extraordinarily angry with Alicia's partner and angry with Alicia (very bold orange), and also empathic with Alicia (pale blue), and also hugely guilty about his anger towards Alicia (heavy zig-zag line from him to half-way to her). This was a dramatic illustration of the huge shift in the therapist's feelings at this point in the therapy (see Figure 5.1*).

John went on to explore his perceptions of what might be happening at this point:

- Feeling so angry he felt out of touch with the client at that point.
- Feeling that he didn't know the client enough yet to process this with them.
- Feeling guilty for feeling angry and then so cut off from a client he had felt great compassion for.
- Feeling worried that the anger might be all his own (from parallels with his own particular difficulties).
- Being aware of the parallels with his client and anxious about how to explore what this might mean.
- Not yet knowing what this might mean for the therapeutic relationship.

John said that he was glad he had done the drawing. Drawing so vigorously—he had pressed so hard that he broke one of the pastels—helped him to reconnect with the strong feelings he'd had in the session, and this had been important to share and explore, at what also felt a deep level, in the supervision. Thus the *process* of doing the drawing was particularly significant here. John also reported that the *content* of the drawing had helped too. He had come to supervision feeling upset and confused by the strong feelings he'd had in the session. He felt that seeing the whole range of different aspects in the drawing made it somehow safer for him to risk exploring the scary bits.

After more time exploring these, John leaned forward and gently rubbed a small gap in the green circle around the client saying: 'I don't feel so cut off from

---

* Figures 5.1 – 10 and 12 are colour plates between pages 58 and 59.

Alicia now and I'm feeling clearer. I'm interested in the angry feelings but not overwhelmed by them. I can be more in touch with her again now. I'm looking forward to exploring more with her and seeing where she is with this.'

Expressive supervision with 'Anne'—Facilitating a therapist who is stuck

In this session, the counsellor, Anne, wanted to explore her process with a client, Bea, and in particular the huge range of feelings she had about the client and the work they had done so far. Anne is an experienced therapist but was saying, 'I feel stuck and I don't know if what I am doing is useful.' Anne is familiar with expressive therapy so, when I asked whether she would like to draw or use colours to explore her feelings, and also her process, with her client, she readily chose to do this. She then spoke as she drew and the supervisor mainly made reflective comments as she explored. The following snapshots of the session show how the supervision session unfolded. As you look at the pictures keep in mind the same non-judgemental quality you would bring to a supervisee's words: do not interpret them. They mean what they mean to Anne. Also how the pictures built up was (and is) probably more important than the final drawings (see Figures 5.2 and 5.3).

Anne: (Draws black box vigorously) *She's like a black box ... closed off ... manipulative ... frustrating ... I have to work so hard to make any contact ... it's even like a battle ... she sits there but she's not present in the room ... at risk ...* (pause) (draws grey lines moving out) *... then she has 'resting' sessions when she comes and just chats about the week ... superficial ... but she's moving on ...* (draws green lines moving out) *... doing a professional training now ... chats about her pregnancy, breast feeding, new friends she's made ... pushes boundaries, phones me, sends letters, moving on ... I feel so frustrated and used.* (Anne draws vigorous lines.)

Supervisor: *Would you like another piece of paper for your feelings?*

Anne: (Draws red and black spiky bits on new paper) *Yes I would. I'm so frustrated and angry when it feels like she's not doing the work ... and she's invading my space ...* (more pressure on the paper) ... (long breath). (See Figure 5.3)

Anne went on to talk more about the frustration of working with Bea over the past four years. Bea wanted to articulate the abuse she had suffered but was unable to. She seemed to struggle to stay present and then 'rest' in apparently superficial chat. Bea was clear that the therapy was important and attended regularly. She wanted Anne to be the perfect mother and, although Anne resisted and they spoke about this, it was a huge relief to her when Anne inevitably failed her. This occurred when Anne took advice from a consultant specialist in the field and acted on his advice. The advice didn't work and Bea perceived Anne as having let her down. However, this was a relief as she learned she could survive the let-down. It became a valuable experience in their relationship.

Anne: (Draws white circle on the black box gently.) *And I know her core is there and I so want to work with her there ...* (pause ... draws gentle ochre and gold soft lines on her own picture). *And actually I know my working with her about her pregnancy, birth and breastfeeding were not just chat. My tenderness and responsiveness to her as a woman were important for her.* (Draws green lines radiating out.) *I can see that she is moving on and growing, making progress in her life, doing things that she thought would be impossible, making friends, being a mother.* (Draws the face with green mouth and tears running down.) *But there is a huge silent scream and tears she is unable to shed from the abuse she cannot speak about ...* (pause). *And I do have very deep empathy and compassion for her.* (Draws ochre/gold soft lines around both bits of the client, and slowly draws soft white lines around her own picture.) *And I feel a tenderness, a sadness and a warmth in me.* (Anne sits quietly, pauses while she looks at both pictures; looks sad.)

Supervisor: *Do you want to stop or pause here?*

Anne: *No. I can see her colours are not right. I need to do more. I need black paper* (takes a small piece of black paper) ... *a blue flower edged with red ... it's her pain ...* (draws firmly and clearly with bright colours against the black) ... *and it's at the centre still and it's unexpressed and blocked ...* (draws white centre and stem of flower) ... *and the white centre of the flower is her core and it's the good core of her ... the heart of her ... and it's so important I know that's there too* (see Figure 5.4). *And as I look at it now I have come full circle back to her closed off black box, but it's more detailed and rich, and I can be aware of her pain and the full range of my tenderness/compassion, and I know I can continue to be here for her. I feel a release having expressed my frustration. It was helpful too to explore where I can firm the boundaries with her, and it was good to share the whole process and see the richness of it all and have the difficulties acknowledged. I need to hang on in there. It's OK for me to be frustrated sometimes ... and she's done a massive amount in four years ... and I really trust in the core of her. I know what I am doing is useful.*

Anne went on to say that the process of doing this had left her feeling exhausted ('I've really gone deep into four years work in one hour!') and also exhilarated, relieved and clearer about her enthusiasm to continue the work.

Expressive supervision with 'Sophie'—Reviewing the work with a long-term client

Sophie had just finished a one year piece of work with a client and wanted to review the client's journey and the impact the ending was having on her.

Her client Zoë had started therapy in a very cheerful state, wanting to clarify a few issues to enhance her successful career. She arrived promptly every week in a smart business-like grey suit and talked enthusiastically about her rapid rise up the career ladder. Sophie's initial reaction was a sense of darkness and concern (grey lines) but an interest (purple lines) in this person so different to the clients with whom she normally worked. She drew the client as green and yellow (bright and enthusiastic) (see Figure 5.5).

She then drew herself and Zoë, the client, as two figures in what she described as a large yellow enthusiastic circle. As she drew she noticed that she seemed smaller than her client and reflected that she struggled with staying present with her. In the drawing, they sat close together, which felt right, and yet they were not touching. This felt respectful and OK. After a few weeks, Zoë began to explore difficulties in her family, and then there was an unexpected crisis as major problems arose in the family. At the same time she had been promoted and was managing a huge load. She was brought down by the family issues. Sophie noted that there was 'a gold thread of respect' running through the journey, a thread which signified her respect for Zoë's courage and resilience. Zoë was able to re-evaluate her whole lifestyle and avoid breakdown. She became more open and made major life-changing decisions about her career, her family and her partner. Sophie drew an explosion of colours at the end of the journey: 'This is Zoë moving forward—lots of red, yellow, blue, bright colours.' Zoë wanted to end the therapy on this positive note and celebrated her final session with warm thanks to Sophie.

Supervisor: *You said at the start that you wanted to explore the impact that the ending was having on you.*

Sophie: *Yes.* (Picks up colours and another piece of paper and draws rapidly starting with a pink felt-tip pen and using it with lots of pressure to make a bold circle with other colours spraying out from it.) [See Figure 5.6] *The pink is my love for her and the pleasure I feel in her growth and enrichment. I know she has been through some really dark and difficult stuff and the red spots are bits of me, like blood and tears, where I also worked so hard alongside her. Important work. The brown is my sadness that I won't know the rest of her journey—I didn't realise this was so much—and there is a navy band of my continuing concern for her. There are question marks with these and that's my wondering. I guess she ended therapy before I felt ready and that's unusual for me. So I both respect her choice to end now and I still have some concern. And I can see that for her, she's full of energy* (yellow glow) (yellow and pink) *and I'm so glad she's happy. She looks like a rocket taking off. I will miss her a lot and it's OK to let her go. She has made huge changes in her life—very rewarding and satisfying work.*

We then explored these issues a little more and Sophie concluded: 'It was so good to review the therapy like this. I've much more of a sense of completion now and an appreciation of our work together. Now I can see where we've been on the journey as a whole.'

Expressive supervision with 'Lucy', a person-centred expressive therapist
Lucy is a counsellor working with a depressed and fragile young client, Rachael. She was finding person-centred expressive therapy especially helpful with her client who had difficulty expressing herself verbally. Rachael had been exploring the time in her childhood when she first became depressed and she had drawn a picture of a tiny figure seated beneath huge green trees. She was then slowly able to describe to Lucy how she had been forbidden by her parents to talk to anyone about her problems, and how she would walk to a nearby copse of beech trees to sit and find comfort with the big trees. This was a place she could be and could feel safe, looking at the sky through the leaves. Lucy wanted to share in the supervision how moved she had been in enabling the client to unfold a little. She explored her perceptions of the content and the process of her work with the client (see Fig. 5.7).

Lucy then said she would like to draw something and very slowly and carefully coloured in a large green circle (see Figure 5.8).

She then wrote at the side the following:

> time and
> gentle stillness
> being here, now
> leafshine
> poetry
> acceptance

Lucy stared at this quietly for a while. She went on to share how calming and centring this had felt for her. It seemed to express something of how she felt she had been in the process with her client. She also explored parallels for herself in how she felt nature was healing for her. Finally, she pointed out that there seemed to be some parallels with the process of the supervision session in that I, the supervisor, had been quieter than usual and quite still. This exploration of the drawings allowed Lucy to reflect on her client's process, her own process, and the process within supervision. At the end, the supervisor checked whether there were any questions which had not been looked at. Lucy replied with a smile that she wasn't aware of anything then, but that she felt she had said so much more than she was even aware she had known about before.

THINKING IN COLOUR—EXPLORING THEORETICAL MODELS

Using colour is particularly important for my own self-expression and often enters my way of thinking about abstract issues. When I paint my impression of theoretical models I find the process and the outcome (i.e. what I produce) helps my understanding. Many people think abstract thoughts in colour or pictorial form.

If I paint a theoretical model, it brings it to life. It also helps me experience where the gaps are for me and to identify the helpful bits. Thus, I start to get a richer experience of the model and how it fits for me. I did this with Proctor's (1988) functional model of supervision in which she suggests that supervision has formative, restorative and normative functions (see Figure 5.9).

I chose soft colours when I painted this, and felt a great harmony as I painted the three functions. Pink was formative, green was restorative and yellow was normative for me. I felt in tune with each function and its importance for me when supervising or being supervised. They seemed to fit well together and to make a harmonious whole—both the egg shape and my feelings about forming, restoring and norming. Then I realised I needed a bit more 'edge' and a bit more energy in this process. I added red streaks using my nails. (I had used fingers to spread the paint rather than a brush and had thus been literally 'hands on'.) This red captured the energy of my excitement and engagement in supervision more fully. Then I decided to use colours to paint the 'reality' of supervision, or of putting the theory into practice. I took a board and began with brighter tones and it quickly became messy and spontaneous, colourful, tough and sparkly (see Figure 5.10).

I then stuck on some found objects: a cube became my institution; a murky magazine picture became the British Association for Counselling and Psychotherapy—remember, don't interpret! I also added bits of fern fronds to suggest the magic of growth and development in ways that are always new and surprising. All this was done spontaneously and the meanings only became clear for me as I looked at it afterwards and explored it verbally with a colleague. By putting theory into practice I feel moved from function to incorporating aspects of process and context. What looked like a total mess became meaningful to me. I could then relate my picture to the complexity of the seven-eyed model of supervision (Hawkins and Shohet, 2000) (see Figure 5.11). When I painted my interpretation of this model it came out rather differently (see Figure 5.12).

In the first volume of this title, Tudor and Worrall (2004) discuss Hawkins and Shohet's process model. Like them, I saw the original model as somewhat hierarchical (supervisor on top, then therapist, then client) and so I put them all on the same level. When I drew the links between them I discovered that one

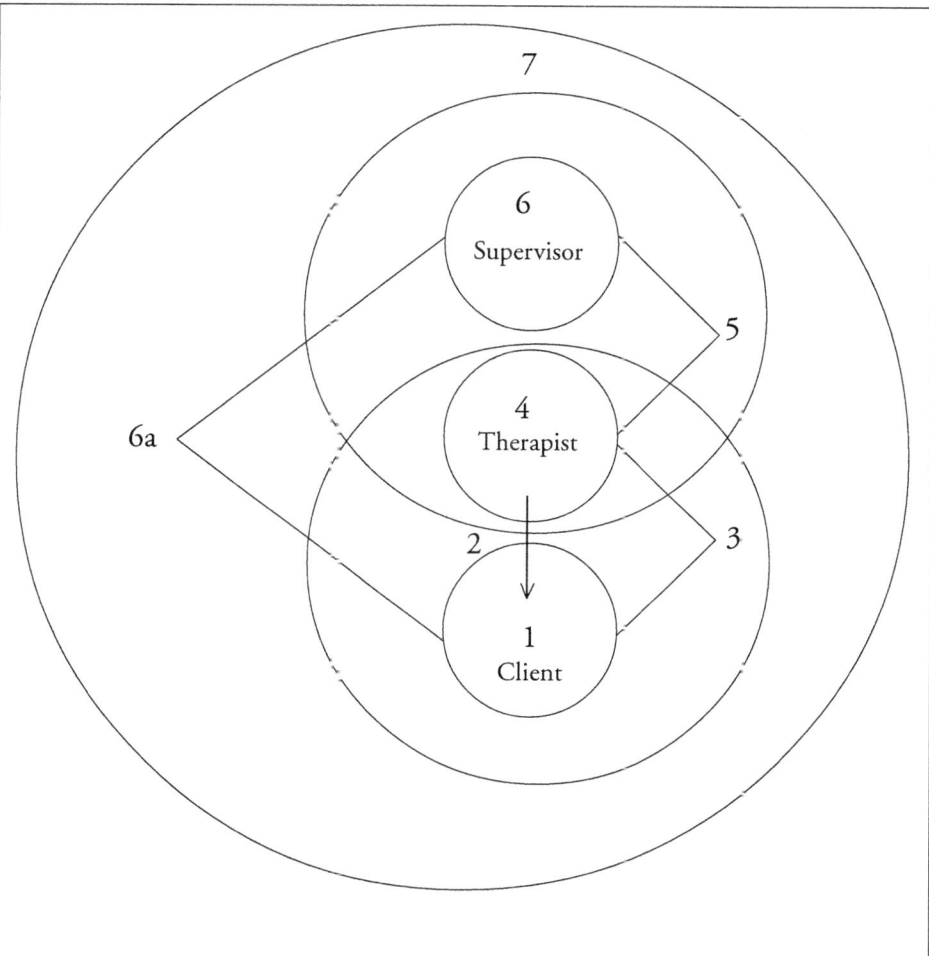

Key:
Mode 1   The content of the therapy session
Mode 2   Focusing on strategies and interventions
Mode 3   Focusing on the therapy relationship
Mode 4   Focusing on the therapist's process
Mode 5   Focusing on the supervisory relationship
Mode 6   Focusing on the supervisor's own process
Mode 6a The (fantasy) supervisor–client relationship
Mode 7   Focusing on the wider context (organisational, professional, economic, social)

Figure 5.11 The seven-eyed model of supervision, 2004 (adapted from Hawkins and Shohet, 2000)

seemed to be missing from the original model. In the original model there is a line between therapist and client representing what Hawkins and Shohet call strategies and interventions. However, there is no similar line between supervisor and therapist. When I came to paint the model I did a very strong line from supervisor to therapist and back again. For me it represents a mutually collaborative engagement. As a supervisee I may come to my supervisor and say: 'I want you to listen to this'; 'I'm feeling stuck and need you to help me explore my stuckness'; 'I'm searching for ideas around X, Y, and Z. What do you think?' or 'I'd be interested to paint the process between me and X and I need you to facilitate this.' I have a sense of mutuality with my supervisor and I find it enormously restorative if she also initiates since it is always clear that I have a choice. This line is my 'eighth eye' to add to the seven-eyed model. I call it 'engagement and interventions' and I draw it as a line with arrows both ways to indicate mutuality in the engagement.

Conclusion

The person-centred expressive approach in supervision enables supervisees to use a variety of non-verbal as well as verbal means of expression. The four examples given above all illustrate different ways in which this has deepened awareness and facilitated the supervision process for these individuals. I have emphasised that it is the process of being expressive (drawing etc.) that is often more important than the final picture or outcome. Having space to explore how they feel while stabbing at the paper or smoothing on the colours can help the supervisee connect with feelings in the therapeutic relationship. Sometimes the final drawing will have significant importance and meaning for the supervisee. Here the skill of the person-centred expressive supervisor will be in staying focused on the meaning and affect for that person. Thus using expressive approaches can be particularly helpful in exploring the therapeutic relationship and process. In the final section I have shared how using expressive drawing has helped me to explore certain models of supervision. One aspect of theory that becomes very clear for me through my drawing is the importance of being fully present and fully engaged in the supervisee/supervisor relationship—this is an active, dynamic, fluid and mutually collaborative relationship.

REFERENCES

Edwards, B. (1989) *Drawing on the Right Side of the Brain: A Course in Enhancing Creativity and Artistic Confidence*. Los Angeles, CA: J.P. Tarcher

Hawkins, P. and Shohet, R. (2000) *Supervision in the Helping Professions* (2nd edn.). Buckingham: Open University

Patterson, C.H. (2000) Is cognition sufficient? In *Understanding Psychotherapy: Fifty Years of Client-Centred Theory and Practice* (pp. 71–9). Ross-on-Wye: PCCS Books. (Original work published in 1968)

Proctor, B. (1988) Supervision A co-operative exercise in accountability. In M. Marken and M. Payne (Eds.) *Enabling and Ensuring*. Leicester: Leicester National Youth Bureau/Council for Education and Training in Youth and Community Work

Rogers, C.R. (1967) A process conception of psychotherapy. In *On Becoming a Person* (pp. 125–59). London: Constable

Rogers, N. (1993) *The Creative Connection and Expressive Arts on Healing*. Palo Alto, CA: Science and Behaviour Books Inc. Republished 2000 by PCCS Books: Ross-on-Wye

Tudor, K. and Worrall, M. (Eds.) (2004) *Freedom to Practise: Person-Centred Approaches to Supervision*. Ross-on-Wye: PCCS Books

CHAPTER SIX

STUDENT-CENTERED SUPERVISION FOR PRE-THERAPY

GARRY PROUTY AND DION VAN WERDE

Pre-Therapy is a way of 'being with' contact impaired clients, such as mentally handicapped, demented, schizophrenic, or traumatized clients, and evolved from the theoretical hints of Carl Rogers (1957) and Fritz Perls (1959). Although Rogers did not develop a Pre-Therapy he pointed the way. He suggested that psychological contact was the *first* condition of a therapeutic relationship and also labelled it a *pre-condition*. Pre-Therapy is, in effect, the theory, practice and science of psychological contact. Its theory and practice are structured in three parts: (1) contact reflections, (2) contact functions, and (3) contact behaviors (Prouty, 1994). The contact reflections refer to the work the therapist does; the contact functions refer to the client's psychological process; and the contact behaviors refer to the measurable aspects of Pre-Therapy (Prouty, Van Werde and Pörtner, 2002).

Since the publication of Prouty's original work on Pre-Therapy in 1976, a number of publications have presented and discussed case material concerning the application of contact reflections (Prouty, 1976, 1990, 2001; Prouty and Kubiak, 1988a, 1988b; Prouty and Pietrzak, 1988; Prouty and Cronwall, 1990; Van Werde, 1990, 1994; Pörtner, 1996; McWilliams and Prouty, 1998; Peters, 1999; Van Werde and Morton, 1999; Zinschitz, 2001; Krietemeyer and Prouty, 2003). However, to date, nothing has been published on the supervision of Pre-Therapy or a Pre-Therapy approach to supervision. This chapter addresses this. By way of an introduction, the first part of the chapter summarizes the basic principles of Pre-Therapy. The second part, written by Garry Prouty, acknowledges Gendlin's student-centered supervision as a significant contribution to the history and development of Pre-Therapy. The majority of Pre-Therapy supervision takes the form of encouraging practitioners to reflect on their practice, in response to which the supervisor takes a supportive and, at times, didactic role. The final part of the chapter describes learnings and reminders from individual applications of Pre-Therapy in the hope and belief that they will be helpful to supervisors of Pre-Therapy practitioners.

PRE-THERAPY

Basic principles

In addition to the basic client-centered attitudes, Pre-Therapy embodies an *ontology* which, consistent with the existential philosophy of Gabriel Marcel, views consciousness as *first and foremost 'being with' a lived experience of presence* (see Koenig, 1992). The second principle to be understood is that the psychotic/brain-damaged organism often symbolizes itself on sub-coherent, pre-expressive levels. The third major principle is the application of non-directive reflections. This is meant as the *empathic* following of the client's process. A case example is offered by Prouty and Kubiak (1988a). The client, diagnosed as retarded and schizophrenic, presented a primary symptom of kissing her erect arm. By the therapist repeatedly reflecting the erect arm, 'Your arm is in the air', the client eventually recovered memories of her mother menacing her arm with a vacuum cleaner as a form of punishment. A fourth principle is that of *concreteness*. In an example, Roy (1991) described the application of contact reflections to a multiple-personality client. Sometimes Roy would literally reflect the position of the client's lips. She would also reflect single words such as 'face', 'dark', 'window', 'cellar door', 'hurt', 'bleeding'. Another concrete reflection of the client's angry face facilitated her getting in touch with another sub-personality.

Contact reflections are used for clients who are often too verbally impaired or psychologically isolated to maintain sufficient communication for a conventional therapeutic relationship. Contact reflections have the theoretical function of developing psychological contact between therapist and client when the therapist *does not grasp the client's frame of reference* (Sommerbeck, 2003). Additionally, contact reflections are extraordinarily concrete to coordinate with the concrete cognitive styles of retarded, schizophrenic and geriatric clients (Prouty, 2003). This enables a more accurate empathic resonance with client expression. In the language of Buber (1964), contact reflections are *'pointing to the concrete'*. This concreteness is manifested in the therapist by a move from a *'listening mode'* to a *'looking mode'*. Traditionally we are taught to listen, but little attention is paid to looking or seeing. We need literally to *look* at the client's situation, the client's face and the client's body to form our reflections as well as listening to the client's verbal expression.

Finally, the issue of '*getting worse before getting better*': Pre-Therapy, because it involves directly processing psychotic content, can open severe pathological reactions very early in the treatment. This early stage can give the impression of '*getting worse*' but is actually a part of processing. The therapist needs to explain this to relevant staff and other carers so they can be prepared, and to parents so they will not become hopeless.

The contact reflections
There are five fundamental contact reflections: situational contact, facial contact, word-for-word contact, bodily contact, and reiterative contact.

Situational reflections (SR)
Existential thinkers, such as Brockleman (1980) often describe humans as being '*in situations*', i.e. concrete manifestations of being in the world. The therapist reflects the client's response to her or his environment, milieu or situation. Examples include: 'John is looking out the window' or 'Mary is sitting on the floor'.

Facial reflections (FR)
Burton (1973) describes the human face as an expressive organ within a phylogenetic context. Facial reflections facilitate the expression of affect. Examples: 'You look sad' or, even more concretely and descriptively, 'There are tears in your eyes'.

Word-for-word reflections (WWR)
Psychotic, retarded and demented clients often present symptoms of incoherence. For example, a client may express 'unintelligible', 'ring', 'unintelligible', 'hat', 'unintelligible', 'mouse'. This makes no sense, but the therapist should reflect the social words.

Body reflections (BR)
The human body can be described as 'bodying forth' (Boss, 1994). This means the body symbolizes itself on a pre-expressive level. For example, schizophrenics often involve themselves in bizarre body posturing such as holding their arms stiffly in the air. The verbal reflection would be: 'Your arm is in the air.' Even more concretely the therapist could reflect by raising their arm.

Reiterative reflections (RR)
These refer to repeating any reflection that succeeds in making contact. There are two types of reiteration: (a) short term, (b) long term. An example of short term would be: A client shows fear in her face; the therapist reflects this; after having reflected other things, the therapist some moments later repeats, 'Just a while ago you looked anxious'. This time the client says 'She scared me'. An example of a long-term reiteration would be: the girl repeatedly points at her stomach for a least half the session. Each time, this pointing is reflected. During the next session, when the same behaviour occurs, the therapist again reflects that this has happened. Finally the story of an unwanted pregnancy emerges.

HISTORICAL INTRODUCTION (GARRY PROUTY)

Pre-Therapy originated between 1966 and 1970 at the Lt. Joseph Kennedy School for exceptional children, a residential and community-oriented facility for mentally retarded and mentally ill children and adolescents, located in Palos Park, Illinois. My role was chief psychologist with treatment responsibility. The treatment population included mentally ill, mentally retarded and dual-diagnosed clients with varying levels of disability. As the work involved frankly psychotic people, the administration thought I should have 'back-up' consultation of my choice. I asked Dr. Eugene Gendlin of the University of Chicago because of his work with Carl Rogers and others (1967) in the treatment of schizophrenics. He volunteered his time.

We agreed to consult once a week with problems I selected from practice. It was a professional relationship at that point and I brought problems such as sexual seduction, violence, and client double-binding. I learned that such things as seduction can be driven by needs of worth; that violence need not be psychotic but can be driven by self-affirmation; and that when the client invites a therapist to be close and then shuts them out, this can be a helplessness–rage function. These types of insights enriched my understanding of what I was being confronted with. Soon, however, a new dimension began manifesting itself. Frequently Gendlin would say that in Wisconsin they could not work this way. 'What did you do?' he asked. 'You are getting results we didn't.' 'What are you doing?' 'This is different.' Although I firmly believed I was just doing 'good' client-centered/experiential therapy, Gendlin's engagement with me permitted entry into a creative dimension that would not have otherwise occurred. It is only because Gendlin provided student-centered consultation in a Rogerian atmosphere that Pre-Therapy was facilitated. This was my basic introduction to 'supervision'. It was Gendlin's valuing and pressing for clarification that eventually led to the statement of the Pre-Therapy method (Prouty, 1976). I was very resistant, and frightened of such a committed step.

In 1970 this student-centered approach took another form. I developed a college-based, para-professional training program that was coordinated with local hospitals. I constructed a program composed of three parts: academics, personal growth and practicums. The academic parts were based on the writings of Carl Rogers (1957), Eugene Gendlin (1968) and the Pre-Therapy method. The personal growth consisted of 100 hours of group process. The practicum for individual counseling consisted of one eight-hour day for each week of a sixteen-week semester. The morning was student ward experience and the afternoon was composed of student-centered 'supervision'. Students presented questions directly from their work on the psychiatric ward. In 1983, at the invitation of the Chicago Counseling and Psychotherapy Center, I ran a post-doctoral supervision for client-centered/experiential counselors and psychologists. It was very practice oriented, since most members had a high degree of client-centered academics and science. The clients were from a local rehabilitation agency and were psychiatrically monitored for diagnosis and medications. Most of the client-centered therapists had little contact with institutional psychiatry and were not familiar with its authoritarian mode. This led to a conflict. One client, whom I knew, was diagnosed as a schizophrenic and labeled himself 'schizo', 'crazy' and 'nutso'. He firmly believed he was psychotic and would need to be on medication for the rest of his life. I had spent years seeing this type of client and he was not psychotic or schizophrenic. I told him he was neither psychotic nor schizophrenic: he was probably suffering from an alcohol-related dysfunction. This made a deep impression on the client and he discussed it with his psychiatrist who said I was wrong, shut down our training program and 'blacklisted' my services all over the local area. Two years later, my wife accidentally met the client. He had left the psychiatrist and the rehabilitation center. He had also stopped drinking and was gainfully employed. He reported that the encounter had changed his sense of self.

In 1995 I directed another student-centered training program at the Chicago Osteopathic Hospital with post-doctoral psychologists. Again, the students formed relationships with patients on the ward and brought their problems to a seminar set for patient review. We used discussion, role-playing, role-reversal and direct patient interviews, but all derived from student needs. Academic lectures were on the practice, theory and early science of Pre-Therapy.

PRE-THERAPY METHOD AND SUPERVISION

In this section, we present you with some points that surface whenever we talk about Pre-Therapy in practice. Pre-Therapy can be done in a 'classical' mode, meaning on a one-to-one basis, with clients functioning on a low-contact level.

They need a systematic and enduring offer of Pre-Therapy. The second way of applying Pre-Therapy is with clients that exhibit a kind of mixed form of functioning: not only pre-expressive functioning but also traces of higher level expressive/congruent contact functioning are present. Elsewhere, we called this 'grey-zone' functioning (Prouty, Van Werde and Pörtner, 2002). A third field of application, which concerns using Pre-Therapy in situations of declining levels of functioning as in dementia and dying, is described elsewhere (see Van Werde and Morton, 1999; Van Werde, 2002; Dodds, Morton and Prouty, 2004).

For the purposes of supervision, these are some of the learnings from individual applications which we have found helpful to us. They serve us and our students as reminders of the basic principles and practices of Pre-Therapy, and help us return consistently to the clarity and discipline of the model. We offer them here in that spirit.

Remember that this is the first time you meet this client

Doing Pre-Therapy demands a non-intrusive phenomenological attitude. Thinking that one 'knows' stands in the way of really putting the client and his or her behavior at the centre of our attention. The way one approaches the client should be fresh: as if everything about the client still has to be learned, so that no previous knowledge can stand in the way of what there is to witness at this given moment. It is necessary to be continuously open to the everyday changing process that the client is.

Value pre-expressive relating and experiencing

The concept of pre-expressive functioning in itself makes us aware of the fact that people who exhibit symptom-like behavior do relate and do express feelings, albeit on a premature, pre-relational and pre-experiential level (Van Werde and Prouty, 2007). As with children who enter the social world, one attunes to it and welcomes every attempt at self-expression even if, from another's perspective, it seems unintelligible, grammatically incorrect or incomplete.

Estimate level and attune to the given level

If pre-expressive functioning is there, use Pre-Therapy reflections to match this level. When the client starts asking questions doubt can arise about the level present. Make a choice either to work with reflections or, maybe, to combine reflection with congruent responding or asking—as long as it stays very close to the here and now given. One can also repeat the question and give an answer in order to avoid blocking the expression of pre-expressive thoughts that are probably also included in the question. How to continue is up to the client: whether to shift up to further expressive functioning or to continue to give more pre-expressive content.

Be with the client
The aim of the contact work is to listen to, to be with, and to relate to the client, even when they are functioning in ways that are initially unintelligible. It can be like dealing with very young children who are speaking their first words or taking their first steps: one is there to support their efforts 'to enter the world'. Because it is done in a non-intrusive and non-judgemental way, the other person is supported and encouraged to continually and freely appeal to their inner strength. When somebody starts to express and relate it shows that he or she is coming out of a protective, pre-expressive cocoon and starting to connect to other people and things. In doing so, and at the same time, the client permits the other, and the world, to come in.

Be empathic without knowing the frame of reference
Closely in accordance with person-centered therapy, Pre-Therapy permits you to be with pre-expressive functioning. This kind of functioning, by definition, means that meaning isn't consciously accessible right away and that one has to stay as close as possible to the concrete behavior given.

Don't think you know
Keep an open mind and open eyes. Don't fill in meaning; not even when it starts unfolding. The client is the one who knows. The therapist or contact facilitator is there as a companion on the road, and is neither interpreter nor judge. This very much refers to the phenomenological attitude. It is about the phenomena as they appear non-symbolically. Prouty (2003) elaborates on the use of reflections as a way of 'pointing to the concrete' and, parallel to Prouty's method, Tao psychotherapy speaks of 'pointing at the moon'. Essentially, this is about the same thing: the pointing (the therapeutic work) is an adjunctive, not the end of the work. Once the moon is seen, the pointing no longer serves. It is about seeing the reality of patients without concepts or assumptions. The finger is merely used to indicate the reality of the moon and after having seen that reality the finger should be discarded. The finger is not the truth, but a method to lead to the phenomenon. It is about the reality of the client (C.H. Huh, 2006, personal correspondence): not the theories of the therapist but the world of the client.

Don't underestimate the strength of the client
Mind the healthy and strong parts of functioning and work with them. By constantly paying attention to the contact-level of the client we have discovered how complex therapeutic progress can be. We now think that a distinction can be made between the level of contact with reality, contact with affect, and contact with others (communicative contact). It is probable that in psychotherapeutic

process these three contact functions do not necessarily have an identical evolution. What is important for us, at this point, is the idea that maybe reality-, affective- and communicative contact can be separately influenced. This is significant— particularly if we think of ward-settings where nurses have numerous daily opportunities to focus on, and work with, reality and communication. This illustrates that contact can be used in a practical way. Theoretically, this also bridges the supposed gap (often complained of in person-centered care) between following individual process ('being with') and working with the given reality ('doing with'). Within the borders of a specific setting—without losing the person-centered attitude, and by always taking the very concrete as a starting point for any action—the two inversely related realities can be synthetically worked with. You reflect in order to restore, or you practice so that poor contact functioning may be strengthened.

Remember that Pre-Therapy is an act of existential empathy
You reach out to somebody who *lives* his symptomatology and who, in so doing, is sheltered and disconnected from the world and from other human beings. Obviously, working with somebody in such a position not only requires empathy for that person's suffering and isolation but also enough presence to be potentially visible and make the difference in the lived world of the other. The client knows best and it is they who must decide whether to allow themselves to be seen and to disclose whatever it is that has made them locked in. To be permitted to enter this protected and secured world of symptomatology and to join the client you need to be empathic, authentic, caring and accepting; playful and deadly serious at the same time; conscious and decisive in your actions; organic and not wooden; to be welcoming, inviting and offering. Everybody lives in a different universe. Our task is to follow the client's track empathically. The guiding principle is the contact rather than the content itself. 'Being with' is, in itself, therapeutic. It is probably what therapy is all about.

REFERENCES

Boss, M. (1994) *Existential Foundations of Medicine and Psychology*. London: Jason-Aaronson

Brockleman, P. (1980) *Existential Phenomenology and the World of Ordinary Experience*. New York: University Press of America

Buber, M. (1964) Phenomenological analysis of existence versus pointing to the concrete. In M. Freidman (Ed.) *The Worlds of Existentialism* (pp. 547–9). New York: Random House

Burton, A. (1973) The presentation of the face in psychotherapy. *Psychotherapy: Theory, Research and Practice*, 10(4), 30

Dodds, P., Morton, I. and Prouty, G. (2004) Using Pre-Therapy techniques in dementia care. *Journal of Dementia Care, 12*(2), 25–28

Gendlin, E.T. (1968) The experiential response. In E.F. Hammer (Ed.) *Interpretation in Therapy: Its Role, Scope, Depth, Timing and Art* (pp. 208–27). New York: Gruen and Stratton

Koenig, T.R. (1992) *Existentialism and Human Existence*. Malibar, FL: Kreiger Publishing Corporation

Krietemeyer, B. and Prouty, G. (2003) The art of psychological contact: The psychotherapy of a mentally retarded psychotic client. *Person-Centered and Experiential Psychotherapies, 2*(3), 151–61

McWilliams, K. and Prouty, G. (1998) Life enrichment of a profoundly retarded woman. *Person-Centered Journal, 5*(1), 29–35

Perls, F.S. (1959) *Ego, Hunger and Aggression*. New York: Random House

Peters, H. (1999) Pre-Therapy: A client-centered/experiential approach to mentally handicapped people. *Journal of Humanistic Psychology, 39*(4), 8–29

Pörtner, M. (1996) *The Person-Centered Approach in Everyday Care for People With Special Needs*. Ross-on-Wye: PCCS Books

Prouty, G. (1976) Pre-Therapy: A method of treating pre-expressive psychotic and retarded patients. *Psychotherapy: Theory, Research and Practice, 13*(3), 290–94

Prouty, G. (1990) Pre-Therapy: A theoretical evolution in person-centered/experiential psychotherapy of schizophrenia and retardation. In G. Lietaer, M. Rombouts and R. Van Balens (Eds.) *Client-Centered and Experiential Psychotherapy in the Nineties* (pp. 645–58). Leuven: Leuven University Press

Prouty, G. (1994) *Theoretical Evolutions in Person-Centered/Experiential Psychotherapy: Applications to Schizophrenic and Retarded Psychoses*. Westport, CN: Praeger

Prouty, G. (2001) Pre-Therapy: A treatment method for people with mental retardation who are also psychotic. In A. Dosen and K. Day (Eds.) *Treating Mental Illness and Behavioral Disorders in Children and Adults with Mental Retardation* (pp. 155–66). Washington, DC: American Psychiatric Press

Prouty, G. (2003) Pre-Therapy—A newer development in the psychotherapy of schizophrenia. *Journal of the American Academy of Psychoanalysis and Dynamic Psychiatry, 34*(1), 59–73

Prouty, G. and Cronwall, M. (1990) Psychotherapy with a depressed mentally retarded adult: An application of Pre-Therapy. In A. Dosen and F. Menalacino (Eds.) *Depression in Mentally Retarded Children and Adults* (pp. 281–93). Leiden: Logon Publications

Prouty, G. and Kubiak, M. (1988a) The development of communicative contact with a catatonic schizophrenic. *Journal of Communication Therapy, 4*(1), 13–20

Prouty, G. and Kubiak, M. (1988b) Pre-Therapy with mentally retarded/psychotic clients. *Psychiatric Aspects of Mental Retardation Reviews, 7*(10), 62–66

Prouty, G. and Pietrzak, S. (1988) Pre-Therapy method applied to persons experiencing hallucinatory images. *Person-Centered Review, 3*(4), 426–44

Prouty, G., Van Werde, D. and Pörtner, M. (2002) *Pre-Therapy: Reaching Contact Impaired Clients*. Ross-on-Wye: PCCS Books

Rogers, C.R. (1957) The necessary and sufficient conditions of therapeutic personality change. *Journal of Consulting Psychology, 21*(2), 95–103

Rogers, C.R., Gendlin, E.T., Kiesler, D.J. and Truax, C.B. (Eds.) (1967) *The Therapeutic Relationship and Its Impact: A Study of Psychotherapy with Schizophrenics*. Madison, WI: University of Wisconsin Press

Roy, B. (1991) A client-centered approach to multiple personality and dissociated process. In L. Fusek (Ed.) *New Directions in Client-Centered Therapy with Difficult Client Populations* (pp. 18–40). Chicago, IL: Chicago Counseling, Psychotherapy and Research Center

Sommerbeck, L. (2003) *The Client-Centred Therapist in Psychiatric Contexts: A Therapists' Guide to the Psychiatric Landscape and its Inhabitants*. Ross-on-Wye: PCCS Books

Van Werde, D. (1990) Psychotherapy with a retarded schizo-affective woman: An application of Prouty's Pre-Therapy. In A. Dosen, A. Van Gennep and G. Zwanikken (Eds.) *Treatment of Mental Illness and Behavioral Disorder in the Mentally Retarded* (pp. 469–77). Leiden: Logon Publications

Van Werde, D. (1994) Dealing with the possibility of psychotic content in seemingly congruent communication. In D. Mearns *Developments in Person-Centred Counselling* (pp. 125–32). London: Sage

Van Werde, D. (2002) Prouty's Pre-Therapy and contact-work with a broad range of persons' pre-expressive functioning. In G. Wyatt and P. Sanders (Eds.) *Rogers' Therapeutic Conditions: Evolution, Theory and Practice. Volume 4: Contact and Perception* (pp. 168–81). Ross-on-Wye: PCCS Books

Van Werde, D. and Morton, I. (1999) The relevance of Prouty's Pre-Therapy to dementia care. In I. Morton (Ed.) *Person-Centred Approaches to Dementia Care* (pp. 139–66). Bicester: Winslow Press

Van Werde, D. and Prouty, G. (2007) Pre-Therapy: Empathic contact with individuals at pre-expressive levels of functioning. In M. Cooper, P. Schmid, M. O'Hara and G. Wyatt (Eds.) *The Handbook of Person-Centered Therapy* (pp. 237–50). Basingstoke: Palgrave

Zinschitz, E. (2001) Understanding what seems unintelligible. In S. Haugh and T. Merry (Eds.) *Rogers' Therapeutic Conditions: Evolution, Theory and Practice: Volume 2: Empathy* (pp. 192–205). Ross-on-Wye: PCCS Books

Part Three

Form

Chapter Seven

Group Supervision

Keith Tudor

Group supervision has been considered the most widely practised form of supervision (see Carroll, 1996). Like a therapy group, a supervision group can be a powerful experience for participants and for its leader or facilitator. In comparison with individual, one-to-one supervision, group supervision offers more opportunities for interaction, more learning from more experience, more possibilities for creativity, a greater sense of community and professional association—and more anxiety! Despite these advantages, my own experience over the last thirty years is that the popularity of this form of supervision is in decline. This chapter aims to reclaim, as Rowan (1976) puts it, 'the power of the group', firstly, by means of a discussion of the phenomenon of 'group' and, secondly, with reference to person-centred approaches to group and to facilitation. Person-centred psychology has specific views about group and about facilitation, views which make it a particularly potent and relevant approach to group supervision. I then discuss the form of group supervision, and conclude the chapter with some consideration of the practicalities, processes and possibilities of supervision groups.

Group

In the West we live in societies and cultures which, in general, value the individual and individualism over the group and collectivism. This is supported by an economic system, capitalism, which drives and thrives on individualism and competition between individuals, a force which often leads to isolation and alienation, not only from our product but also from our neighbour. This, in turn, is supported by Western psychologies which emphasise autonomy, independence, and individual resilience, happiness, and subjectivity. When we think about going to see a therapist or a supervisor we tend to think about an individual: one-to-one therapy and supervision is, as it were, our default setting. Yet, our biological, neurological, developmental and social 'settings' are, if anything, relational, not individual, and the logic of being relational is to be in relationship with others (plural).

Against this background there are some psychologists, therapists and others who think and write more about relationship and take a more relational approach to life:

- Angyal (1941, 1965/1973), whose work influenced Rogers, for instance, writes about the trend towards *homonomy*, alongside the trend towards autonomy. He describes homonomy (1941, p. 172) as 'a trend to be in harmony with superindividual units, the social group, nature, God, ethical world order, or whatever the person's formulation of it may be.' One manifestation of this trend is to be in group, and to have a sense of belonging to a group (family, social group, neighbourhood, community) and profession.

- As an alternative to what sometimes appears as an obsessive concern with independence, some people emphasise *interdependence*. These include figures as diverse as Karl Marx, Mahatma Gandhi and the American philosopher, Will Durant, who, in 1945, launched a *Declaration of Interdependence*. Groups provide perhaps the best opportunity to explore and work through the personal and social psychology of interdependence.

- In Western societies in particular, individual resilience is highly valued. Stories in myth, legend and daily newspapers tell of the trials and fortitude of the individual, battling 'against the odds'. Writing about mental health, Joubert and Raeburn (1998) place the concept of individual resilience in the context of the need for *supportive environments*. This perspective proposes a necessary balance between the individual and the environment—and offers a challenge to promote the mental health both of the individual and of the environment. A number of Yalom's (1995) therapeutic or curative factors in group therapy fulfil this function of providing a supportive environment: the instillation and maintenance of hope, for example, group members observing the improvement of others; universality, the notion that we are not unique, alone or isolated; altruism, the notion that people receive through giving support, reassurance, suggestions, insight, and so on; the development of socialising techniques and social learning; as well as existential factors, including responsibility and contingency.

- Whilst human happiness is universally viewed as a good thing, it is predominantly presented as a quality of and outcome for the individual. At present, at least in UK social policy, there appears to be an 'agenda for (individual) happiness', largely fuelled by Layard's (1995) research on the subject, as well as his political influence. In a separate strand of research and development, Keyes (2003) has developed a perspective on mental health in which he identifies a number of dimensions of subjective well-being, including five on *positive social well-being*, which includes: social acceptance, social actualisation, social contribution, social coherence, and social integration (having a sense of belonging to, and comfort and support from a community). Such social well-being is not possible outside a social context such as a group.

- Subjectivity refers to a process which proceeds from or takes place in a person's mind rather than the external world. In psychology and psychotherapy it refers to the therapist's use of their own subjective experience, usually of the client. This, again, focuses on the individual, whether therapist or client, in what Stark (2000) refers to as 'one-person psychology'. However in the last fifteen years, there has been an increasing interest in *intersubjectivity*, which Atwood and Stolorow (1996) describe as 'reciprocal mutual influence' and which represents a 'two-person psychology'. They go on (p. 181) to describe the implications of such reciprocity:

  > from this perspective, the observer and his or her language are grasped as intrinsic to the observed, and the impact of the analyst and his or her organising activity on the unfolding of the therapeutic relationship itself becomes the focus of ... investigation and reflection.

  Groups provide a rich source of interactions, relational possibilities, and intersubjectivity. This perspective also supports Yalom's (1995) research that altruism is an important therapeutic factor, and Giesekus and Mente's (1986) observation that clients' empathic understanding of each other is the most important therapeutic factor in therapy groups.

These examples suggest that, compared with individual encounters, groups provide more opportunities for us to experience a sense of belonging, of having colleagues, and of professional association—and a more immediate one than simply being a paid-up member of a large, but perhaps largely anonymous, professional organisation. Groups offer an experience of interdependence and intersubjectivity. Thus, in a supervision group, colleagues may more realistically support or stand by each others' work, and more effectively challenge each other, thereby taking up some of the responsibilities of being colleagues (see Chapter 3). Indeed, such a group is a microcosm of a larger professional community, and may encompass experiences and issues of diversity, norms, responsibilities, power, authority and influence. Also, a supervision group may be experienced as especially relevant for practitioners who themselves are running groups (see Houston, 1985; Tudor, 1999).

Before considering the form of group supervision, I briefly discuss three aspects of person-centred approaches to group: group encounter, group as organism, and group facilitation.

Person-centred approaches to group

Person-centred psychology is an organismic psychology (see Rogers, 1939, 1951; Barrett-Lennard, 1998; Tudor and Worrall, 2006). As such it emphasises a view of the person as interdependent with, and within, his or her environment. It follows that this interdependence, and the interrelationship or interchange between individual and environment, is central to any understanding of the person, and that a group is probably the most effective forum in which to experience and work with this. This is why there is a strong tradition of group work within the person-centred approach, including encounter groups, large groups and community groups.

According to Buber (1937, p. 11): 'All real living is meeting' or encounter. Rogers (1962/1973) equates encounter with relationship. Encounter is sometimes defined as 'meeting face-to-face' and, from its etymology (*contra*), there is an implication that such meeting involves some sense of being 'against' (see Schmid, 1998). Encounter is also a form of group and was, for a period in the 1960s and '70s, a social movement. This reflected the strong counter-cultural influence of encounter which was, at the time, an influential social experience. In his book on the subject, Rogers (1970/1973) wrote that:

> the trend towards the intensive group experience is related to deep and significant issues having to do with change ... in persons, in institutions, in our urban and cultural alienation, in racial tensions, in our international frictions, in our philosophies, our values, our image of man himself. It is a profoundly significant movement. (p. 169)

When we experience difficulties in establishing and maintaining a group—whether a social, therapy, supervision or any other kind of group—we may consider that people's sense of individuality and isolation is stronger than their desire for group and community. Given his interest in encounter groups as a social phenomenon, it is not surprising that, in the later years of his life, Rogers became more involved in the resolution of conflict and intercultural tension, and in peace initiatives through facilitating encounter groups in several of the world's 'hot spots' (see McGaw, 1973; Rogers, 1978, 1986).

According to Wibberley (1988), Rogers was one of the key influences on encounter and brought to it a particular perspective on a less structured group, with more emphasis on communication between members of the group, and on congruence or genuineness on the part of the participants. Although Rogers (1970/1973) suggests that encounter groups go through a number of phases of development, Barrett-Lennard (1979) argues that these may be summarised in three phases of: engagement; trust and process development; and encounter and change. Given the emphasis in the person-centred approach on personal development and, specifically, in the training and continuing professional development of therapists (see Chapter 12), encounter groups and group encounter remain important. This extends to experiences of large groups and community groups, for example, community meetings as part of a course, and at conferences (see Bozarth, 1982; Wood, 1984, 1999; Natiello, 2001).

The second aspect and contribution of person-centred approaches to group theory is the view that a group is an organism. Bion (1961), the founder of group dynamics theory, first regarded the group *as* an organism in its own right, and this is a common metaphor in person-centred approaches to groups. Rogers (1970/1973, p. 50) also likens the group to an organism, 'having a sense of its own direction even though it could not define that direction intellectually'. As the group has a sense of direction, so it develops its own potential and that of its members. Equally (ibid.), 'a group recognizes unhealthy elements in its processes, focuses on them, clears them up or eliminates them, and moves on towards becoming a healthier group', a view which leads Rogers (ibid.) to state that: 'This is my way of saying that I have seen the "wisdom of the organism" exhibited at every level from cell to group.' Wood (1982) takes this conceptualisation further and talks about the group being an organism. There is a parallel debate in organisational theory about the nature of organisations, in the context of which Wheatley and Kellner-Rogers (1996) assert that: 'organisations are living systems. They too are intelligent, creative, adaptive, self-organising, meaning-seeking.' Embleton Tudor et al. (2004) elaborate this concept of the group being an organism with regard to certain qualities of the organism:

- That the group tends to actualise, which includes its interactions with perceived external 'reality'.

- That the group behaves and functions as an organised whole, and cannot be understood without reference to its environmental field or context.
- That the group engages in and develops an organismic valuing process.
- That the group is always in motion.

Both with regard to large groups and the concept of group as organism, person-centred approaches and the group analytic traditions are, perhaps surprisingly, close (see Sturdevant, 1995).

The third, important aspect of person-centred approaches to the group is their perspective of the role and relationship of the group leader as a facilitator. This perspective follows from the belief that human beings—and groups—are organisms which tend to actualise, in relation to which the facilitator adopts a non-directive attitude, and what Rogers (1970/1973, p. 52) refers to as a 'climate-setting function'. The person-centred facilitator is genuinely free of a desire to control the outcome, and respects the capacity of the group to deal with problems. The term 'facilitator' means to make easy, and it is the task of the person-centred facilitator to ease relationships: to be and to encourage others to be in contact, authentic, acceptant, empathic, and receiving or experiencing each other as acceptant and empathic. In effect, the facilitator helps to co-create these therapeutic, or climatic, environmental conditions. That the person-centred facilitator embodies a non-directive attitude does not mean that he or she does not, or cannot, set structure or boundaries. Indeed, there are times and groups when it may be necessary to provide a high degree of structure. Coghlan and McIlduff (1990) offer a useful distinction between those facilitative behaviours which are directive and those which facilitate structure and, consequently, they argue that it is legitimate and congruent within a person-centred approach for a facilitator to offer to a given group low directivity with a high degree of structure.

These perspectives on groups and facilitation make person-centred approaches particularly potent and collaborative approaches to group supervision.

Supervision Group

Early forms of group supervision of counsellors in training included case presentations, some focus on group dynamics within the supervision group, as well as some didactic input from the group supervisor/trainer (see Orton, 1965). This early report highlights the range of possibilities which makes group supervision potentially a richer experience for all involved.

Group supervision combines two phenomena or sets: group and supervision. If we think about these in terms of a Venn diagram (Figure 7.1), we may clarify something about the purpose of group supervision. In Figure 7.1, Set A: *Group* represents an interest a person may have in being in a group; Set B: *Supervision* represents that same person's interest and need to be in supervision. This individual could meet these needs by being in individual supervision and, for instance, joining a choir. It is only where the two sets or needs overlap or intersect, as in this example, that there is a purpose in that person being in group supervision.

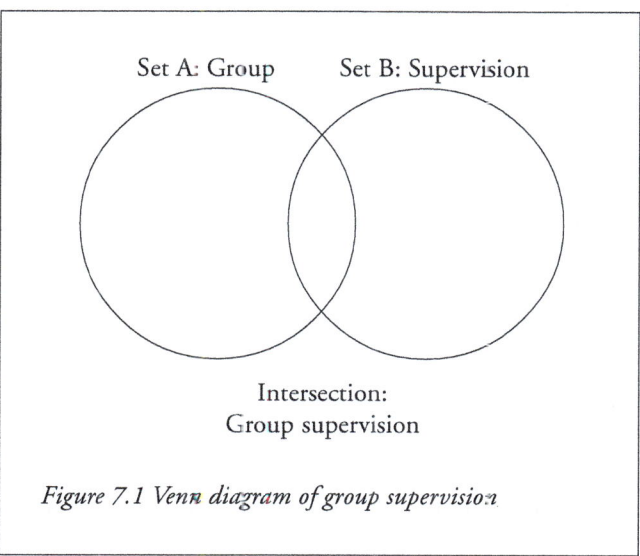

Figure 7.1 Venn diagram of group supervision

So what is the purpose of group supervision? In his work on large groups Kreeger (1975) identifies three different types of large group: problem-centred, experience-centred, and therapy-centred. I apply these to supervision groups in an order which I think is most relevant:

- Supervision-centred. This type of group meets with the express purpose of doing supervision. The group supervisor takes a structured, supervisory approach and tends to do more supervising than facilitating.
- Experience-centred. The principal purpose of this type of supervision group is to provide an experience of group supervision. There is usually a minimum of structure and formal leadership, held (if at all) by a group facilitator, such as that in facilitated groups, non-facilitated peer groups, and supervision groups which encompass continuing professional development. Given the focus on experience, these groups tend to meet for a longer period of time than supervision-centred groups.
- Problem-centred. This type of group, or the focus of a group at a particular point, is concerned with the problems of interrelationships in the

supervision group. The group supervisor facilitates the communication between members and the resolution of problems.

Of course, these types and purposes may overlap. Also, I consider that there is a clear distinction between person-centred supervision, in which the focus of supervision is on the person of the supervisee/practitioner, and client-centred supervision, in which the focus is on the supervisee's clients or client work (see Introduction). This perspective cuts across all three 'types' of groups.

Just as there is a purpose for the practitioner to meet his or her needs for group and for supervision in one place (represented by the intersection in Figure 7.1), so, too, the group supervisor needs to be clear that he or she wants not only to supervise but to supervise *and also* to facilitate a supervision group. There are a number of different ways in which to think about and to do this. To some extent this is represented in the different emphasis (as in the above descriptions) between supervision and facilitation. In an article about Foulkes' concept of the group matrix, Roberts (1982) identifies three ways of conceptualising the relationship between the group facilitator (conductor/leader/therapist) and the group: working *in* the group, working *through* the group, and working *of* the group. This conceptualisation is equally applicable to the facilitation of group supervision:

- Working *in* the group. In this approach to groups the supervisor supervises the individual therapist in the context of the group. Proctor (2000) refers to this as the 'authoritative group'. One specific example of this type of group is the Balint group (Balint, 1964), which is a dynamic work–discussion group comprising general practitioners with, originally, the doctor–patient relationship as the focus. Generally the participants in a Balint group do not work together as a team outside the discussion seminar and, therefore, the group meets in the service of clinical supervision, not of the group or even a practising team. This approach to supervision *in* the group may even be realised by individual supervisees coming forward to be supervised in front of the group, rather like Perls' model of individual therapy in the 'hot seat' in front of the group. The other group members may or may not contribute some comments or feedback, usually at the end of the individual 'piece of work'. In this approach to working in groups, the participants tend to make bids for time and/or their agenda, which the group supervisor manages. Whilst participants in this kind of supervision group may acknowledge that they learn something from their observation of other people's supervision, they also often experience having only a certain amount of time. Indeed, this may even be represented by the equation: the total time of the group, for example three hours, divided by the number in the group, say six, equalling thirty minutes each. This way of working emphasises the individual and only pays attention to group process and dynamics if they are interfering in individuals' supervision.

- Working *through* the group. Here the supervisor/facilitator focuses on the relationships between the group members themselves and between them and him or herself as facilitator. Historically, this approach to providing a facilitative space for exploration of intersubjective experience and relationships was developed by Foulkes (1964), and is applied to supervision groups in a number of ways. The facilitator may encourage participants to comment on each other's presentations; he or she may comment on parallel processes between relationships within the group and those outside the group, i.e. between the therapist and clients. One of the benefits of group supervision—and of supervision training (see Chapter 16)—is that supervisees have the opportunity not only to observe but also to take part in live supervision, often with the opportunity and time to reflect and process afterwards. In this approach to group supervision, the supervisor is both supervisor and group facilitator and, in terms of counting supervision hours, individual participants tend to count the whole or much of the time of the group.

- Working *of* the group. This model, developed by Bion (1961), in its therapeutic form treats the group-as-a-whole, with interventions directed at the whole group in an attempt to analyse the group's 'basic assumptions' (i.e. dependency, fight or flight, pairing, and the work group). The application of this approach to supervision groups is rare, the principal example being that of working with staff sensitivity groups in the context of therapeutic communities. In these groups the external group facilitator/consultant works with the staff group as a whole in order that it can work more effectively with the client group (see Bramley, 1990; Haigh, 2000). The facilitator responds to staff concerns about particular clients, about the client group as a whole, about the community and its internal and external relations, and to any conflicts between staff. Whatever the content, the facilitator focuses on the processes and dynamics of the staff group as a whole and thus this is distinct from client-centred supervision which, in the context of a therapeutic community, is usually undertaken by a separate supervisor.

The type of group and the approach to groups taken by the group supervisor/facilitator are 'field sensitive'. In other words, they are sensitive to, and dependent on, the environmental context of the group (professional, organisational, social) and of its participants. Also, they are meta-models in that they describe an overview of, or approach to, groups and group supervision within which specific models may fit. There are numerous models of supervision which describe the functions, roles, responsibilities, tasks, process and context of supervision, as well as the development of the supervisee (for a summary of which see Tudor and Worrall, 2004a, 2004b). Some of these are generic, some are informed by specific theoretical orientations and some are specific to those orientations. There is only one that I know of which is specific to group supervision and that is Proctor's (2000) 'group supervision alliance model'.

Having discussed groups, person-centred approaches to groups, and different approaches to group supervision, I now turn to the practicalities, processes and possibilities of supervision groups.

PRACTICALITIES, PROCESSES AND POSSIBILITIES

From the above, it is obvious that both or all parties to group supervision need to be clear about the purpose of the group, the type of group, and the approach taken by the facilitator. There are also other practical considerations to establishing and maintaining a supervision group which may simply be decided by the supervisor, or may be the subject of discussion, negotiation and contracting between the group supervisor, group participants and, where appropriate, third parties such as funding organisations. Points to consider could include:

- Type of group. Open or closed membership, fixed term or ongoing.
- Group membership. Mixed (heterogeneous) or selected (homogeneous), by experience for example, in which case the supervisor needs to be clear and consistent about the entry requirements for membership.
- Size of group. Usually related to the duration of each group meeting.
- Time factors. Duration and frequency of meetings, lifetime of the group; also, both group supervisor and participants need to be mindful that different professional associations have different formulae for calculating and counting hours of supervision which take place in the context of a group.
- Setting. Where the group is held. This is particularly important when working with a work group or team for whom there are distinct advantages in being 'off site'.
- Commitment. What's involved and required of the participants in terms of time, attendance, and fee.
- Responsibilities. The collaborative and respective responsibilities of the facilitator and participants (see Chapter 3).

For further discussion of these practicalities in the context of group therapy see Tudor (1999). Other writers discuss the practicalities and implications of group supervision:

- In each of the editions of their book Hawkins and Shohet (1989, 2000, 2006) discuss group supervision, its advantages and disadvantages, group styles, contracting, setting the climate and structuring, as well as a number of techniques for group supervision. They also discuss group dynamics and draw heavily on the work of Rioch, Coulter and Weinberger (1976) who write about the interface between supervision and group dynamics. Hawkins and Shohet (2006) argue that group supervisors should understand the stages of groups and how to facilitate group development especially with regard to power, competition and authority.
- Carroll (1996) discusses the strengths and weaknesses of various forms of group supervision: facilitated groups, peer groups and team or staff group supervision.
- Lammers (1999) discusses the differences between group supervision and team supervision.
- In the first book on the subject of group supervision Proctor (2000) presents her own model and discusses a number of practicalities in establishing and running supervision groups. The chapters on sharing responsibilities, on peer groups, and on creativity are particularly useful.
- Lockett (2001) discusses the responsibilities of the group supervisor from a managerial perspective. However, apart from the fact that Lockett is somewhat conservative and uncritical about issues of responsibility (for a response to which see Chapter 3), she also perpetuates inaccuracies about the supervisor's responsibilities, asserting, for example, that supervisors have a duty of care towards the supervisees' clients (for a response to which see Chapter 12). Working as a group supervisor and supervising group supervisors I find the following a useful way of reflecting on, checking and deconstructing responsibilities (see Table 7.1 over).

The process models of supervision, notably Casement (1985, 1990) and Hawkins and Shohet (1989), describe processes primarily in the context of individual supervision. These models can be applied to group supervision and, indeed, in their discussion of group supervision, Hawkins and Shohet (1989, p. 96) specifically refer to the concept of 'paralleling' in groups 'because the variety of responses of different members can be used to good effect'. They continue, 'If members of the group can be aware of what they are experiencing, or have been

Basis for responsibility	Group supervisor's responsibilities	Group participants' responsibilities
2	1 The group supervisor identifies, reflects on and checks his or her responsibilities ...	3
... against specific and identified responsibilities, as set out, for instance, in a framework or code of ethics and professional practice ...	⟵	
	⟶	... and discusses and shares these with the group.

Table 7.1 Group supervisor's responsibilities—a collaborative method

asked to swallow, this can be an extremely useful clue for clarifying what is undigested by the supervisee and client.' Proctor (2000) offers an example of applying Hawkins and Shohet's process model to group supervision. However, there are few process models of group supervision. In this context, group supervisors/facilitators are likely to draw on their experience and knowledge of group dynamics and group process to inform their facilitation of supervision groups. Thus, when a participant in a supervision group says that he might like to talk about someone but doesn't actually do so, this may reflect the supervisee's own process, or a parallel process between the therapist and the client, or be part of a group process concerning issues of worth, shame, or scarcity. A participant runs over the time to which they've agreed and someone else responds: 'It's alright. What I was going to talk about doesn't matter.' This may be an authentic response, and it may be indicative of a group process about contracts and contracting, mutual respect, self-worth and so on. Supervisors who are trained in theoretical orientations which are group approaches (such as group analysis), or which have a strong tradition of group (such as psychodrama, person-centred therapy, gestalt therapy, and transactional analysis), may be more confident about the translation from therapy group process to supervision group process. Of course, the extent to which the group supervisor focuses on and works with group process depends on the purpose and type of the group as well as their theoretical orientation. Proctor (2000) has a useful chapter on group process under the title of the 'hot issues of group life'. Another author by the same name (Proctor, 1997) addresses a supervision group process whereby a supervisee presents a case/client to the group. The other group members make various comments, contributions and suggestions, with the result that the original supervisee feels overwhelmed, stupid, and ashamed, and believes that his or her client has somehow been taken away and become 'owned' by everyone else in the group. To avoid this, Proctor suggests a particular supervision group process, involving the supervisee as presenter, with other supervisees designated as consultants and as observers, with the group supervisor holding the whole process as facilitator. Whilst this model is not new (for instance, with regard to training therapists), it is a rare example of a group process model of group supervision.

Finally, in terms of the possibilities which supervision groups afford, a number of authors advocate group supervision as offering the opportunity for participants to engage, and to be engaged, more actively than in individual supervision. Houston (1990/1995), for instance:

1. Facilitates group members to use the psychodramatic technique of 'doubling', whereby the person presenting role-plays his or her client, and another group member 'stands in' for the therapist. This can help the presenting therapist gain some insight into, and empathy for, his or her client and, in any case, experiencing another supervisor can give the therapist another angle on their own work with his or her client.
2. Sets up what she refers to as 'triangle exercises' in which participants in the group take different roles—those of client, therapist, and supervisor—and ask questions of each other.

Other authors specifically focus on the creative possibilities that group supervision offers:

- Wilkins (1995) describes a stage-model of group supervision which draws on a creative therapies approach, which is especially informed by psychodrama, and includes art work, role reversal, role-training and role-play.
- Proctor (2000) devotes a chapter to creativity and gives various examples of creative practice including one where the supervisee talks to other members of the group as if they were his client, and another exercise which helps to engage the senses and to heighten the sensory acuity of supervisees. She also makes the point that, if supervision includes experiential work, then time should be allowed for debriefing and processing this.
- Hawkins and Shohet (2006) suggest a number of techniques to support the exploration of group dynamics including dream work, sculpting, and an exercise on estrangement which helps explore unconscious dynamics.

Other creative options I have used include:

- Asking questions. One group member thinks of one of his or her clients but does not say anything. The others in the group ask questions, preferably individually and quickly, to which the supervisee responds in kind without too much left-brain analysis. Examples of questions asked might include: 'What do you find difficult about this client?', 'How does he or she smell?', 'What do you know about their social life?', 'Who does this client remind you of?', 'What food would this client taste like?' and 'What question would you like us to have asked you?' This process often produces interesting results. For instance, I have experienced groups do this without reference to the gender of the client. The process usually gives the supervisee food for thought in terms of questions they haven't thought about or questions which they realise they never dared to ask themselves. It is also interesting for the participants to reflect on the questions they asked—and, with regard to the person-centred approach, it challenges a common myth that person-centred practitioners don't or shouldn't ask questions. Also, as an exercise, it can enliven the supervision group, and can be done quickly.

- 'Lucky dip'. This exercise came about when one member of a supervision group had asked for some time to talk about clients but couldn't decide which of her clients to present. As she sat looking at her diary, I had the thought that someone else could choose for her. I put this to her and she agreed, with the result that she talked about a client that she hadn't brought to supervision before. Both the supervisee and the group got so much from the supervision and from the process that 'lucky dip' became a regular option of choice.

- Cascade supervision. This refers to a particular way of supervising the supervisor. One member of the group (A) presents, another (B) supervises A for an agreed period of time, after which another member (C) supervises B with regard to her supervision of A. In a supervision group this is usually done in the context that C has seen the original piece of supervision. In training groups it is possible to organise this differently and creatively (see Chapter 16).

- Separating into two groups. As with the 'lucky dip', this came about through a particular experience. It was near the end of a day-long meeting of a supervision group and two supervisees still wanted a reasonable amount of time to discuss a particular client. Until that point the group has always stayed together for the duration of its meetings. We had discussed the possibility of splitting the time or of negotiating who would have all the time. As I looked around the group, I saw experienced practitioners and mostly experienced supervisors. I suggested the option that, if someone else was willing to supervise, we might split into two groups for half an hour and then come back together for the last ten minutes of the day. I felt a little nervous and quite bold, as if I'd broken a taboo or, at least, an assumption. The option was taken up, the group split into two, everyone got something from the experience and, when we came back together, said that it had been liberating.

These are some of the creative options that supervision groups allow. Working creatively with a group encourages fluidity, spontaneity, engagement, participation, responsibility, and economy. This supports the argument that group supervision rather than individual supervision should be the default setting or the form of choice.

REFERENCES

Angyal, A. (1941) *Foundations for a Science of Personality*. New York: Commonwealth Fund
Angyal, A. (1973) *Neurosis and Treatment: A Holistic Theory*. New York: John Wiley and Sons. (Original work published 1965)
Atwood, G. and Stolorow, R. (1996) *A Meeting of Minds: Mutuality in Psychoanalysis*. Hillsdale, NJ: Analytic Press
Balint, M. (1964) *The Doctor, His Patient, and the Illness* (2nd edn.). London: Pitman
Barrett-Lennard, G. (1979) The client-centered system unfolding. In F.J. Turner (Ed.) *Social Work Treatment: Interlocking Theoretical Approaches* (pp. 171–241). New York: Free Press
Barrett-Lennard, G.T. (1998) *Carl Rogers' Helping System*. London: Sage
Bion, W. (1961) *Experience in Groups and Other Papers*. London: Tavistock
Bozarth, J.D. (1982) The person-centered approach in the large community group. In G. Gazda (Ed.) *Innovations in Group Psychotherapy* (2nd edn.). Springfied, IL: Charles Thomas
Bramley, W. (1990) SSGs: A conductor's field experiences. *Group Analysis*, 23, 301–16.
Buber, M. (1937) *I and Thou* (R.G. Smith, trans.). Edinburgh: T. and T. Clark
Carroll, M. (1996) *Counselling Supervision: Theory, Skills and Practice*. London: Cassell
Casement, P. (1985) *On Learning from the Patient*. London: Tavistock
Casement, P. (1990) *Further Learning from the Patient: The Analytic Space and Process*. London: Routledge
Coghlan, D. and McIlduff, E. (1990) Structuring and nondirectiveness in group facilitation. *Person-Centered Review*, 5, 13–29
Embleton Tudor, L., Keemar, K., Tudor, K., Valentine, J. and Worrall, M. (2004) *The Person-Centred Approach: A Contemporary Introduction*. Basingstoke: Palgrave
Foulkes, S.H. (1964) *Therapeutic Group Analysis*. London: George Allen and Unwin
Giesekus, U. and Mente, A. (1986) Client empathic understanding in client-centered therapy. *Person-Centered Review*, 1, 163–171

Haigh, R. (2000) Support systems. 2. Staff sensitivity groups. *Advances in Psychiatric Treatment, 6,* 312–19

Hawkins, P. and Shohet, R. (1989) *Supervision in the Helping Professions.* Buckingham: Open University Press

Hawkins, P. and Shohet, R. (2000) *Supervision in the Helping Professions* (2nd edn.). Buckingham: Open University Press

Hawkins, P. and Shohet, R. (2006) *Supervision in the Helping Professions* (3rd edn.). Buckingham: Open University Press

Houston, G. (1985) Group supervision of groupwork. *Self & Society, 8*(2), 64–68

Houston, G. (1995) *Supervision and Counselling* (2nd rev. edn.). London: The Rochester Foundation. (Original work published 1990)

Joubert, N. and Raeburn, J. (1998) Mental health promotion: People, power and passion. *International Journal of Mental Health Promotion, 1,* 15–22

Keyes, C.L.M. (2003) Complete mental health: An agenda for the 21st century. In C.L.M. Keyes and J. Haidt (Eds.) *Flourishing: Positive Psychology and the Life Well-Lived* (pp. 293–312). Washington, DC: American Psychological Association Press

Kreeger, L. (Ed.) (1975) *The Large Group: Dynamics and Therapy.* London: Maresfield

Lammers, W. (1999) Training in group and team supervision. In E. Holloway and M. Carroll (Eds.) *Training Counselling Supervisors* (pp. 106–29). London: Sage

Layard, R. (2005) *Happiness: Lessons from a New Science.* New York: Penguin

Lockett, M. (2001) The responsibilities of group supervisors. In S. Wheeler and D. King (Eds.) *Supervising Counsellors: Issues of Responsibility* (pp. 153–67). London: Sage

McGaw, W. (Producer and Director) (1973) *The Steel Shutter* [Film]. La Jolla, CA: Center for Studies of the Person

Natiello, P. (2001) From group to community. In *The Person-Centred Approach: A Passionate Presence* (pp. 121–40). Ross-on-Wye: PCCS Books

Orton, J.W. (1965) Areas of focus in supervising counselling practicum students in groups. *Personnel and Guidance Journal, 14,* 167–70

Proctor, B. (2000) *Group Supervision: A Guide for Creative Practice.* London: Sage

Proctor, K. (1997) The bells that ring: A process for group supervision. *Australian and New Zealand Journal of Family Therapy, 18*(4), 217–20

Rioch, M.J., Coulter, W.R. and Weinberger, D.M. (Eds.) (1976) *Dialogues for Therapists.* San Francisco, CA: Jossey-Bass.

Roberts J.P. (1982) Foulkes' concept of the matrix. *Group Analysis, 15,* 111–26

Rogers, C.R. (1939) *The Clinical Treatment of the Problem Child.* Boston: Houghton Mifflin

Rogers, C.R. (1951) *Client-Centered Therapy.* London: Constable

Rogers, C.R. (1973a) The interpersonal relationship: The core of guidance. In C.R. Rogers and B. Stevens *Person to Person: The Problem of Being Human. A New Trend in Psychology* (pp. 89–103). London: Souvenir Press. (Original work published 1962)

Rogers, C.R. (1973b) *Carl Rogers on Encounter Groups.* New York: Harper and Row. (Original work published 1970)

Rogers, C.R. (1978) *Carl Rogers on Personal Power.* London: Constable

Rogers, C.R. (1986) The Rust workshop. *Journal of Humanistic Psychology*, 26(3), 23–45
Rowan, J. (1976) *The Power of the Group*. London: Davis-Poynter
Schmid, P. (1998) 'Face to face': The art of encounter. In B. Thorne and E. Lambers (Eds.) *Person-Centred Therapy: A European Perspective* (pp. 74–90). London: Sage
Stark, M. (2000) *Modes of Therapeutic Action: Enhancement of Knowledge, Provision of Experience, Engagement in Relationship*. Northvale, NJ: Jason Aronson
Sturdevant, K. (1995) Classical Greek 'koinonia', the psychoanalytic median group, and the large person-centered community group: Dialogue in three democratic contexts. *The Person-Centered Journal*, 2(2), 64–71
Tudor, K. (1999) *Group Counselling*. London: Sage
Tudor, K. and Worrall, M. (2004a) Person-centred perspectives on supervision. In K. Tudor and M. Worrall (Eds.) *Freedom to Practise: Person-Centred Approaches to Supervision* (pp. 43–64). Ross-on-Wye: PCCS Books
Tudor, K. and Worrall, M. (2004b) Process in supervision: A person-centred critique. In K. Tudor and M. Worrall (Eds.) *Freedom to Practise: Person-Centred Approaches to Supervision* (pp. 65–77). Ross-on-Wye: PCCS Books
Tudor, K. and Worrall, M. (2006) *Person-Centred Therapy: A Clinical Philosophy*. London: Routledge
Wheatley, M.J. and Kellner-Rogers, M. (1996) *A Simpler Way*. San Francisco, CA: Berrett-Koehler
Wibberley, M. (1988) Encounter. In J. Rowan and W. Dryden (Eds.) *Innovative Therapy in Britain* (pp. 61–84). Milton Keynes: Open University Press
Wilkins, P. (1995) A creative therapies model for the group supervision of counsellors. *British Journal of Guidance and Counselling*, 23(2), 245–57
Wood, J.K. (1982) Person-centered group therapy. In G. Gazda (Ed.) *Innovations in Group Psychotherapy* (2nd edn.). Springfied, IL: Charles Thomas
Wood, J.K. (1984) Communities for learning: A person-centered approach. In R.F. Levant and J.M. Shlien (Eds.) *Client-Centered Therapy and the Person-Centered Approach: New Directions in Theory, Research and Practice* (pp. 297–316). New York: Praeger
Wood, J.K. (1999) Towards an understanding of large group dialogue and its implications. In C. Lago and M. Macmillan (Eds.) *Experiences in Relatedness: Groupwork and the Person-Centred Approach* (pp. 137–66). Ross-on-Wye: PCCS Books
Yalom, I.D. (1995) *The Theory and Practice of Group Psychotherapy* (4th edn.). New York: Basic Books

CHAPTER EIGHT

E-MAIL SUPERVISION

COLIN LAGO AND JEANNIE WRIGHT

Supervision via e-mail is a relatively recent professional development in counselling and psychotherapy. This chapter explores supervision online via e-mail and with particular reference to the person-centred approach. The authors have for some time, both separately and jointly, been interested in the potential opportunities offered for self-expression and exploration through writing in general and, more specifically, through online applications. Despite our interest and searches, we have to date found no research publications on online supervision other than the work of Fenichel (2003) who provides a very thorough and practical overview of what online supervision is and how an online supervisory relationship is developed. He also provides a well-informed perspective and introduction to the pioneering work of the International Society for Mental Health Online (ISMHO) (see www.ISMHO.org). The ISMHO has led the way in ethical practice in online therapy and supervision and its website provides a wealth of case studies and reported experience of practitioners who have been in the forefront of the use of technology in counselling and psychotherapy.

Despite this minimal research data, online supervision is currently being practised in the United Kingdom and other parts of the world. This chapter is thus based on:

1. Previous awareness of and studies in the potential of creative writing within therapy and self-development (see Bolton et al., 2004).

2. Previous considerations of and experiences in e-mail counselling (Lago, 1995, 1996a, 1996b, 1997; Lewis, 1999).
3. Consultations with users and colleagues within this electronic medium.
4. Membership of an online study group.
5. Our own direct experience of mutual online supervision.

In this chapter we have adopted a style and structure that is consistent with the developing forms of e-mail communication, where e-mail has become a 'voice' somewhere between speaking and writing. We hope that the following text thus communicates our personal experiences, our thoughts and considerations, and our working communications in a form that demonstrates some of the implications of supervising electronically.

A BRIEF HISTORY OF OUR INTEREST IN THIS ALTERNATIVE MEDIUM

Colin: I can't remember now if it was something that one particular client said to me or if it was an accumulation of various conversations with student clients, counselling colleagues and university committee proceedings, but I recall feeling strongly that the emerging world of electronic communications and possibilities had to be considered carefully by our profession. I was not aware of any publications, or of much in the way of professional discourse on the subject. Yet, there I was, working in a university environment where, already (in the mid-1990s), students and staff had twenty-four hour access to computer terminals 364 days of the year, and students were reporting their powerful experiences of connectedness and intimacy achieved through e-mail, 'chat rooms', internet resources and so on. In its lack of response to this explosion of new methodology for communication, I really wondered if our profession was burying its head in the sand.

Writing this now, just ten years later, seems quite extraordinary. There are many online therapy services now available; it is possible to qualify as an online therapist; and substantive mental health information and many interactive self-help programmes are available on the internet. Colleagues even conduct supervision by e-mail.

Let me return, briefly, to those origins of my awareness referred to above. Parallel to the practice of therapy, where we gain our knowledge through our clients, I came to appreciate the existence of this electronic landscape through talking with students and staff in the university in which I was working. My professional concerns were:

- Why is no one in our profession writing about these issues?
- Why is no one in our profession talking about these issues?
- When I have tried to raise it for discussion, how can I understand the 'throwing up of hands' response I seem to be getting from colleagues?
- Was it fear of new technology I was encountering?
- Was it the apprehension of facilitating what was perceived to be the demise of human contact by encouraging these modes of connection?
- Were colleagues concerned that this might spell the end of counselling services, particularly within further and higher education?

As may be seen from the following references, I became impassioned to communicate to colleagues and our professional associations, that it was incumbent upon us to address this phenomenon and to adopt a considered professional response to it (Lago, 1995, 1996a, 1996b, 1997). Eventually, as a consequence of the deliberations of a working party within the Association for University and College Counselling (AUCC) that I had chaired, in 1999 the British Association for Counselling (BAC) published a study by Lewis titled 'Counselling Online'.

The above 'historical' stepping-stones had both seemingly paralleled Jeannie's experience and led to further developments that she now describes.

Jeannie: Meanwhile between 1997 and 1999 I was working at the University of the South Pacific, in Fiji, which was wonderful, but professionally isolating. I had used e-mail to supplement the group supervision with colleagues at the University in Fiji and learned a lot about 'practice at a distance'. I had also begun to research the literature on the benefits of writing in therapy and how writing is used in various modalities (Wright, 2002, 2004a). Joining the team at Sheffield as Staff Counsellor in 1999 provided an opportunity to be a part of the conversation about online provision, which Colin has outlined above. With support from other colleagues, the conversation at Sheffield eventually developed into a working group and then into a project designed to both offer a service to staff and to research the experience from both the clients' and the practitioners' point of view.

The pilot project offering online counselling to staff at the University where Colin and I were both working in 1999 was a little before its time. We struggled to find examples of practice in the UK and found Ethical Guidelines via the American Counseling Association (ACA, 1989). However, some of the findings from the International Society for Mental Health Online in the USA and the 'writing paradigm' based on Pennebaker and his associates' research (see, for example, Francis and Pennebaker, 1992) were very relevant to our proposed online service. In an experiment replicating others that had shown positive outcomes for writing about hitherto undisclosed, emotionally distressing experience, Francis and Pennebaker asked one group of university staff volunteers to write about the stressful, or emotionally difficult areas of their lives. A control group was asked to write about trivial events. Positive changes across a range of measures were observed in the group writing about emotional upheavals. The written word is powerful, as novelists and poets have known throughout the ages. The scientific research on writing and health (see Lepore and Smyth, 2002) has been applied successfully to 'real world' therapeutic contexts. Text-based communication, as in e-mail supervision, can draw on the findings of both those interested in expressive and reflective writing as a therapeutic vehicle (see www.lapidus.org) and the growing body of scientific 'gold standard' research on the 'writing paradigm' (i.e. an intervention which encourages open writing as distinct from a structured writing intervention).

In the person-centred approach Brice (2000) had clearly found it possible to offer the core conditions using e-mail with a client who was temporarily unable to use a face-to-face service. Other therapeutic orientations have used writing and its application via the internet. The narrative approach has been called 'a practice of writing' (see Speedy, 2004) and Ryle (2004), for example, describes the specific uses of writing online in the supervision of cognitive analytic therapists.

Being open then to the possibilities of electronic therapy and supervision (and as a consequence of being invited to write this chapter), we conducted our own co-supervision for some months via e-mail, some extracts of which we reproduce here (in italics). I (Jeannie) also had had a first taste of supervision via asynchronous e-mail messages when working with clients online in Sheffield. (In asynchronous messages, one person sends a message and then waits for the other to reply, similar to correspondence by post or 'snail mail'. In synchronous e-mailing, both people, or a group of people, are online at the same time and can 'converse' in real time.)

This joint process has further enabled us to experience, first hand, the joys and challenges of this approach to supervision. In addition, as we have always engaged in both individual and group supervision, we have also been able to note and appreciate some of the differences between live supervision and online approaches.

The rest of this chapter now addresses different aspects of e-mail supervision. In the first part we suggest that this medium can facilitate the supervisee's capacity for reflectivity. The second part acknowledges the lean amount of research to support this mode of professional engagement. Notwithstanding this, our editorial contributions to the text by Bolton et al. (2004) underline our conviction of the many values of 'personal writing' in terms of self-development and exploration, and it is this underlying valuing of the writing format that underpins our belief of the possible values inherent in e-mail supervision. These are briefly acknowledged in the third section. The field of electronic based communications is, in relative terms, a young field. Young people, who have been schooled in computers and digital technology, have embraced this medium enthusiastically and used it ingeniously. For older therapists (like ourselves) the fourth part addresses both the challenges and opportunities inherent in the delivery of electronic therapy and supervision. In the following part, e-mail supervision in practice, we offer a series of points addressing specific aspects of practice, contained within which are direct and indirect allusions to person-centred practice. We conclude by listing the advantages, as we currently apprise them, of the use of e-mail as a form for supervision.

SUPERVISION AS PART OF REFLECTIVE PRACTICE

In common with other 'human services' such as social work, nursing and teaching, counselling promotes reflective practice as a central part of initial training and continuing professional development. Writing as part of, or as a vehicle for reflective practice is also widely used in a variety of settings and across disciplines (Bolton, 2005). Here we are concerned with how the writing involved in e-mail supervision may contribute to a reflective capacity, a form of ongoing 'internal supervision', within the supervisee, particularly from a person-centred point of view.

Pennebaker (2002), a social psychologist and pioneer of the 'writing cure', suggests that:

> To me the essence of the writing technique is that it forces people to stop what they are doing and briefly reflect on their lives. It is one of the few times that people are given permission to see where they have been and where they are going without having to please anyone. (p. 283)

Despite the fact that words such as 'forces' and 'given permission' in the above quotation are not consistent with the person-centred approach, we do believe that using writing is a most useful medium to develop thinking and expression. As an adjunct to this, perhaps it is no surprise that a great number of counselling and psychotherapy courses recommend to their students that they maintain reflective diaries during their studies. In addition, recent moves in a range of disciplines towards valuing subjective experience and personal narrative adds to the argument for more phenomenological research into the subject of writing in therapy, and in online supervision:

Evocative stories activate subjectivity and compel emotional responses. They long to be used rather than analyzed; to be told and retold rather than theorized and settled; to offer lessons for further observation rather than undebateable [sic] conclusions; and to substitute the companionship of intimate detail for the loneliness of abstracted facts. (Ellis and Bochner, 2000, p. 744)

Research base

The research base for online therapy and supervision is growing, but is still very limited (see Grohol, 2004). Goss and Antony (2003) provide an overview of developments in online counselling and supervision. Work has been conducted and published online in the USA by the International Society for Mental Health Online (www.ISMHO.org) as indicated earlier. Within the person-centred approach there has been some interest in the possibility of working online therapeutically (Brice, 1999), but our searches have drawn a complete blank in terms of research specifically about e-mail supervision, let alone within the person-centred approach.

Our pilot project, as outlined previously, drew from a different but linked body of research around the benefits of expressive and reflective writing. This chapter does not focus on that research directly (for reviews of US-based research see Lepore and Smyth, 2002), but some of the experiments (e.g. Pennebaker and Seagal, 1999) and other studies (Wright, 2004a) certainly informed the online work in Sheffield.

The psychological values of electronic writing

In the text by Bolton et al. (2004) Colin analysed the uses of writing by international students at one university in the UK (Lago, 2004). There was very clear personal evidence offered by respondents as to the value of writing as a therapeutic mechanism. This was illustrated in the variety of ways in which the participants in the study used their writing:

- As a psychological container—writing helped them manage and contain difficult and sometimes anxiety-provoking circumstances.
- As a personal route to understanding—through the writing process their own reflective capacities were stimulated and, consequently, their own understanding of events was enhanced.
- As having an interpersonal value—as one interviewee said: 'Writing helps me to work out what I'm feeling about someone or what I need to say to

them ... and these "sample letters" then really help me to work out what to say when I actually do write to them.' (Lago, 2004, p. 101)
- Writing and thinking go hand in hand—each of the interviewees in this survey paid tribute to the connection between writing and thinking.

Together with research and experience from those using creative and reflective writing in practice (e.g. Bolton et al., 2004), the whole body of 'writing paradigm' research, pioneered by Pennebaker, supports the specific elements featured above from Colin's chapter. The extraordinary psychological values of writing—and, by implication, writing via e-mail—are therefore examined from both the scientific and the humanities ends of the research spectrum (see Wright, 2004b). E-mail supervision is a further step on this journey, a further usage to which writing might be harnessed for the sake of the supervisee who, for whatever reasons (distance, convenience, preference, cost, etc.), might prefer to conduct their supervision via this medium.

THE POTENTIAL AND FRUSTRATIONS OF TECHNOLOGY IN THE COMMUNICATION PROCESS

The current rapid advancement of computer-driven technology means that there are increasing systems through which supervisors and supervisees might communicate. For example, one such system is Skype (www.sykpe.com), a phone service which operates via the internet at the cost of the internet connection and, therefore, makes it much cheaper to talk long distance and internationally. This opens up more possibilities for on-line supervision. When used in conjunction with a web camera, it means that both participants can talk and see each other on their computer screens. As time unfolds we conjecture that e-mail systems might decrease in usage in favour of 'sound and sight' systems such as Skype.

By contrast, however, many colleagues in counselling and psychotherapy experience immense frustration with and are, indeed, relatively or completely unaware of the increasing technological possibilities associated with digital communication. The following expresses how some ageing counsellors feel about technology!

> *Dear Computer,*
> *I need to finish this writing. You are very old now and beginning to behave erratically. Sometimes fonts change without me doing anything. Sometimes underlining appears, sometimes not. Installing that database that was supposed to make referencing easier was the most desperate mistake. I can't work it. I panic about losing all that I've already done. Sweat breaks out on my scalp. It seems to make you crash. Now I don't know how to uninstall it.*

> *The feeling of not being able to fix it, to be in control of how the finished writing looks upsets me out of all proportion to the problem. Is this to do with age? Gender based? Having to use you and other newer computers has contributed to the stress of this writing in untold ways. So, I'm telling those ways now. It has taken all the joy of writing out of it. Yes, you have made Tipp-ex and other whiting-out tools obsolete but I prefer paper and pen/pencil. Maybe newer technology—voice activated?—will help; maybe, maybe not.*
> *Yours truly, Jeannie.*
> (E-mail communication between the authors, 11th January, 2006)

Inevitably, over time, this situation will change and increased computer literacy and competency on the part of the therapist will be accompanied by developments in the electronic medium.

E-MAIL SUPERVISION IN PRACTICE

This section of the chapter reports and reflects on the various points of learning and discovery that we made during our trial of supervision by e-mail. We and other authors have made some of the following points in different publications, but their continued significance within our own correspondence emphasises their value.

On issues of time, frequency, and contracting

Drawing a comparison with live supervision, we tried to adopt the use of an hour as a guide to writing our messages. We experienced time passing very quickly when we were writing, and our texts often noted this:

- *I can't believe that 23 minutes had gone already!!!* (Colin)
- *Like you I'm going to time this. One thing I've noticed about the writing-therapy client I have is that I spend rather longer than the 50-minute hour, and as you say, that has to be watched. Well, here goes…* (Jeannie)
- *I've been up early and thought I'd make a start but, as you've said, the time this takes is surprising.* (Jeannie)

We were often surprised at how apparently little 'wordage' we had written (as supervisees) within an hour's session. In that time it was possible to outline one, perhaps two, supervision dilemmas. This raises interesting questions in terms of the extent to which:

(a) The supervisee uses only an hour for their writing and composition, thus maintaining the boundaried parallel with live supervision; or

(b) The supervisee focuses much more on the content of the concerns that they wish to have discussed in supervision and, consequently, take more time to compose their message. This approach ignores the extent of time that the supervisee takes but enables them to strive for an accuracy of expression of their material.

Further, in using the written word, it is possible to optimise the reflected learning from it through rereading it at different times. This facility obviously relates to both the original writing of the supervisee and then that of the supervisor and their comments. Clients have reported how useful this element of working electronically is for them, indicating that such revisiting of the joint writings (of themselves and their therapists or supervisors) has furthered their own considerations and emotional comfort with difficult issues.

In consideration of the frequency of agreed supervisory e-mails (weekly, monthly, etc.) the limit on time dedicated to writing may really only be of concern to the supervisor and as such may be reflected in the contract agreed between supervisee and supervisor. The supervisor necessarily has to have some regard for their other professional commitments and might wish to schedule their e-mail supervisory work into their daily diary of face-to-face work. In such cases the supervisor might, for example, schedule an hour's session to reply to the supervisee's last e-mail/s.

In the staff-counselling online project (Wright, 2001) each client was informed that their message/s would be responded to at a specific time each week. The client was free to write one or many messages in the intervening time-frame between sessions, but knew that the e-mail therapist would only reply on the regular agreed dates. This system thus reflected face-to-face work simulating weekly appointments and was, therefore, asynchronous. This mechanism both respected and facilitated the therapist's own capacity to determine their workload, and enabled the client to explore at length their particular concerns. Whether working as an e-mail therapist or supervisor, the respondent has both to read the text and to construct and compose an appropriate response to the issues raised, which raises the issue of competence in both reading and writing.

On becoming a wordsmith

Good morning Colin!
Thank you for starting things off—it was lovely to read your words, your 'voice' is very much the same when you speak and write. (Jeannie)

This point is, of course, closely related to the absence of non-verbal cues. Communication by e-mail requires a certain fluency and competence with the written word. The clearer that the supervisee can write about the critical incident or issue/s that they wish to discuss in supervision, the clearer will be the communicated meaning of the incident or issue to the supervisor. Such clarity on the part of the supervisee obviously deserves to be reflected in the quality of the supervisor's text in response.

At its most basic the essence of e-mail supervision is conducted through what appears on the computer screen. In addition to words, sentences and paragraphs, there are other signs and symbols to be included. These can be loosely compared to the whole area of paralinguistics in communication where accent, tone, volume, emphasis, pitch, sounds other than words, (sighs, groans, and so on), and message convention (what is said, when) are profoundly determined by personality, emotional arousal, situation and culture. The 'para-symbolic' equivalent on screen is composed of the use of punctuation marks, font choice, upper or lower case, italics, brackets and the vast array of computer developed shorthand and constructed symbols ('smiley' faces being one such example). Such stylistic options, used creatively, can provide further shades and extensions to meaning.

The further challenge of communicating online is to realise that we are missing between seventy-five and eighty per cent of the expressed communication through the loss of perception of each other's non-verbal behaviour. The suggestion is that, in working online, we are only really working with perhaps twenty per cent of communication potential: in other words, that we are reduced to making and inferring meanings from words, symbols and sentence structures alone.

Having a fluent capacity for composing written messages (being a 'wordsmith') is obviously a desirable skill in any written communication, including e-mail (Lago, 1996b). The e-mail format is one that was designed for, and lends itself to, the transmission of direct, brief messages. Supervisors who use e-mail regularly in their everyday work, and are thus used to transmitting brief, succinct answers to normal correspondence may have to be extremely disciplined in their use of e-mail for what is often an extensive response to the supervisee. They may have to avoid the abbreviations, clipped sentences or one-word responses they employ in their everyday business e-mails. Alternatively, they could tailor an appropriate Word document to send as an attachment to the supervisee.

On becoming a person-centred (supervisor) wordsmith

When the task of e-mail supervision is considered within the theoretical perspectives of the person-centred approach, it is inevitable that the e-mail supervisor's way of being, represented by their writing style, needs:

- to convey the attitudinal qualities of the approach (congruence, unconditional positive regard, empathy);

- to convey the philosophic position of the approach (trusting the supervisee in their choice of material they present, respecting the supervisee's capacity to process the challenges they are facing, etc.); and
- to incorporate an embodied model of person-centred supervision (see Villas-Boas Bowen, 1986; Patterson, 2000).

Similar to face-to-face work, the e-mail supervisor's way of being, conveyed through their written communication style, is a critical component in the formation and maintenance of a 'good enough' working relationship with the supervisee.

On using the font and the keyboard creatively!

> *Your first para on the following page raises an extraordinary paradox:* 'Each time something is offered, something is taken away.' *I agree with you so much ... the task of* 'being there' *and* 'staying out of the way enough' *seems the most difficult and delicate tightrope going ...* (Colin)

In the above extract from a supervisory response by Colin, he has used italic for his writing and then offered an original statement made by the supervisee (Jeannie) in plain text, thus drawing a distinction between the two writers. Similarly, in the same text response he writes:

> *My 'notes in the margin' that I wrote when reading [the printout of] your attachment, specifically to the lines ...* 'It's been fascinating observing the parallels between this work—as close to home as I can get, and previous experience of counselling with people from SUCH different backgrounds, races, religions, languages.' ... *say 'I'd love you to expand on this so that I COULD CATCH YOUR FULL MEANING.'* ... *(Please excuse these capitals, I hadn't intended them, but when I looked up I realised that my finger must have caught the caps key ... a sort of electronic Freud slipping here!!! ... and as I do wish to catch your full meaning—I've left it in, in capitals.) ... Do you mean something like even apparently counselling people who are* 'close to home' *can prove extremely challenging ... that geographically/ethnically close clients can seem so different, so* 'other' *... (Jeannie, I hope you can read the meaning into this that I intended ... it's a bit cumbersome as a sentence/statement!)*

An analysis of this suggests:

- that the supervisor has carefully read and reflected on the supervisee's text.
- that the supervisor, in using the supervisee's exact words—which is a value of written communication—provides evidence of having both noted and 'mulled over' the text, which will help to reassure the supervisee that:

The supervisor takes her work and concerns seriously.

The supervisor genuinely wishes to understand her experience.

The supervisor is human / congruent.

- that the supervisor has demonstrated their wish to comprehend the supervisee, and to facilitate/stimulate the supervisee's continued reflectivity on their original text.

DIVERSITY, PERCEPTION AND PROJECTION

The medium of e-mail messages, where communication is restricted to the exchange of verbal texts, offers a unique opportunity for meaningful exchanges between two people who are not visible to each other. This absence of visual clues offers interesting opportunities for relationships to grow unencumbered by the complex perceptual and judgemental criteria that impact each of us in the social world. Visible difference and the diversity of the 'other' in face-to-face circumstances can, and frequently does, constitute an initial barrier to relationship formation and, at worst, may lead to discriminatory outcomes. The natural tendency to appraise and judge others based on our initial perceptions occurs within moments of meeting. In the 'face-to-face' meeting our initial judgements are impacted by our attitudes, prejudices, projections and previous experiences of people.

Of course, when we receive e-mails, we may well fantasise about the sender of the message if we do not already know them. We might wonder about their name (if they have included it in the message) and develop our own vision of what it means, where it comes from, what it might say about the writer and so on. Also, a writer's language style might make us curious; their sentence structure, word selection, formal presentation as opposed to 'stream of consciousness', spelling and so on. Our perceptual senses and curiosity may continue to be aroused and heightened but our own experience, and thus our contention, is that the 'words only' focus of the e-mail medium both facilitates and focuses the supervisor's attention upon the meanings of the message and consequently reduces the tendency to evaluate/judge the other. In short, we contend that the effect of the initial impact of people's difference and diversity upon the subsequent relationship is substantially lessened within the e-mail relationship.

ON INTERNAL AND EXTERNAL LOCUS OF EVALUATION

Jeannie: *I'm currently supervising the online counsellors of a pilot project and have been fascinated by how closely their experience is mirroring my own in the Sheffield pilot. We are meeting face-to-face at present but may soon move to online supervision. One member* of the supervision group, Geraldine, who has consented to her voice being added to this chapter, illustrates some of the key points about reflecting on practice online.[1]

Geraldine: *My concern is that I may have ended up becoming more of an 'agony aunt' and less of a person-centred counsellor and I'd like to explore this a bit in supervision. When I read over the transcripts I find that there are some instances where I have approached things in a way that I don't think I would have done in a face-to-face session. 'C' initially approached us for counselling because, as she put it: 'At times I sit and worry what people think of me and what they are saying about me behind my back.' In person-centred terms I see this as an external rather than an internal locus of evaluation. I believe that if I am genuine in the relationship and the client experiences my empathic understanding and unconditional positive regard then, through the process of therapy, the client will become more self-referrent. To encourage the client's autonomy I will want to avoid any suggestion that 'I know best', and I am aware that it is more helpful to try to understand things from the client's point of view than to attempt explanations from mine.*

Concerns about directivity

Jeannie: *In online supervision, as well as online counselling, I have found myself using questions much more than in face-to-face practice. I also had a tendency to give advice in some of my early responses to clients, which was picked up by my online supervisor at the time. One clear advantage of online supervision and online therapy is that the text between you and your client is available for full analysis and reflection, at any time (assuming you have saved it on the computer). Re-reading Mearns and Thorne (2000) reassured me that I was not moving too far away from the spirit of the person-centred approach: 'The importance of directivity is not in what the counsellor does but in what the client experiences.' (p. 191)*

On owning one's own material

(Please note that I have introduced this latter point—you weren't making it ... The comments are based on my experiences recently in both the large and small groups in Austria.) (Colin)

Colin: This statement, deliberately appended in brackets at the end of a paragraph, sought to suggest support for something that Jeannie had been exploring in terms of group process and facilitation, but also recognised, in its sentence structure, that my own comments were also influenced by my recent experiencing in other groups and therefore may not have applied fully to Jeannie's text.

We contend that this medium requires the writer to be very explicit in communicating the exact sense that they are striving to convey: a demanding task. For example, the writer must find a written equivalent to the skilled use, in

---

1. Geraldine Wilkes is part of a pilot project online counselling service in a university setting.

face-to-face contact, of a saying, perhaps accompanied by a shrug or other appropriate non-verbal sign.

On intentions, communication and meaning!

> Dear Jeannie,
> Further to your last notes sent to me, written on the 18*th* Nov, please find some thoughts below.
> I have gone immediately to your second paragraph discussing empathic following. You go on to talk about the challenge/difficulty of catching such nuances online. This complexity of communicating, particularly online, was highlighted for me the following day when I did a workshop on Cultural Awareness. I shared with them 5 principles of perception/communication ... which included the points that (a) each of us perceives differently, (b) we each see things which don't exist and (c) we do not see things which do exist. Given these phenomena, the demands of attempting to communicate with accuracy and clarity (and maybe elegance—but this might put too high a demand on writing anything!!!), either in writing or speaking, are formidable ... recognising, all the time, that others may not catch our meaning that we intend. (Meanings being in people, not words, sort of thinking!) (Colin)

This extract from our e-mail communications is deliberately included to, yet again, emphasise the importance we are placing on the challenge of accurately understanding and interpreting the supervisee's written messages. The three principles of communication listed in the above quote point us to just how easy it is to misunderstand online communication. Supervisor-written responses, seeking understanding and clarification, are likely to figure frequently in the person-centred e-mail supervisor's responses to their supervisees.

SOME ADVANTAGES OF E-MAIL SUPERVISION

It has been suggested that it is disappointing that online counselling has not progressed as it was predicted to do (Grohol, 2004). This could also be said for online supervision. Nevertheless, the benefits can be summarised as follows:

- Writing as part of reflective practice facilitates the development of the 'internal supervisor' and reflexivity in the practitioner—writing and thinking go hand in hand.
- It offers access for those with mobility disabilities or for whom geographical distance is an issue.

- Time may be used differently. That is, the supervisee might choose to write about their concerns or issues immediately after a session, while it is fresh in their minds and at some point send that account, or several of these, to the supervisee.
- If e-mail supervision is conducted asynchronously then the supervisor can choose his or her own moment to construct a reply. This, of course, might have to conform to the 'working contract' that both parties have previously agreed.
- The focus and pace is essentially within the writer's control. As one person using writing therapy put it: 'it allows me to articulate fully without being distracted by physical surroundings, or time pressure, or either party's mood/mind set at that particular time'.
- Availability—writing for online supervision is available anywhere, anytime, subject to access to a computer with an internet facility.
- Clarity—some people record how writing enables them to be clearer in their communication with self and others. Thus, a supervisee will already have started on their work on the issues/cases they present in their writing process.
- For some people the writing/electronic medium is less shaming and facilitates more openness than face-to-face contact. It has long been recognised that some people are more open on screen than in person when expressing shaming experiences and inhibited emotions——and the same is likely to be true of tentative reflections on difficult aspects of therapy.
- There is a written record of process and progress—by rereading and reflecting on their writing, some people suggest that they gain a sustained sense of their own achievement and frequently come to appreciate the multiple nuances and complexities the original situation evoked.

In summation, in this chapter we consider that the medium of e-mail for counselling supervision has considerable potential. Supervision may be conducted at a distance, even internationally, via this method. Individual choice may be fully exercised in terms of when the writing is done, thus optimising those moments when, as a supervisee, you might be so anxious about your last client that writing down some initial reflections might prove relieving and illuminating. This is in contrast to having to wait, perhaps up to a month, for your next face-to-face supervision session. A clear and permanent record of the electronic dialogue between supervisee and supervisor can serve as a focus for consolidating learning, in contrast to spoken dialogues, some aspects of which might easily disappear from memory. These factors supportive of supervision by e-mail do need, however, balancing alongside the willingness and wish of both partners (supervisor and supervisee) to engage in electronic supervision. Recognition must also be made of the usage of time, and direct parallels with live supervision are unlikely to be helpful in developing this alternative form. Additionally, in the absence of non-verbal behaviour, attention to and efforts towards accurate understanding and transmission of messages is a necessity in practice.

Though the absence of supportive theoretical and research evidence in this field might dissuade many from engaging with it, we contend that it is a viable, credible and useful form for supervision and would encourage colleagues who do implement this format to seek to monitor, reflect and indeed, research the work they carry out. Publication and other forms of dissemination of such experiences will, over time, contribute to refined and improved supervisory practices.

REFERENCES

American Counseling Association (1989) *Ethical Guidelines*. Alexandria, VA: ACA

Bolton, G. (2005) *Reflective Practice: Writing and Professional Development* (2nd edn.). London: Sage

Bolton, G., Howlett, S., Lago, C. and Wright, J. K. (2004) *Writing Cures: Introductory Handbook of Writing in Counselling and Psychotherapy*. Hove: Brunner-Routledge

Brice, A. (1999) A case study of therapeutic support using e-mail. *Person-Centred Practice*, 7(1), 27–32

Brice, A. (2000) Therapeutic support using e-mail: A case study. *Counselling*, 12(2), 100–1

Ellis, C. and Bochner, A. (2000), Autoethnography, personal narrative, reflexivity: researcher as subject. In N.K. Denzin and Y.S. Lincoln (Eds.),*Handbook of Qualitative Research*. London: Sage

Fenichel, M. (2003) The supervisory relationship online. In S. Goss and K. Anthony (Eds.) *Technology in Counselling and Psychotherapy: A Practitioner's Guide* (pp. 75–88). Basingstoke: Palgrave

Francis, M.E. and Pennebaker, J.W. (1992) Putting stress into words: The impact of writing on physiological, absentee and self-reported emotional well-being measures. *American Journal of Health Promotion*, 6, 280–287

Goss, S. and Anthony, K. (2003) *Technology in Counselling and Psychotherapy: A Practitioner's Guide*. Basingstoke: Palgrave

Grohol, J. (2004) Online counseling: A historical perspective. In R. Kraus, J. Zack and G. Stricker (Eds.) *Online Counseling: A Handbook for Mental Health Professionals* (pp. 51–68). San Diego, CA: Elsevier

Lago, C. (1995) *Computer Therapeutics*. Paper delivered at the 6th International Forum of the Person-Centered Approach, Thessaloniki, Greece

Lago, C. (1996a) Computer therapeutics: A new challenge for counsellors and psychotherapists. *Counselling*, 17(4), 287–9

Lago, C. (1996b) *Future Shock: Electronic Connections and Human Disconnectedness*. Paper delivered at the 1st World Conference of Psychotherapy, Vienna, Austria

Lago, C (1997) Electronic therapies: Possibilities and limitations. *Person-Centered Journal*, 4(1), 53–8

Lago, C. (2004) 'When I write I think': Personal uses of writing by international students. In G. Bolton, S. Howlett, C. Lago and J.K. Wright (Eds.) *Writing Cures: Introductory Handbook of Writing in Counselling and Psychotherapy* (pp. 95–105). London: Brunner-Routledge

Lepore, S.J. and Smyth, J.M. (2002) *The Writing Cure: How Expressive Writing Promotes Health and Emotional Well-being*. Washington DC: American Psychological Association

Lewis, K. (1999) *The View of the British Association for Counselling: Counselling Online—Opportunities and Risks in Counselling Clients via the Internet*. Special Report. Rugby: BAC

Mearns, D. and Thorne, B. (2000) *Person-Centred Therapy Today: New Frontiers in Theory and Practice*. London: Sage

Patterson, C.H. (2000) *Understanding Psychotherapy: Fifty Years of Client-Centred Practice*. Ross-on-Wye: PCCS Books

Pennebaker, J.W. (2002) Writing about emotional events: From past to future. In S.J. Lepore and J.M. Smyth (Eds.) *The Writing Cure: How Expressive Writing Promotes Health and Emotional Well-Being* (pp. 281–91). Washington, DC: American Psychological Association

Pennebaker, J.W. and Seagal, J.D. (1999) Forming a story: The health benefits of narrative. *Journal of Clinical Psychology*, 55, 1243–54

Ryle, A. (2004) Writing by patients and therapists in cognitive analytic therapy. In G. Bolton, S. Howlett, C. Lago and J.K. Wright (Eds.) *Writing Cures: Introductory Handbook of Writing in Counselling and Psychotherapy* (pp. 59–71). London: Brunner-Routledge

Speedy, J. (2004) The contribution of narrative ideas and writing practices in therapy. In G. Bolton, S. Howlett, C. Lago and J.K. Wright (Eds.) *Writing Cures: Introductory Handbook of Writing in Counselling and Psychotherapy* (pp. 25–34). London: Brunner-Routledge

Villas-Boas Bowen, M.C. (1986) Personality differences and person-centered supervision. *Person-Centered Review*, 1(3), 291–309

Wright, J.K. (2001) Developing online counselling in the workplace. *Counselling at Work*, No. 34, pp. 4–6. Rugby: British Association for Counselling and Psychotherapy

Wright, J.K. (2002) Online counselling: Learning from writing therapy. *British Journal of Guidance and Counselling*, 30, 285–98

Wright, J.K. (2004a) Developing online text-based counselling in the workplace. In G. Bolton, S. Howlett, C. Lago and J. K. Wright (Eds.) *Writing Cures: Introductory Handbook of Writing in Counselling and Psychotherapy* (pp. 142–50). London: Brunner-Routledge

Wright, J.K. (2004b) The passion of science, the precision of poetry: Therapeutic writing: A review of the literature. In G. Bolton, S. Howlett, C. Lago and J.K. Wright (Eds.) *Writing Cures: Introductory Handbook of Writing in Counselling and Psychotherapy* (pp. 7–17). London: Brunner Routledge

PART FOUR

DEBATES, DEVELOPMENTS AND DOMAINS

CHAPTER NINE

SUPERVISION AND TRAINING OF 'ROGERS-1' AND 'ROGERS-2' THERAPISTS: BASIC CONCEPTS AND METHODS

MARVIN FRANKEL AND LISBETH SOMMERBECK

The authors discuss the training and supervision of therapists in the light of radical changes in Rogers' descriptions of therapy from 1951 to later descriptions, a change which we distinguish as 'Rogers-1' and 'Rogers-2' (Frankel and Sommerbeck, 2005, in press). This distinction may be seen in therapeutic practice and, we argue, should be identified and elaborated in the training and supervision of therapists. Indeed, we think that the training and supervision of both Rogers-1 and Rogers-2 therapists must make the distinction between Rogers-1 and Rogers-2 explicit. The first part of the training of therapists would entail helping them to recognize the differences between the therapeutic conduct of Rogers-1 and Rogers-2. For this purpose, critical assessments from both perspectives of selections from Rogers-1 and Rogers-2 therapy sessions would constitute a serious part of the training of therapists from both of these schools of thought. Examples of this are included in the first part of the paper. It seems these examples demonstrate the incompatibility between Rogers-1 supervisors and Rogers-2 supervisors. The second part discusses the issues for training and supervision that are implied by the distinction between Rogers-1 therapy and Rogers-2 therapy. The authors do not focus solely on the individual supervision relationship because they regard training, in a broader sense, as being intimately connected with supervision. Both training and supervision must be appropriate for a therapist's preferred approach (Rogers-1 or Rogers-2) to be of optimal value in enhancing a therapist's competence.

THE DISTINCTION BETWEEN ROGERS-1 AND ROGERS-2

In a recent paper the authors distinguish between Rogers-1 and Rogers-2 (Frankel and Sommerbeck, 2005). We contend that Rogers-1 was presented in the classic text *Client-Centered Therapy* in which Rogers (1951) identifies two conditions required for therapeutic change: unconditional positive regard and empathy. Unconditional positive regard was conveyed by a compassionate tone and manner and the utter *absence* of any comment on the therapist's part that expressed his or her tastes, attitudes, values, guidance or prejudices. The hypothesis was—and is—that clients, on hearing an empathic understanding of their narratives in the context of unconditional positive regard, are able to provide their own insights and direction. While Rogers-1's empathic reflections succeed in capturing the critical themes of the client's narrative as he himself sees it (from the client's internal perspective), Rogers-1 also attempts to convey unconditional positive regard to the client. However, this aspect of the communication is not empathic, in that the client does not view himself with unconditional positive self-regard. In effect then, the client is being valued by Rogers more than he (the client) values himself until, of course, the therapy is brought to a successful close when the client's positive self-regard is unconditional as well. In every other respect, the empathic understanding of Rogers-1 always remains within the internal frame of reference of the client. Consequently, Rogers-1 consistently evokes the client's own narrative. The exclusive referencing of the internal frame of reference of the client becomes abundantly clear in considering this fragment of Rogers-1 with Gloria (Shostrom, 1965) as she speaks of her conflicting attitudes about sex outside of marriage:

Gloria: *Yeah, I feel like you're going to say, 'Now why do you think they're wrong.' And, uh, I have mixed feelings there too. Through therapy I'll say: 'Now look, I know this is natural. Women feel it; sure we don't talk about it a lot socially. But all women feel it, and it's very natural.' I've had sex for the last eleven years, I'm of course going to want it, but I still think it's wrong unless you're really, truly in love with a man. And my body doesn't seem to agree. And so I don't know how to accept it.*

Rogers: *It sounds like a triangle to me, doesn't it. You feel that I or therapists in general, or other people say 'It's alright, it's alright, it's natural enough, go ahead.' Um, and I guess you feel your body sort of lines up on that side of the picture, but something in you says, 'But I don't like it that way, not unless it's really right.'*

This simply provokes Gloria to accept her dilemma more fully:

Gloria: *Right.* (Pause, long breath.) *Uh, I have a hopeless feeling. I mean these are all the things I sort of feel myself. And I feel, oh now what.*

Gloria has accepted her hopelessness and Rogers' comment reveals his acceptance of the hopelessness as well:

Rogers: *And you feel, this is the conflict and it's just insoluble and therefore it's hopeless and here you've looked to me and I don't seem to give you any help, to ..*

In this response Rogers-1 does not offer any consolation, any grounds for hope, any questions that challenge Gloria's sense of despair. Gloria must live with that despair until she finds her own way.

In stark contrast, for Rogers-2, the external frame of reference of the therapist's reactions is a crucial aspect of effective psychotherapy. This encourages therapists to express freely their own judgments, attitudes, guidance and even challenges. The notion that such statements may reflect nothing more than the neurotic limitations of the therapist was never addressed. Since these non-empathic responses were now an encouraged aspect of the psychotherapeutic exchange, a new term entered the lexicon of Rogers-2 therapists: congruence. The Rogers-2 therapist must always be true to his own feelings and judgments, but in a way that does not produce conditions of worth. Thus, congruence was added to empathy and unconditional positive regard as necessary for positive therapeutic outcome.

For these and related reasons, the authors assert that, after 1951, Rogers in fact created a new therapy better called 'we'-centered or relationship-centered therapy in contrast to client-centered therapy (see Bachelor and Hovarth, 1999; Frankel and Sommerbeck, 2005, in press). Whereas Rogers-1 evokes the narrative of the client through his empathic reflections, Rogers-2 provokes the client's narrative by offering ideas that emanated from his own frame of reference. We can also see this in Rogers' interview with Gloria:

Rogers: *Or I guess I hear it a little differently ...*

Here Rogers-2 offers an interpretation of Gloria and acknowledges it as such. Gloria's narrative, which, up until that time, had been evocative in nature, is altered as she rejects the interpretation:

Gloria: *Gee, I don't feel like I'm saying that, no that isn't what I feel, really ...*

Later in the interview Rogers-2 offers another interpretation that is not reflecting Gloria's internal frame of reference:

Rogers: *I guess, uh, I'm sure this will sound elusive, but it seems to me, perhaps the person you're not being fully honest with is you?*

And once again the evocative nature of Gloria's narrative is broken as she responds to the attempt of Rogers-2 to help her from his external frame of reference:

Gloria: *Right. Alright. Now I hear what you're saying ...*

Gloria's attention has been diverted from self-narration to Rogers' perspective on her narration. On another occasion Rogers-2 offers his own judgment of Gloria's state of mind:

Rogers: *You don't sound so uncertain.*

Again Gloria's evocative narrative is short-circuited as she responds:

Gloria: *I don't? What do you mean?*

A moment later Rogers attempts to soothe Gloria by telling her that her apprehensions are normal when he states:

Rogers: *I understand, it's, I guess one thing that, uh, I feel very keenly is, it's an awfully risky thing to live ...*

Gloria's rather personal attempt to own and confess her apprehension about taking risks is undermined when her fear is homogenized by the aphoristic statement of Rogers that 'it's an awful risky thing to live'. Gloria, who does not feel normal, receives the unempathic reassurance that she most definitely is quite normal.

In this interview with Gloria, Rogers never noted the major departure he had made with his former stance on therapy. Indeed, at the present time, most Rogers-2 therapists see their view as evolving and consistent with Rogers-1. For example, Mearns and Thorne (2000, p. 89) write: 'We will suggest that Rogers' development of theory was not advanced during his "California" period, but it is worth emphasizing that the approach genuinely found its "heart" during that time.' Consequently, the supervision of Rogers-1 and Rogers-2 therapists during and after training requires that students from each school of thought recognize just how central their differences are. This is not an easy task since the vocabularies of Rogers-1 and Rogers-2 are the same. Both Rogers-1 and Rogers-2 write of empathy, unconditional positive regard, conditions of worth, the actualizing tendency, organismic valuing process, and so on. People who speak the same language are inclined to believe that they mean the same things. But, as Einstein noted, the meaning of a concept can only be understood in light of the actions that are taken with respect to that concept (see Rapoport, 1953). Thus, we hope that students training to become either Rogers-1 or Rogers-2 therapists would, in the course of their training, learn that their respective understandings of unconditional positive regard, empathy, conditions of worth, and the therapeutic relationship have little, if anything, in common. The fact that the distinction between Rogers-1 and Rogers-2 remains in any way controversial demonstrates how a common vocabulary can obscure differences. Consequently, it seems important that therapists in training and in supervision recognize rather profoundly these differences lest they carelessly and unwittingly slip from one school of thought to the other in their therapeutic practice. We think that such consistency is important. Rogers-1 (1951, p. 49) denounced the consequences of a confused eclecticism on the part of therapists: 'The more completely he [the therapist] acts upon his central hypothesis the more convincing is the evidence that the hypothesis is correct.'

Ideally, Rogers-2 students will appreciate that their perspective is not the product of an evolution of theory or the result of research on the key elements of effective psychotherapy but is, instead, a complete rejection of Rogers-1 and the creation of a 'we'-centered approach: the logic of which is that therapist and client could embark on a friendship, qualified only by the fact that it is a client-purchased friendship intended primarily to be helpful to the client. In contrast, Rogers-1 students would have to recognize that Rogers-2 bears less resemblance to Rogers-1 than orthodox psychoanalysis does. For example, it could be argued that the neutrality of the psychoanalyst has more in common with the unconditional positive regard offered by Rogers-1 therapists than the unconditional positive regard of Rogers-2 therapists. Like a Rogers-1 therapist, the orthodox psychoanalyst never expresses his frustrations, expectations or personal evaluations of the client's character as Rogers-2 therapists might (see below; Frankel and Sommerbeck, 2005).

In order to underline the difference between these divergent understandings and schools of thought, a critical part of the training curriculum for all 'person-centred' therapists would be the critical assessment of Rogers-2 from a Rogers-1 perspective, and vice versa. The following selections from therapists, whom we identify as Rogers-2 therapists, are themselves self-evident criticisms of Rogers-1 in that the therapist consistently offers critical commentary from an external frame of reference. We follow these selections with a critical analysis from a Rogers-1 perspective. This can also be read as examples of the incompatibility of a Rogers-1 supervisor with a Rogers-2 supervisee and vice versa. We will also show, specifically, how the training and supervision of students from these two schools of thought can be conducted, and we will pay particular attention to the training and supervision of Rogers-2 students so that their personal communications[1] to clients entail as little risk of conveying conditions of worth as possible. Hopefully, this kind of training will encourage both Rogers-1 and Rogers-2 therapists to go

---

1. Throughout the chapter 'personal communication' is taken to mean communication that is not guided by any conceptualization of appropriate and/or inappropriate therapeutic discourse.

their separate ways and engage in research efforts that distinguish the comparative efficacy of these two independent schools of psychotherapeutic thought.

CRITIQUE OF ROGERS-2 SUPERVISEES BY ROGERS-1 SUPERVISORS

Example 1 (from Bozarth, 2001, p. 194–195)

> Rose was a graduate student and client in a university counseling center … I noticed that I was not interested in some of her discussions and continuously had to re-establish my attention to her discourse … While I was pondering our interactions after one session, I became aware that I had been staring at her breasts during part of the session … I did talk with a colleague and felt clear that I was not reacting to Rose with sexual desire. My behavior continued the next session leading me to think that I might have to discuss the matter with her … Several sessions later, Rose discussed in detail her household budget. As she presented her detailed budget in a steady monotone, I was suddenly aware that I was again staring at her breasts. I rather abruptly interrupted her budget delineation to tell her about my behavior … As I finished telling her and was contemplating what else to say, Rose continued by switching from a discussion of her budget to a discussion of her bisexual feelings … It was when I expressed this 'persistent feeling' (really persistent self-observation) to Rose that we were both free to pursue her open struggle of sexual identity … I accepted my organismic experience and behavior without distortion and denial. My awareness in this instance was expressed to Rose.

Critical analysis of Example 1 by Rogers-1

'*Rose was a graduate student and client in a university counseling center … I noticed that I was not interested in some of her discussions and continuously had to re-establish my attention to her discourse.*'

Bozarth seems not to accept that every movement, every word, every act of the client is to realize a way to overcome their defensiveness and fear of disapproval. Instead of accepting a Rogers-1 perspective which is *always* counterpointed by the thought: 'You're really trying to struggle toward normality, aren't you?' (Rogers, 1951, p. 34), it strikes us that Bozarth does not view Rose in this light when he states: '*I noticed that I was not interested in some of her discussions and continuously had to re-establish my attention to her discourse.*' A psychoanalyst might suggest that Rose is resisting the therapy in light of psychoanalytic theory, which informs the analyst when the interpretation is suggested. Bozarth, and indeed Rogers-2 therapists, offer no such overarching understanding of personality that can justify their personal responses. Below we suggest the kind of training Bozarth and other Rogers-2 therapists would have to undergo so that their personal reactions are viewed by clients as just that—personal. Rogers-1 therapists wish to create the conditions which nurture clients to have an understanding of themselves based on their organismic valuing process. This is an intrapersonal and non-normative understanding. For Rogers-1 therapists, the display of any impatience would seduce a client into considering how others relate to *them*, thus inducing him to meet the conditions of worth suggested by such a display. In this case, the Rogers-2 therapist is telling clients to understand themselves in light of the reactions of others, not in the light of their organismic valuing process. The approach of Rogers-2 is thus interpersonal and normative.

'While I was pondering our interactions after one session, I became aware that I had been staring at her breasts during part of the session ... I did talk with a colleague and felt clear that I was not reacting to Rose with sexual desire. My behavior continued the next session leading me to think that I might have to discuss the matter with her.'

As a Rogers-2 therapist, Bozarth is not upset at his lack of attention to the internal frame of reference of the client, within which the client presumably did not refer to her breasts. Nevertheless, Bozarth does feel it is necessary to make sure that his feelings are not erotic in nature. But why? If it is therapeutically acceptable to attend to breasts without desire why isn't it equally acceptable to attend to breasts with desire? It might even be more acceptable, in that a client might feel empowered to learn she had the power to inspire such desire and, in contrast, feel rather disempowered to learn that her breasts did not attract erotic desire! This is not an attempt on our part to be amusing or ironic, though it may not escape the reader that the situation is both amusing and ironic—and, from a Rogers-1 perspective, quite sad. Bozarth states (p. 194) that he 'might have to discuss the matter with her'. Here we see that Bozarth, as a Rogers-2 therapist, is not prepared to be *necessarily* transparent as a Rogers-1 therapist, who is consistently transparently absorbed in attempting empathically to understand the client and to communicate this understanding to the client. Instead, Bozarth must make a decision to be open, but on what basis does he decide? Rogers-2 therapists have not addressed this significant point. In attending to Rose's breasts, Bozarth, from the point of view of Rogers-1, is simply unable to concentrate on the job in hand. Consider this quote from Raskin (1947/2005, pp. 330–1), a Rogers-1 therapist and enthusiast, who describes the therapist's efforts to follow the internal frame of reference of the client's narrative:

> At this level, therapist participation becomes an active experiencing with the client of the feelings to which he gives expression, the therapist makes

a maximum effort to get under the skin of the person to whom he is communicating, he tries to get within and to live the attitudes expressed ... to catch every nuance of their changing nature: in a word, to absorb himself completely in the attitude of the other. And in struggling to do this, *there is no room for any other type of therapist activity or attitude.* (our emphasis)

One can only suspect that the Raskin of Rogers-1 vintage would regard Bozarth as perhaps an inappropriate candidate for practicing client-centered therapy, particularly when Bozarth regards his attention to the client's breasts as empathic in nature as the following excerpt indicates.

'Several sessions later, Rose discussed in detail her household budget. As she presented her detailed budget in a steady monotone, I was suddenly aware that I was again staring at her breasts. I rather abruptly interrupted her budget delineation to tell her about my behavior ... As I finished telling her and was contemplating what else to say, Rose continued by switching from a discussion of her budget to a discussion of her bisexual feelings ... It was when I expressed this "persistent feeling" (really persistent self-observation) to Rose that we were both free to pursue her open struggle of sexual identity ... I accepted my organismic experience and behavior without distortion and denial. My awareness in this instance was expressed to Rose.'

Bozarth discovers that his disclosure of his preoccupation with Rose's breasts provokes the client to discuss 'her bisexual feelings' rather than her budget. Bozarth considers his preoccupation to be empathic since it seems to release Rose to discuss her sexual identity and, as a Rogers-2 therapist, Bozarth regards this as a positive outcome. A Rogers-1 therapist would assume that whatever the content under discussion (budget, sexuality), the client is seeking to develop their own valuing system, and that either topic is 'legitimate'. From this, we see that Rogers-2 therapists comfortably reinforce the client's need to ask permission to have the right to pursue his or her trajectory. The entire premise of Rogers-1 is thus destroyed since it contends that it is the need for others to grant them this right that led the client to be estranged from their own valuing system in the first place.

Since he calls his confession 'empathic', Bozarth would deny that his statement gave Rose permission and would feel that he simply joined hands with Rose in her effort to find a sexual identity. However doubtful Rogers-1 would be of such an interpretation of empathy, Rogers-1 would also be concerned that in joining hands the Rogers-2 therapist reinforces Rose's need for sexual identity and, in so doing, reinforces the social convention that sexual identity is indeed important to have. The reader may be surprised by this statement and simply assume that it is axiomatic that all human beings require a sexual identity. But sexual *activity* does not require a sexual *identity*. People are not generally worried about their food preference identity though they are very discriminating about the foods they eat. (A vegetarian might be concerned about 'his food preference identity', as might a vegan, or anyone devoted to organic wholefood, real meat or real ale.) In short, a Rogers-1 therapist would never think normatively about a client: for him or her the client is utterly unique.

Example 2 (from Mearns, 2000, pp. 17–20)
Mearns, another therapist we would identify as a Rogers-2 therapist, offers the following illustration:

Andrea: (looks at therapist, expecting some response)
  (Silence)
Therapist: (fidgeting and looking uncomfortable) *I feel strange … uncomfortable … cold … What you are saying makes perfect sense and yet I feel uncomfortable … In fact, a little voice in me is saying 'That's a pity she needs to be so hard on herself'.*

Critical analysis of Example 2 by Rogers-1
Once again a Rogers-2 therapist communicates an external frame of reference and, in our view, risks imposing conditions of worth on his client by, in effect, telling her that she is making him or her (the therapist) uncomfortable when she (the client) is self-critical. Rogers-1 would feel that the client can learn only that her propensity for being self-critical will be aversive for the therapist. Rogers-1 could easily imagine Andrea wondering: '*How can the therapist accept me if I make him uncomfortable and even "cold"? Moreover he thinks I am pitiful.*' And, of course, Andrea may go on the attack and think, if not say: '*What a patronizing ass!*' Like Bozarth, this Rogers-2 therapist uses a contextless self as a source of therapeutic feedback and, in doing so, abandons the internal frame of reference of the client, showing minimal concern with creating conditions of worth. In stark contrast to both Bozarth and Mearns, consider Rogers (1951, p. 35):

> The therapist says in effect, 'To be of assistance to you I will put aside myself—the self of ordinary interaction—and enter into your world of perception as completely as I am able. I will become, in a sense, another self for you—an alter ego of your own attitudes and feelings—a safe opportunity for you to discern yourself more clearly, to experience yourself more truly and deeply, to choose more significantly.'

Example 3 (from Lietaer, 2001 pp. 46–47)
All these influences [Gendlin, May, Whitaker] have made client-centered therapy into a more interactional one, with the therapist not only functioning

as an alter ego, but also as an independent pole of interaction, who expresses, at times, to the client his own feelings about the situation ... In such an authentic mutual encounter, there may be moments in which the therapist almost relinquishes his professional role and encounters the client in a very personal and profoundly human way.

Critical analysis of Example 3 by Rogers-1

'*All these influences [Gendlin, May, Whitaker] have made client-centered therapy into a more interactional one, with the therapist not only functioning as an alter ego, but also as an independent pole of interaction, who expresses, at times, to the client his own feelings about the situation.*'

For the Rogers-2 therapist 'more interactional' means *less* attending to the client's internal frame of reference and relying more on the external frame of reference of the therapist. Rogers-2 thus confuses a quantitative judgment with a qualitative judgment. It would be absurd to say that, by following the internal frame of reference of the client one hundred percent of the time, the Rogers-1 therapist is less *interactional* than the Rogers-2 therapist who spends considerable time speaking from an external frame of reference. These are two different *kinds of interactions*, so one could only speak of *more* or *less* within the context of each of these interactions. In comparing apples and oranges would it make sense to say that apples are more of a fruit than oranges? Moreover, the Rogers-2 therapist believes, we presume, that the expression of his personal feelings will have positive therapeutic impact. Rogers-2 authors do not offer a theoretical understanding as to why a therapist's personal perspective has therapeutic value. Why should a client care about what a therapist feels? For Rogers-1, who was always aware of power differentials between therapist and client, teacher and student, the answer may be quite simple. The Rogers-2 therapist is often a graduate from an accredited university, and it is reasonable to assume that whatever he or she personally states would be seen by the client as being informed by his or her training and education, thus lending it considerable prestige and clout. Of course, Rogers-1 therapists also have considerable status, but they do not speak from their own frame of reference, and thus negate the possibility that the client will take their comments as being informed by a wisdom that stems from their clinical training. When a Rogers-2 therapist states his impatience or frustration, the client may perceive or evaluate such reactions as reasonable since they are being uttered by a graduate, master or doctor of philosophy. In fact, such personal therapeutic reactions may reflect nothing more than the immaturity of the therapist or be informed by nothing more than a neurotic burst of temper.

'In such an authentic mutual encounter, there may be moments in which the therapist almost relinquishes his professional role and encounters the client in a very personal and profoundly human way.'

The Rogers-2 therapist does not view the Rogers-1 therapist as engaging in an authentic encounter, since Rogers-1 maintained a strict observance of remaining within the internal frame of reference of the client. We see also that Rogers-2 separates the personal and professional and separates the latter from the 'profoundly human way'. We argued above that it makes little sense to differentiate Rogers-1 and Rogers-2 in terms of more or less *interaction*. Similarly, they cannot be compared in terms of more or less *authenticity*. From a normative point of view Rogers-2 might strike most people as more 'authentic' but, as we have noted above, the normative perspective was anathema for Rogers-1. Once again, in offering unsolicited personal effusions, the Rogers-2 therapist shows little concern for imposing conditions of worth and, in so doing, abrogates the giving of unconditional positive regard. The Rogers-2 therapist seems to feel that the rules which guide everyday conversations are more 'human' than the conversations that guide unusual relationships. Would the Rogers-2 therapist regard the medical examination of a patient by a doctor as less human, since the doctor does not engage in a more ordinary interaction with the patient? The questions asked and the answers given do not have the same meaning for each of these participants as they might in everyday conversation.

CRITIQUE OF ROGERS-1 BY ROGERS-2

The shift from the Rogers-1 client-centered therapy to a we-centered therapy is captured in this quotation by Monte (1987, p. 519): 'The focus had … shifted by 1975 to a mutual expression of feelings by client and therapist.' Whittaker (in Rogers, 1967, pp. 510–11), a Rogers-2 therapist, offers the following evaluations of a Rogers-1 therapy session:

> If one assumes the process of therapy is in the person of the *therapist* then the life theme of the therapist should be an essential characteristic and visible in any segment of verbal recording, I would formulate our theme as: the therapist says by his total functioning, 'I am trying to grow, come we'll both work at it together.' I cannot see the personal theme of these therapists [Rogers-1 therapists]. I expect to enjoy the patient. I expect to respond only if I feel emotionally spontaneous or if there is some necessity for restructuring the relationship. The Rogerians here [Rogers-1 therapists] seem committed to respond at each point of the patient's verbalization. I

watch and wait for the encounter. They seem to make an effort to start an encounter with each move of the patient. I feel that therapy is an opportunity and a responsibility for joining with the patient in an interaction around my convictions, possibly not in moral issues but in the issues of interpretation and evaluation of the current experience and possibly even of his historical experience. I feel free to challenge the patient if I feel personally related to what is going on. I do not feel this is true of the therapists here portrayed ... The lack of spontaneity and the lack of flexibility in the therapist-as-a-person seemed an orientation very much like analysis. The therapist is standing behind the patient, unseen and almost non-existent. Does this denial of self actually imply an acknowledgment of the 'other'? Is it possible that the patient is being taught to be more on guard because the therapist is so on guard? What is the effect of the therapist not enjoying his relationship with his patient; of not being able to express himself personally?

The Rogers-2 therapist regards Rogers-1 as being less than spontaneous and flexible, and failing to express him or herself in a personal way. As we have stated before, the Rogers-2 therapist fails to realize how spontaneously expressive empathic reflectivity can be and fails also to realize that all social interactions are guided by particular rules of discourse. When I pick up my mail and wish the clerk a 'goodday' and offer a smile, I am not being less personal than when I say the same to someone I love dearly. This is captured in a letter one of the authors (MF) wrote to a good friend when interning at the University of Chicago's (Rogers-1) Counseling Center in 1963:

> *Dear E.*
> *Your colleague Paul (the psychologist), wonders why I would want to intern at the Counseling Center and engage in client-centered counseling. He offers the kind of criticisms that circulate here at the U. of C. as well, especially in the school of psychiatry. I can't deny I felt similarly when I entered the program here. How can repeating what a client says be helpful?*
>
> *Well, I heard a tape recording of Rogers doing therapy. I was stunned on several counts.*
>
> *First, Rogers was more present in that interview (session? conversation?) than anyone I have ever experienced. He hung on every word, every nuance of feeling, every gesture of the client. Nothing the client said was irrelevant. By his words and tone Rogers showed how deeply and compassionately he was involved in the client's narrative. The confusions of the client seem to dissolve whenever Rogers related to them. I imagined the immense freedom I would feel if I had*

the opportunity to speak to Rogers precisely because he would be so present and yet so unintrusive. I was so taken aback by the client's lack of awareness that he was indeed speaking to Carl Rogers, this extraordinarily famous figure. He could have been speaking to anybody, but an 'anybody' with an ability to listen in an unimaginably kind way. I was struck also by Rogers's humility. He never once offered the kind of insight or statement that could lead the client to respect him in a conventional way. I ask myself whether I could be so humble? New Yorkers are not often seen as inclined to be humble, and for good reason. After all, wasn't the opportunity to demonstrate how perceptive, how insightful I could be a major reason for wanting to be a psychotherapist in the first place. Was I prepared to be so invisible and anonymous from a conventional perspective, of course? There is a story that circulates here at the counseling center—purportedly true—although it may be apocryphal. Supposedly, Rogers had been seeing a railroad worker at the counseling center a few years previously and, at the conclusion of the therapy, the railroad worker wrote to the director of the counseling center and thanked the institution for providing him with a therapist who knew so much about the railroads! That story sums up my experience as I listened to the tape recording of the Rogers interview and is my answer to your psychologist friend Paul.

This letter would simply baffle the Rogers-2 therapist. How could Rogers be more present when he doesn't offer a single challenge or a single judgment from an external frame of reference? How could this author have claimed to witness an authentic relationship? Whitaker, Mearns, Bozarth and Carl Rogers (post-1951) would have difficulty appreciating the experience of this author (MF). We hope that this makes it clear how important it is for supervisor and supervisee to be aware whether they are engaged in a Rogers-1 or Rogers-2 supervision relationship. Otherwise, they will not be able to appreciate in an empathic way the experience of each other.

The supervision and training of Rogers-1 therapists

Because of their emphasis on being non-directive, Rogers-1 students in particular would have to engage in training that opened up the question as to when it was appropriate to conclude that unconditional positive regard and empathy were simply ineffective. Certainly, there is considerable research (see for example Lambert and Bergin, 1994) that shows that, when a client is phobic, the very directive behavioral approach—as directive as Rogers-1 therapy is non-directive—has been significantly more effective than any other approach. There is little reason to believe that empathy and unconditional positive regard will have much effect on an agoraphobic. Indeed Rogers-1 students would have to ponder and discuss the following conclusion of two well-known psychotherapy researchers:

> Ratings of therapist attitudes such as empathy, regard, warmth and genuineness are far from perfectly correlated with outcome. Thus, research has identified a certain limit or boundary to the effects of therapist attitudes, casting doubt on the accuracy of Carl Rogers' bold attempt at specifying the necessary and sufficient conditions for positive personality change. Obviously these conditions are much more relevant to Axis 1 and milder disorders than they are to Axis 2 and more severe disorders.[2] Rogers' indifference to diagnosis precluded a clear demonstration of where these relationship factors did or did not make a major impact. Had research results clearly supported his hypothesis there would be many more client-centered practitioners and the search for active ingredients would be over. (Lambert and Bergin, 1994, p. 174)

Rogers-1 was dedicated to discovering whether there was indeed any empirical support for client-centered therapy and these results would have most certainly inspired him to investigate rather than ignore such findings.

Rogers-1 students would also have to discuss other dimensions than psychiatric diagnoses that could indicate that Rogers-1 therapy might be more useful to some clients than to others. The apparent effectiveness of cognitive-behavioral therapy shows that many clients are comfortable speaking to expert psychotherapists. Furthermore, Rogers-1 students should confront why the much more directive cognitive-behavioral approach has dominated the field of psychotherapy. Such discussions might yield alterations in Rogers' theory of personality and psychotherapy or more sophisticated research that showed more clearly the positive results of Rogers-1 therapy (see Rogers, 1959). The changes in client-centered therapy were not the result of a single investigation that showed that the communication of an external frame of reference constituted by the therapist's attitudes was more effective than attending entirely to the internal frame of reference. Imagine if one drug was discontinued and a new one introduced as better, without a single study to demonstrate the superiority of the latter. The

---

2. One of the authors (Lisbeth Sommerbeck) couldn't bear to let this quotation pass without a comment. What Lambert and Bergin find obvious is contrary to Lisbeth's experience of more than 30 years' work in psychiatric hospitals, where she has found client-centered therapy to be at least as useful as other psychotherapeutic approaches and, in combination with Pre-Therapy, the only approach that has a potential for reaching the most disturbed people in the backyards of psychiatry, those who are often regarded as being 'beyond psychotherapeutic reach' (see Sommerbeck, 2003, 2005).

authors suggest that the change in emphasis took place when clients demanded the more typical doctor–patient relationship. Rogers-2 succumbed to this need. The authors believe that this traditional model (expert doctor and patient) is ubiquitous in different schools of psychotherapeutic systems.

After listening to a therapeutic training tape, a Rogers-1 supervisor might ask the student to offer his or her view of the session. In listening to the student the supervisor should offer unconditional positive regard and empathy and remain entirely within the framework of the student. Once this is completed the supervisor should give his assessment of the therapy session and the student should offer his or her empathic understanding and unconditional positive regard. In this way the student experiences the effectiveness of empathy and unconditional positive regard, or the lack thereof. This method of supervision would enable the student to learn to convey unconditional positive regard to a supervisor (or client) who may have just been negatively critical of the session in question.

THE SUPERVISION AND TRAINING OF ROGERS-2 THERAPISTS

Unlike the Rogers-1 therapist, we have seen that the Rogers-2 therapist offers his or her personality as a therapeutic tool. Whittaker (in Rogers, 1967) wants his clients to know *him*. Other Rogers-2 therapists want to express their frustration, impatience and boredom when such judgments and feelings are present. But these Rogers-2 therapists wish to accomplish this without coercing the clients to repress their experience in order to satisfy the therapists. Yet, as we have discussed above, the therapist is not just anyone the client may encounter during the day but a purported expert on human conduct. Since human conduct often has a moral dimension, the psychotherapist can be viewed as an expert on ethical matters. Pervasive feelings of guilt and shame are often the reasons people seek psychotherapy. Consequently, clients may feel obliged to heed the significance of the personal statements of a Rogers-2 therapist. It is thus incumbent on Rogers-2 therapists to disempower themselves of the influence of their status. At present, a Rogers-2 therapist who immodestly states, 'I feel free to challenge the patient if I feel personally related to what is going on' seems not to be aware of the arbitrariness of his limitations and how such limitations may present a low ceiling for the client. It should be noted that the Rogers-2 therapist is not offering behavioral directions that have some basis in scientific research. Such directions from an external frame of reference would be based on the education of the therapists in question. Instead, these challenges emanate from the 'personal' perspective of the therapist; in effect his or her character. As we have shown, Rogers-1 would never be guilty of challenging a client, whereas the Rogers-2 therapist is anxious to display his insights. Consequently, a major part of the training of Rogers-2 therapists would be spent discovering the arbitrariness of their personal responses. This can be accomplished in graduate seminars. Rogers-2 therapists might read biographies, by different authors, of the same historical figures, say Hemingway or Lincoln; this will illustrate the fact that, like a biographer, a therapist constructs the figure under consideration with the consistent bias of their own outlook. Rogers-2 therapists might also profit from reading novels and analyzing, in discussion, the central characters. Biographies and novels are simply offered as one possible way for students of a Rogers-2 persuasion to encounter the arbitrariness of their own characters. The diversity of perception demonstrated by such a project might inspire sufficient humility in the Rogers-2 therapist to caution against offering a personal and biased perspective—and one which may bear little relevance to training in psychology in general, and to psychotherapy in particular.

We have seen in the above examples how Rogers-2 therapists can feel bored, impatient, uninterested, cold, and pitiful, towards their clients; and this is only a very small selection of examples we could have offered of the range of feelings towards their clients that Rogers-2 therapists disclose. It is likely that the negative judgments of Rogers-2 therapists towards their clients stem from their belief that the clients have freely chosen to be non-cooperative, tedious, or angry. Consequently, Rogers-2 students could discuss their views on free will and the issue of personal responsibility. The discussion of various biographies would also illuminate the difficulty in seeing the trajectory of a life in terms of such choices.

If moments of choice are difficult to underline, or agree upon, then in what sense can a Rogers-2 therapist justify impatience and hostility towards their clients? Seminars that revolved around such issues might humble Rogers-2 students and serve them well when seeing clients. In addition to a curriculum of biography and novels, Rogers-2 therapists must be prepared to offer clients scenes from their own lives that illuminate their less-than-proud moments. Such narratives would enable clients to see their Rogers-2 therapists' reactions in the context of *their* (the therapists') lives as distinct from their (the client's) own lives. Rogers-2 students ought to learn to share their less than optimal actions during the training period with their peers. Since clients often discuss their failures in love relationships, family, and work, and since the emotions of anger, resentment, pride, shame, ingratitude and guilt are principal themes in these dramas, Rogers-2 therapists can learn to recount such incidents during their training and thus have them ready at hand to offer them to clients when they feel they are relevant to the client's narrative.

Rogers-2 students should also consider how any outcome research could be performed with an approach that relies so heavily on the personalities of the therapists. Are the personal reactions of Rogers-2 therapists sufficiently alike to put them into the same therapeutic category? This is not a problem for Rogers-1 since the empathic reflections of one therapist would significantly resemble those of another therapist. Rogers-2 students should also discuss why directing the client's attention to the therapist's frame of reference by making personal responses is better than offering clients clear behavioral directions that have been shown to be effective (Bartow et al., 1989, 1993).

After attending to a recording of a Rogers-2 student, and to the student's view of their session, the supervisor ought to proceed exactly as he or she would proceed with a client. In other words, the supervisor should respond to the internal frame of reference of the student and offer, as well, their own personal judgments and feelings of the student and the session in question. If, for example, there are feelings of respect, respect should be expressed; if there are sexual feelings, sexual feelings should be expressed; if the supervisor is impatient with the student's progress, impatience should be expressed. However, the supervisor should humbly and clearly relate these feelings to his own history, at least as much as to the behavior of the supervisee. In this way, the student will discover what it is like to relate to the external frame of reference of a supervisor who insists on his or her good intentions to provide empathy, unconditional positive regard and the authenticity that is too often absent in conventional relationships. Following the supervisor's statement, the student ought then to offer his or her assessment of the supervisor. In this way the 'we' relationship of the two would evolve, or not, as the case may be. In addition, the Rogers-2 student will have to deal with the challenges of providing unconditional positive regard to a supervisor (or client) with whom he or she is engaged in a 'we-centered' or 'personal' or 'I–Thou' way.

REFERENCES

Bachelor, A. and Horvath, A. (1999) *The Therapeutic Relationship.* Washington, DC: American Psychological Association

Bartow, D. (1993) *Clinical Handbook of Psychological Disorders* (2nd edn.). New York: Guilford Press

Bartow, D., Craske, M., Cerny, J. and Klosko, J. (1989) Behavioral treatment of panic disorder. *Behavior Therapy, 20,* 261–282

Bozarth, J. (2001) Congruence: A special way of being. In G. Wyatt (Ed.) *Rogers' Therapeutic Conditions: Volume 1: Congruence* (pp. 184–99). Ross-on-Wye: PCCS Books

Frankel, M. and Sommerbeck, L. (2005) Two Rogers and congruence: The emergence of therapist-centred therapy and the demise of client-centred therapy. In B. Levitt (Ed.) *Embracing Non-Directivity* (pp. 40–61). Ross-on-Wye: PCCS Books

Frankel, M. and Sommerbeck, L. (2006) *Non-Directive Therapy: In Name Only.* Unpublished paper

Frankel, M. and Sommerbeck, L. (in press) Two Rogers, congruence and the category error: The change from client-centered therapy to we-centered therapy. *Person-Centered and Experiential Psychotherapies*

Lambert, M. and Bergin, A. (1994) The effectiveness of psychotherapy. In S. Garfield and A. Bergin (Eds.) *Handbook of Psychotherapy and Behaviour Change* (4th edn.) (pp. 143–189). New York: Wiley

Lietaer, G. (2001) Being genuine as a therapist: Congruence and transparency. In G. Wyatt (Ed.) *Rogers' Therapeutic Conditions: Volume 1: Congruence* (pp. 36–55). Ross-on-Wye: PCCS Books

Mearns, D. (2000) *Developing Person-Centred Counselling*. London: Sage Publications

Mearns, D. and Thorne, B. (2000) *Person-Centred Therapy Today*. London: Sage Publications

Monte, C. (1987) *Beneath the Mask*. New York: Holt, Rinehart and Winston

Rapoport, A. (1953) *Operational Philosophy*. New York: Harper

Raskin, N. (2005) The nondirective attitude. In B. Levitt (Ed.) *Embracing Non-Directivity* (pp. 329–48). Ross-on-Wye: PCCS Books. (Original work published 1947)

Rogers, C.R. (1951) *Client-Centered Therapy*. Boston: Houghton Mifflin

Rogers, C.R. (1959) A theory of therapy, personality, and interpersonal relationships as developed in the client-centered framework. In E. Koch (Ed.): *Psychology: A Study of a Science, Vol. 3: Formulations of the person and the social context* (pp. 184–256). New York: McGraw-Hill

Rogers, C.R. (1967) A dialogue between therapists. In C.R. Rogers, E.T. Gendlin, D.J. Kiesler and C.B. Truax (Eds.) *The Therapeutic Relationship with Schizophrenics* (pp. 507–20). Wisconsin: The University of Wisconsin Press

Shostrom, E. (Ed.) (1965) Client-centered therapy. In *Three Approaches to Psychotherapy* [Film]. Orange, CA: Psychological Films

Sommerbeck, L. (2003) *The Client-Centred Therapist in Psychiatric Contexts: A Therapist's Guide to the Psychiatric Landscape and its Inhabitants*. Ross-on-Wye: PCCS Books

Sommerbeck, L. (2005) An evaluation of research, concepts and experiences pertaining to the universality of client-centred therapy and its application in psychiatric settings. In S. Joseph and R. Worsley (Eds.) *Person-Centred Psychopathology: A Positive Psychology of Mental Health* (pp. 317–36). Ross-on-Wye: PCCS Books

Chapter Ten

Hoops, Hurdles and Thresholds: Supervising Therapists Through Training and Qualification

Geraldine Thomson

To be original, or different, is felt to be 'dangerous'. (Carl Rogers)

During the last decade or so I have had the privilege of accompanying many supervisees through part of their learning, from their preparation for and earliest encounters with clients to their final preparation for certificates, diplomas, degrees and beyond. My contact with them has taught me much about person-centred ways of learning, working and living, and has consequently enriched my life. It is to these supervisees that I would like to dedicate this chapter, which is a product of my supervision work with both unqualified and qualified practitioners, and of my inclination to consider and reconsider my experiencing, witnessing and understanding of learning. My supervisees and this process of consideration have helped me make more sense of my role as supervisor, the tasks I undertake and the potentially developmental nature of the supervisory relationship. In my writing here, I hope to convey some of what I have learnt specifically in working with supervisees nearing qualification. Along with my experiences 'on the job' I have also found it useful to refer to some of what Rogers said about learning and creativity. Both sources of information have proved inspirational and challenging and I have generally enjoyed 'checking out' in practice the received wisdom of the founding father of the person-centred approach.

Before I continue I need to 'come clean'. As I write I am once again aware of the unease I experience when using terms such as 'supervisor', 'supervisee', 'qualified' and 'unqualified'. Before expanding on my learning regarding final external evaluation I think it best to say something about my difficulty with these words. Whilst recognising that such terms are commonplace within the field and that they signify particular roles and relationships between practitioners, I have to own that they 'stick in my craw'. They suggest the opposite of the mutuality I hope to establish with those 'unqualified' practitioners who are new to the exploration of their practice. They appear at worst to militate against and at best to obscure a person-centred recognition that experiencing and knowing reside in the individual, and a valuing of that. The working relationship under discussion here includes both supervisor and supervisee, and the terms can suggest that one is more knowing and qualified and one is less so. Now while that may bear some relation to the fact that one has a certificate on the wall and the other has not, and whatever that may then imply, it does not to my mind overtly encourage equal valuing of all the knowledge the respective parties bring to the relationship and their therapeutic work. So, from my person-centred perspective, these terms are misleading, suggesting expertise and lack of expertise when, in fact, what is present is difference.

I am not at this point, however, going to suggest a change of terminology, although I am considering terms more congruent with the approach. In my experience, mutuality, if jointly valued and desired, can be created within the intimacy of a relationship that welcomes transparency of thoughts, feelings and experiencing, respect and freedom, where learning is collaborative and reciprocal, where personal responsibility is accepted and where the acknowledged focus of the work stems from, and remains with, the new practitioner's experience of therapeutic practice.

It would seem to me, and to those supervisees with whom I have discussed this, that such a way of being, working and learning can eventually 'get behind' the misnaming of a relationship that for me is married to a trust in Rogers' two essential propositions: the organism and its innate tendency to actualise. I agree with Tudor and Worrall (2004, p. 13) who hold that:

> In the context of supervision, this belief in an organism and its tendency to actualise reminds supervisors that both their supervisees, and the clients or patients with whom their supervisees work, are tending innately towards actualising their potential as fully as possible, given inner and outer circumstances. This helps free supervisors to hold a high level of trust in the work that their supervisees are doing, and in the capacity of their supervisees' clients to make the most of and take the best from that work. It follows that supervisors do not normally need to assess, monitor or police the work of their supervisees, and can instead devote their attention to helping supervisees explore their own thoughts and feelings about their work. Seen in isolation, this stance may seem naïve or even negligent,

and is open to criticism ... We think, though, that the stance we're describing is an attitudinal and behavioural manifestation of a belief in the organism's innate tendency to actualise.

In adopting this stance myself I am consciously placing my feet firmly on the bedrock of Rogers' philosophy, and because I would consider it unethical to mislead new practitioners who 'knock at my door' for 'supervision' I am overt in my description of how I choose to work and the beliefs and experiences that inform my practice. I have no desire to work in any other way and hope that those with whom I have the opportunity to learn will settle for nothing less, and that those who wish to be assessed, monitored or policed will go elsewhere. At this point some do. For those who remain I have found I can hold, like Rogers (1967/1989a, p. 313), 'a profound trust in the human organism and its potentialities'. Rogers (ibid.) continues:

> If I distrust the human being, then I *must* cram her with information of my own choosing lest she go her own mistaken way. But if I trust the capacity of the human individual for developing her own potentiality, then I can provide her with many opportunities and permit her to choose her own way and her own direction in her learning.

The only problem I have with Rogers here is his use of the word 'permit'. I have noticed that when I experience myself as a supervisor giving 'permission' to supervisees I have already moved away from a position of trust. When I trust them it is more a matter of recognising their entitlement to make choices in learning than of permitting them anything.

So, now to those ideas and experiences that help me understand my work with supervisees approaching final assessment and evaluation. In looking at my own experience, the experiences of my supervisees, and much of what Rogers said on learning and creativity, I have found it helpful also to reflect on the context in which the supervisory learning experience occurs. What strikes me is that, along with many supervisors, I encounter supervisees who are new to practice within a wider, often quite traditional, educational context, as they seek out learning and support and the accumulation of required learning credits for certificates, diplomas and degrees. I find it useful to stay mindful of this wider educational context as it appears to impact the learning relationships I seek to establish with my supervisees.

With only a few exceptions, I have yet to encounter a supervisee who has not experienced increasing anxiety during the latter stages of preparation for assessment or examination and becoming 'qualified'. I cannot always know for sure what causes this, though supervisees have connected it with conditions of worth, fear of failure and worries about whether they belong and where they fit in 'the person-centred world'. What seems most common is a temporary loss of confidence in internal valuing when, as one supervisee said, 'external evaluation's looming large on my horizon!' At this time, in my experience, most supervisees experience more or less acutely what Rogers (1954/1961a, p. 357) acknowledges: 'Evaluation is always a threat.'

I know for sure that I don't fully learn anything when I am anxious or feeling threatened, even though I might, in my incongruence, appear to function well and prove capable of completing given learning 'tasks'. In such instances, however, I don't enjoy the learning process as the expanding, integrative and creative experience that I know it can be: an experience that leaves me confident about what I know. Neither do my supervisees. Given that I consider my task as supervisor to be the facilitation of learning and creative practice, this has led me to question and examine the learning process within supervision, and supervision within its wider educational context. I have reflected upon my experience as supervisor and supervisee, and the experiences my supervisees describe, along with much of what Rogers said on learning and creativity, with a view to identifying those factors that might minimise anxieties and those that can awaken creativity and maximise what I most value and understand as 'integrated learning'. By 'integrated learning' I mean a more holistic process of learning that values primarily the wisdom of the organism alongside more commonly valued 'parts' such as intellectual understanding. Essentially, I have been asking myself the question: 'How can I facilitate the integrated learning and development of supervisees who are constructively creative, unconstrained, original and responsible in their work, especially as they approach final evaluation?' My answer, informed by Rogers' ideas on the facilitation of learning and creativity, is to start my supervisory relationships as I mean to go on.

ROGERS ON LEARNING

Much of what Rogers said about learning within the wider context of formal education is consistent with his view of the non-directive facilitation of change and learning in the therapeutic relationship and speaks to me also of learning in supervision. This is particularly so if I think of education as a gaining of experience rather than as instruction or training. Rogers' thinking on education and learning was, and often is, considered radical and controversial. He was concerned (1977/1989b, p. 325) that there was 'no place for the whole person in the educational system, only for her intellect'. His views were influenced by his experiences in the classroom, in groups and in individual therapy, and he tentatively described the goal of education (1967/1989a, p. 304) as 'the facilitation of change and learning'. He talked with enthusiasm (ibid.) of being able to

> free curiosity; to permit individuals to go charging off in new directions dictated by their own interests; to unleash the sense of enquiry; to open everything to questioning and exploration; to recognise that everything is in a process of change.

He suggests (ibid.):

> Out of such a context arise true students, real learners, creative scientists and scholars, and practitioners, the kind of individuals who can live in a delicate but ever-changing balance between what is presently known and the flowing, moving, altering problems and facts of the future.

He described what he termed a 'community of learners' (ibid.) and placed himself firmly within their midst when he said (1957/1961c, p. 276): 'I realize that I have lost interest in being a teacher ... I realise that I am only interested in being a learner.'

Whether I am working one-to-one or with a group of supervisees I have often experienced and relished being part of such 'a community of learners'. My supervisees tell me that they do too. Increasingly, I experience my continuing learning as a supervisor and the learning of supervisees as a process akin to what Rogers described. I think of it as a learning with and from one another, a joint venture prompted by the concerns of the supervisee involving an ongoing co-creative process of transforming and recreating our respective understanding and experiencing. When I am learning at my best as a supervisor I am living a continuing personal process of researching and experimenting, a movement through coming to know and then again 'not knowing', when I am sometimes experiencing what Keats, in a letter to his brothers in 1817, called 'negative capability'. He described this (Gittings, 1970, p. 43) as 'the capacity of being in uncertainties, Mysteries, doubts, without any irritable reaching after fact and reason'. When I am engaged in this process I find I am not inclined to impose understanding on myself or supervisees. They in turn often express a willingness to sit with their own 'muddle' or to 'wait and see'. One supervisee put it beautifully. Speaking of her client, she said, 'I guess I don't need to know. I just need to trust he'll know for himself.' Receiving this kind of wisdom is levelling and inclines me toward a broad view of learning in which I can understand myself, supervisees and their clients as part of a wide community of learners choosing to live as evolving persons in the continuous and widespread educational process of life.

When as a supervisor I think of myself as a facilitator of learning and change, Rogers' experience has pointed to the qualities and attitudes I need to embody in my working relationships. He writes (1967/1989a, p. 321):

> Those attitudes that appear effective in promoting learning can be described. First of all is a transparent realness in the facilitator, a willingness to be a person, to be and live the feelings and thoughts of the moment. When this realness includes a prizing, a caring, a trust and respect for the learner, the climate for learning is enhanced. When it includes a sensitive and accurate empathic listening, then indeed a freeing climate, stimulative of self-initiated learning and growth exists. The student is trusted to develop.

Checking out for myself, as both supervisee and supervisor, whether these attitudes are as potent as Rogers claims has been important for me; a slow process of 'sucking and seeing'. In feeling entitled to question them, and my experience of them, I have moved from holding them as tenets of faith, in relation to cherished beliefs about human potential, to a firm conviction of their truth and worth.

In the context of education and, I argue, by implication also in the context of supervision, Rogers (1967/1989a, p. 306) regarded realness or genuineness to be the most basic of these essential attitudes:

> When the facilitator is a real person, being what she is, entering into a relationship with the learner without presenting a front or a façade, she is much more likely to be effective. This means that the feelings that she is experiencing are available to her, available to her awareness, that she is able to live these feelings, be them, and able to communicate them if appropriate. It means that she comes into a direct personal encounter with the learner, meeting her on a person-to-person basis. It means that she is *being* herself, not denying herself.

I find, in all relationships, that being real is potentially levelling as I experience both the internal sense of power in being authentic and the vulnerability of being transparent. When facilitating reflection on practice with supervisees I experience this as promoting mutuality, surely a prerequisite to establishing the communality in learning that Rogers described. I can concur with Rogers (1967/1989a, p. 308) that this is sometimes difficult, for 'to be real is not always easy, nor is it achieved all at once, but it is basic to the person who wants to become that revolutionary individual, a facilitator of learning'.

In practice, this means that I can have any number of responses to supervisees including curiosity, enthusiasm, sensitivity, boredom, frustration and anger. It means that when I can accept my experience and responses as my own and not impose them on supervisees (although I might express them) I am being genuine and I am more likely to facilitate integrated learning. Feeling responses are not all that is involved, given that for at least some of the time we will be thinking, and also talking 'person-centred language', making sense of practice, codes and frameworks of ethics and the like, in person-centred terms. To differing extents supervisees will need to develop confidence in their ability to dialogue in this way if they are to go forward and gain certificates, diplomas, or degrees. If I am real I may find I am confused by a supervisee's understanding or take a different view to them regarding key person-centred concepts. If I am transparent and own this as my confusion or difference of opinion, I offer them, and myself, an opportunity either to acknowledge that we have a different intellectual understanding or to clarify a confusion one or both of us may be experiencing.

Working with supervisees close to qualification I have learned to resist the temptation to value intellectual understanding at the expense of organismic experiencing. My transparency about this, if and when I notice it happening, seems to facilitate integrated learning in the relationship. This can become more difficult both for myself and for my supervisees as qualification approaches and with it what appears to be, and sometimes is, an invitation to revert to old ways of being and learning that may, in certain respects and at other times, have proved effective. In response to supervisees' requests I have on occasion offered additional sessions where we agree to explore and clarify intellectual understanding of ethics, practice and theory. In doing this I don't jettison the rest of what I know about learning. It is more a case of responding to an individual learner's expressed and particular need and it appears to be of benefit in that it reveals where we come from in our thinking. One supervisee described this as 'learning person-centred shorthand' as she became more adept at using key terms to convey her understanding of complex ideas and experiences that had previously left her feeling 'exasperated and long-winded' and ill equipped for her viva.

Rogers also believed (1967/1989a, p. 308) that successful facilitators of learning embody an attitude of 'prizing the learner, prizing his feelings, his opinions, his person'. He describes this prizing (ibid., p. 309) as 'a basic trust—a belief that this other person is somehow fundamentally trustworthy' and says that it 'is an operational expression of her essential confidence and trust in the capacity of the human organism'.

As a supervisor, I prize and accept 'unqualified' supervisees as 'imperfect practitioners'. (I use this term in relation to myself also and in relation to 'highly qualified' practitioners.) Prizing and accepting supervisees in this way demands that I trust their potential. This runs counter to the culture of traditional education:

prizing the learn*er* alongside the learn*ed* is not what many of us experienced as we stumbled or sailed through schooling and professional trainings. Accepting and prizing the wisdom of the new practitioner, their fresh insights and challenging ideas, demands that I am humble in the face of difference. I will not always understand or like the experiences, thinking and practice supervisees describe. I will, though, be prepared to honour them in their process of learning and becoming.

For Rogers (1967/1989a, p. 310)

> A further element that establishes a climate for self-initiated, experiential learning is empathic understanding. When the teacher has the ability to understand the student's reactions from the inside, has a sensitive awareness of the way the process of education and learning seems *to the student*, then again the likelihood of significant learning is increased.

For *teacher* in this passage, I substitute *supervisor*, and for *student* I substitute *supervisee*. What prompts me to empathise in relationships is the belief that another's experiencing, though different from mine, is as valid and as worthy of acceptance. When I follow my inclination to empathise with supervisees I am following a curiosity about them. This is not an intellectual curiosity, of which an outcome might be greater understanding, but a wanting to experience as closely as I can 'how it is' for them. This is fed by a respect for difference that holds within it a respect of my truth and their truth and the awareness that we are equals in experiencing and learning. This curiosity may be further fuelled by the knowledge that I stand to learn from my supervisees and their experiencing, and that rather than allowing their different worlds and ways of being to threaten all or some of what I hold to be true, I stand to gain from my awareness of their experiences and perspectives. I can allow their experiencing to inform and educate me. What can block me in this learning process is my own vulnerability and subsequent defensiveness. For example, as they move closer to final evaluation this might involve a wondering about how they will be perceived and received and how this might reflect upon me and my worth as a supervisor. At these times in my vulnerability I notice I am inclined to impart knowledge, to 'teach' supervisees rather than to stay undefended and open to learning with them.

ROGERS ON CREATIVITY

If I accept that to learn is to come to know, or to become aware of, then I can think of learning as an ongoing process that carries within it discrete yet related creative acts as I come repeatedly into new awareness and new knowing. To create can be understood as 'to bring something new into being'. This fits for me with this active process of continually bringing into being new awareness and meaning. Increasingly, I consider the activity of learning within the context of creativity, and creative activity within the context of living and actualising as when learning at my best I am allowing, first, an undistorted awareness of my organismic experiencing and second, a wondering and meaning-making process to occur. This newness of awareness and making of meaning allows me to create and re-create my reality, so that in the act of continually learning I am continually and constructively creative. This process is something I witness in my supervisees and something they express in their own individual ways and is akin to living 'the good life' which Rogers (1957/1961b, pp. 186–87) described as the direction 'which is selected by the total organism, when there is psychological freedom to move in *any* direction'. For Rogers, the individual living this good life is increasingly open to experience, engages in increasingly existential living, increasingly trusts the organism and is (ibid., p. 193) 'a creative person. With his sensitive openness to the world, his trust of his own ability to form new relationships with his environment, he would be the type of person from whom creative products and creative living emerge.'

Clearly Rogers' take on creativity sits well within his philosophy of learning and life: a broad view that recognises the inherent creative potential of the organism. 'The mainspring of creativity', he suggests, (1954/1961a, p. 350)

> appears to be the same tendency which we discover so deeply as the curative force in psychotherapy—*man's tendency to actualize himself, to become his potentialities* … It is this tendency which is the primary motivation for creativity as the organism forms new relationships to the environment in its endeavour to be most fully itself.

Rogers avoids making a subjective distinction between 'good' and 'bad' creativity or imposing a hierarchy of creativity and, given his scientific background, owns there must be, for him, 'something observable, some product of creation' (ibid., p. 349). He is not meaning only tangible products however: a new idea or understanding would qualify as product. These products are novel constructions springing

> out of the unique qualities of the individual in his interaction with the materials of experience. Creativity always has the stamp of the individual upon its product, but the product is not the individual, nor his materials, but partakes of the relationship between the two. (Ibid.)

For Rogers, creativity was not restricted to content. He saw little difference between painting, composing music, devising new instruments for killing, developing scientific theory, 'discovering new procedures in human relationships, or creating new formings of one's own personality as in psychotherapy' and he explained that his 'knowledge of the way individuals remould themselves in the therapeutic relationship, with originality and effective skill, gives one confidence in the creative potential of all individuals' (ibid., pp. 349–50). He defined the creative process (ibid., p. 350) as 'the emergence in action of a novel relational product, growing out of the uniqueness of the individual on the one hand, and the materials, events, people or circumstances of his life on the other'. In my experience as a supervisor most new supervisees define creativity more narrowly, limiting it to the arts and occasionally to scientific research and discovery. They often perceive it initially as something 'other people' do. I notice their understanding of learning and creativity changing over time as they begin to experience and recognise their own learning and creative potential unfolding, as they allow new awarenesses to emerge, perhaps about their own process in relation to a client, which on reflection they can form into a new understanding of the therapeutic relationship. I am happy to say I have also witnessed this process when the events, people and circumstances in question have impending vivas with panels of external evaluators who may or may not award qualifications.

Rogers' hypothesis about the inner conditions of constructive creativity—of being open to experience, trusting an internal locus of evaluation and being able to play with ideas—certainly fits with my experience of myself as a creative practitioner and with the self-descriptions supervisees sometimes give me. For Rogers, openness to experience involved the opposite of psychological defensiveness and he suggested (1954/1961a, pp. 353–4) that it could mean 'lack of rigidity and permeability of boundaries in concepts, beliefs, perceptions, and hypotheses. It means the ability to receive much conflicting information without forcing closure upon the situation. It means what the general semanticist calls the 'extensional orientation'. Rogers accepted that creative activity was possible without this complete open awareness to what exists in any given moment, but he believed (ibid., p. 354) that if

> the openness is *only* to one phase of experience, the product of this creativity may be potentially destructive ... The more the individual has available to himself a sensitive awareness of all phases of his experience, the more sure we can be that his creativity will be personally and socially constructive.

This is the kind of creative activity that I want to help facilitate in supervisees: not a degree of openness that may be easier for me (or perhaps for both of us) to accept, but that is to some extent distorted. An example may prove useful here.

One supervisee felt she was 'blocked somewhere' in her acceptance and empathy with a client who experienced herself as psychologically abused in her marriage. She made what she termed a 'breakthrough' when she voiced in supervision a response she believed she had denied to awareness and then held back from expressing: 'I might as well spit it out. If I'm totally honest there's part on me wants to give her a good shake, tell her: wake up and smell the coffee … get out.' This openness to all of her experiencing in relation to her client was indeed a learning breakthrough. In being able to accept it, she allowed herself the opportunity to reframe, constructively and creatively, her understanding of herself, of her relationship with her client and of her thinking about, and experiencing of, relationships between men and women.

Rogers goes on to say (1954/1961a, p. 354):

> Perhaps the most fundamental condition of creativity is that the source or locus of evaluative judgment is internal. The value of his product is, for the creative person, established not by the praise or criticism of others, but by himself.

He was not suggesting that we ignore the evaluation of others but rather that:

> the basis of evaluation lies within himself, in his own organismic reaction to and appraisal of his product. If to the person it has the 'feel' of being 'me in action' of being an actualization of potentialities in himself which heretofore have not existed and are now emerging into existence, then it is satisfying and creative, and no outside evaluation can change that fundamental fact. (Ibid.)

Rogers describes this third inner condition as:

> the ability to play spontaneously with ideas, colors, shapes, relationships— to juggle elements into impossible juxtapositions, to shape wild hypotheses, to make the given problematic, to express the ridiculous, to translate from one form to another, to transform into improbable equivalents. It is from this spontaneous toying and exploration that there arises the hunch, the creative seeing of life in a new and significant way. It is as though out of the wasteful spawning of thousands of possibilities there emerges one or two evolutionary forms with the qualities which give them a more permanent value. (Ibid.)

He believed that the ability to toy with elements and concepts, though probably less important than the two conditions mentioned above, seems to be a condition of creativity. I've been toying with this idea myself and I'm not sure I experience this condition as 'probably less important', although it does seem to be an outcome of the other two conditions, and can be conceived of as a 'final' condition.

To recreate can be understood as to put fresh life into something, and it seems to me that that is precisely what is happening when as learners we toy with the freshness of our new experiencing and understanding, revitalising old ways of being and conceptualising that have become tired or obsolete. When I experience myself or witness supervisees 'toying' in this way I sometimes notice the presence of fun in the learning process. It is as if by allowing creativity to meld with learning, the process of learning can also become recreational. I hear from supervisees that in contrast to more traditional ways of learning it is in this recreational re-creating and learning that they are more likely to risk 'getting it wrong'. If we can trust an internal locus of changing evaluation within the context of a supervisory relationship, and toy creatively with what does and doesn't fit, it seems we are better equipped to harvest the understanding that can be gleaned from what we and perhaps others would term a mistake. To my mind this can only benefit our clients.

Rogers (1954/1961a, p. 356) notes: 'From the very nature of the inner conditions of creativity it is clear that they cannot be forced, but must be permitted to emerge.' He states that this is most likely if we provide conditions of 'psychological safety' and 'psychological freedom'. As a supervisor I consider it important to remind myself of the two conditions Rogers describes, as they create an environment within which I and my supervisees are more likely to develop potential and be constructively creative: where we can all as practitioners claim freedom to practice.

Rogers (ibid. p. 358) argues that we may establish the first, psychological safety, by three associated processes:

- accepting the individual as of unconditional worth;
- providing a climate where external evaluation is absent; and
- understanding empathically, which for Rogers 'provides the ultimate in psychological safety, when added to the other two'.

Rogers (ibid. p. 357) suggests that whenever a 'person with a facilitating function feels basically that this individual is of worth in his own right and in his own unfolding, no matter what his present condition or behaviour, he is fostering creativity.' For Rogers (ibid.) that attitude could probably only be genuine when the facilitating person 'senses the potentialities of the individual and thus is able to have an unconditional faith in him, no matter what his present state'. A supervisee who perceives this attitude will sense a climate of safety within which she can learn to drop façades, be less rigid, discover what it means to be herself and actualise 'in new and spontaneous ways' thus 'moving toward creativity' (ibid.).

Regarding the absence of external evaluation Rogers (ibid.) states: 'When we cease to form judgments of the other individual from our own locus of evaluation, we are fostering creativity. For the individual to experience this is "enormously freeing"'. For Rogers (ibid.) external evaluation is always a threat and 'always creates a need for defensiveness, always means that some portion of experience must be denied to awareness'. When new supervisees first cross my threshold they will, more or less acutely, be experiencing this sense of threat. This has sometimes left me wanting to alleviate their anxiety, although I know from experience that this does not foster learning or creativity. What I can do, that proves helpful, is to refrain from evaluating them or the myriad of thoughts, feelings and experiences they bring. Nevertheless, if I wish to foster integrated learning and constructive creativity I must remain real in my reaction to them. I am as entitled to my reaction to them as they are of their reaction to me, and my intention will be to communicate my responses honestly and sensitively. If I can stay with my reactions to them, rather than stray into evaluations, I have some hope of communicating my willingness to honour their internal valuing processes along with my own. A number of supervisees have reminded me of those early encounters as they approach qualification. They recall 'taking the plunge' or 'testing the water' and explain how they are using their recollections of crossing the threshold into supervision to inform and support themselves in new ways as they go forward.

Rogers was clear that the first essential process of accepting the worth of the individual unconditionally amounts to little and would be unlikely to foster constructive creativity unless accompanied by empathic understanding. He was uncompromising when he stated (1954/1961a, p. 358) that: 'If I say that I "accept" you, but know nothing of you, this is a shallow acceptance indeed, and you realise that it may change if I actually come to know you.' I certainly do not expect those who choose to learn with me to trust my acceptance of them other than when they experience me as empathising with them. It is only then that I witness them, and myself, accepting and sometimes revelling in our similarities and differences, being and learning creatively alongside one another.

For Rogers creativity was fostered when a second condition of psychological freedom was also present. He believed this could be experienced when facilitators permitted individuals 'complete freedom of symbolic expression'. He described this permissiveness as neither soft, nor indulgent or necessarily encouraging, but simply as:

> permission to be *free*, which also means that one is responsible. The individual is as free to be afraid of a new venture as to be eager for it; free to bear the consequences of his mistakes as well as of his achievements. It is this type of freedom responsibly to be oneself which fosters the development of a secure locus of evaluation within oneself, and hence tends to bring about the inner conditions of constructive creativity. (Ibid.)

All of this marries with what I sometimes witness supervisees experiencing. However, as a facilitator, I don't view myself as granting permission. I may be splitting hairs here but I find it more helpful to consider constructive creativity as fostered by a recognition, acceptance and prizing on my part of a supervisee's entitlement to freedom of symbolic expression than the direct and directive use of permission.

Supervisees generally take into final evaluation tangible products of their creative practice: tapes of client work, therapeutic studies, perhaps materials for presentations. Their confidence in these tangible products appears to depend on whether they have been able to make, what Tudor and Worrall (2004, p. 27) describe as, 'meaningful and appropriate relationships between philosophy, theory and practice'. There is often evidence of their development from 'theory-bound' to more 'experience-sensitive' practitioners (ibid., p. 28) in these tangible products, as well as in their manner of being. In their authorship, and increasingly in expressions of personal authority, they reveal a willingness to communicate. The reality and significance of deadlines, dwindling funds, or perceived career opportunities may motivate them to take the last steps toward final external evaluation, and yet what they often also describe as prompting them is this desire and readiness to communicate. Having spent some considerable time, money, effort and energy in preparing for qualification, many supervisees, whilst recognising a degree of anxiety, want to share what they have learnt and all they have become as practitioners. By way of respecting and caring for themselves they generally wait until they feel confident enough to encounter the opinions and evaluation of others who may award or withhold qualifications. A supervisee who had at times experienced herself as 'a square peg trying to fit in a round hole' in relation to the person-centred approach, described herself before qualifying as 'a bit more rounded. This whole process ... I've changed. I still don't know if I fit but I want to find out. I like the shape I am'.

The key factor in determining confidence seems to me to be a sense of personal authority, a reliance on, and trust in, internal valuing. As I change and develop, this trust is something I want to test in myself and one way I get the measure of it is to invite the experience and opinion of another. Over time, in their work with me, supervisees also invite this kind of dialogue. It may be about theory, practice, ethical codes and frameworks, or whatever else they need to bring. At times these dialogues have been challenging, even painful, for one or other, or both of us. What I notice in them and myself as an outcome is increased robustness, a knowledge that we can both hold our own. When this robustness is present I hear supervisees' perceptions of the process of qualifying changing. It seems to me they experience the prospect less as a jumping through hoops, or a clambering over hurdles, and more as a natural progression, the crossing of another threshold.

I can say, in conclusion and in answer to my earlier question, that when I have begun a supervisory relationship by offering a climate for learning and creativity such as Rogers described—and when I have continued to offer this consistently—the anxiety a supervisee might expect to experience, as the time for written and oral evaluation approaches, appears to diminish. When I have been genuine, accepting, prizing and trusting of a supervisee's potential as a person and as a practitioner, when I have empathised and recognised his entitlement to complete freedom of symbolic expression, and have somehow managed to convey all of this to him, then what I witness is the development of a practitioner who integrates his learning and is constructively creative. The manner in which supervisees express themselves as people and practitioners indicates openness to experiencing, a deep-rooted and habitual trust in their internal evaluating, and an ability to toy, and even to play, with elements and concepts.

REFERENCES

Gittings, R. (Ed.) (1970) *Letters of John Keats: A Selection.* Oxford: Oxford University Press

Rogers, C.R. (1961a) Toward a theory of creativity. In *On Becoming a Person* (pp. 347–59). London: Constable. (Original work published 1954)

Rogers, C.R. (1961b) A therapist's view of the good life: The fully functioning person. In *On Becoming a Person* (pp. 183–96). London: Constable. (Original work published 1957)

Rogers, C.R. (1961c) Personal thoughts on teaching and learning. In *On Becoming a Person* (pp. 273–8). London: Constable. (Original work published 1957)

Rogers, C.R. (1989a) The interpersonal relationship in the facilitation of learning. In H. Kirschenbaum and V.L. Henderson (Eds.) *The Carl Rogers Reader* (pp. 304–22). Boston: Houghton Mifflin. (Original work published 1967)

Rogers, C.R. (1989b) The politics of education. In H. Kirschenbaum and V.L. Henderson (Eds.) *The Carl Rogers Reader* (pp. 325–34). Boston: Houghton Mifflin. (Original work published 1967)

Tudor, K. and Worrall, M. (2004) Person-centred philosophy and theory in the practice of supervision. In K. Tudor and M. Worrall (Eds.) *Freedom To Practise: Person-Centred Approaches to Supervision* (pp. 11–30). Ross-on-Wye: PCCS Books

CHAPTER ELEVEN

SUPERVISING A THERAPIST THROUGH A COMPLAINT

WENDY TRAYNOR

For a therapist, the experience of a complaints procedure can be stressful and even traumatic. Despite, or perhaps because of, this stress the process of receiving and responding to a formal complaint can often catalyse in the therapist a dramatic process of personal and professional development. A person-centred supervisor can offer the necessary and sufficient conditions to hold a therapist through this process, and may support a therapist emotionally and practically in their efforts to deal with the demands of the complaint process.

I have experienced complaints procedures from a variety of personal and professional angles. This includes supervising person-centred therapists who have been the subject of complaints. I have also had dialogues with a number of practitioners who have experienced institutional and professional complaints, paying particular attention to their experiences of supervision. I have anonymised the details of any of those experiences that I have written about in this chapter.

Various texts exist which explicitly explore complaints in therapy. Palmer Barnes (1998) explores psychotherapy complaints and grievances including legal and practical advice, whilst Casemore (2001) explores the personal, practical and legal issues relating to complaints. Other issues such as ethics and boundaries pertinent to complaints are explored by Mearns and Thorne (2000), and Wilkins (2003). This chapter focuses on supporting in supervision the therapist who is the subject of a complaint, and on some of the important elements of supervision which a complaints process may highlight. These include: an awareness of the psychological responses to a complaint, offering containment, the supervisor's authenticity, the supervisor embodying the core conditions, and the procedure itself. Other themes explored include issues relating to the supervisor's responsibility and maintaining a person-centred perspective in the context of legalistic thinking. I explore false complaints, transgressions and misunderstandings, power issues and how the therapist moves on.

THE PERSON-CENTRED THERAPIST IN A COMPLAINTS PROCESS: POSSIBLE PSYCHOLOGICAL RESPONSES TO A COMPLAINT

Person-centred therapy is distinct from many other models, often being referred to as a 'way of being' (Rogers, 1980) in the relationship, rather than one based on expertise or the application of 'interventions'. Rogers advocates an encounter in which the therapist attends to the client as a whole person, not from behind a professional façade (see Rogers, 1967). Since then, much has been written about the use of self in person-centred psychotherapy (see, for example, Bozarth, 1998). A complaint against a person-centred therapist is likely, then, to challenge their whole way of being. It may leave the therapist feeling attacked in terms of personal values and personal integrity, a process which can result in a loss of self-worth. Supervision, whilst not a substitute for, and having a different overall focus from, personal therapy, may therefore focus on self-preservation as well as professional restoration.

At each stage (accusation, procedure, adjudication or judgement) a complaint can engage with a therapist's own introjects and almost inevitably seeks out the weak points in the self-structure of the person/personality. Responses to complaints are, of course, unique to each person. However, certain themes seem to recur. Feelings of shame, self-blame and self-doubt are common when, regardless of the nature and severity of the complaint, the therapist can feel that they are holding a shameful secret and fear the repercussions of disclosure. They may also fear or experience the judgement or pre-judgement of others: 'There's no smoke without fire.' The therapist may simultaneously feel the need to be 'reasonable' and demonstrate acting ethically and responsibly. Whether the complaint is upheld or not, several practitioners whom I supported spoke of fear of loss of income or damage to reputation.

Palmer Barnes (1998) discusses complaints from a practical and legal perspective. She also highlights the possible feelings of shock, outrage, hurt, fear, shame, confusion, anger and guilt which a practitioner may experience. She comments: 'However rational your view may be of the value of standards for professional practice and the accountability that goes with membership of a profession, receiving a complaint about one's professional practice is shocking'

(p. 70). She emphasises the significance of support from colleagues just to *think*. Palmer Barnes suggests that personal therapy as well as supervision may be appropriate to help the practitioner focus on the practical elements of the procedure, since many therapists are extremely distressed by the procedure itself.

The therapist may look at themselves and unravel their worst fears. They may then need to attend to unresolved issues. Colleagues and others may 'take sides'. This can affect the therapist's trust in self and others. The procedure may also have a direct or indirect impact on significant others on an emotional and practical level. It is therefore important that the supervisor should strive to create the safest environment possible. Weaks' (2002) study identifies the importance of safety in the supervisory relationship. This includes the freedom and permission to discuss all aspects of work including difficult areas. Person-centred supervisors and therapists might best understand this requirement in terms of Rogers' (1957) conditions for therapeutic change. Since a person-centred practitioner's therapeutic life is likely to be an integral part of their self-structure, any review of practice requires revision of the self-structure and is best conducted in what Rogers (1951) describes as 'complete absence of any threat' (p. 517). This is a basic requirement of supervision if the practitioner is to be enabled to face issues of ethics, accountability, and professional and personal development honestly; to make difficult decisions, and to process the feelings evoked by a complaint.

In my discussions, comments on this have included:

- 'My supervisor helped me to get in touch with my anger after I was initially being concerned only with the well-being of the complainant.'
- 'People who did not understand the approach were ready to judge and condemn me, and many ran away in fear like I was contaminated by something dangerous. In supervision I felt understood, accepted and deeply valued and respected.'

Another therapist said that, on receiving the complaint, the organisation where she worked told her: 'You're on your own with this' as they went into 'litigation avoidance mode'. Her supervisor supported her through a difficult process to a positive outcome. She was able to use supervision not only to explore the specific practice issues raised but also to review her understanding of what person-centred therapy means. She also dealt with her own feelings of anger and betrayal regarding the organisation. Following the completion of the complaints process, she regained her confidence and eventually spoke openly to her manager.

The supervisor as offering containment

Containment within the supervisory relationship appears to be an important issue. One supervisee felt that her supervisor's containment enabled her to be open, to think more clearly, and to hold a professional stance during hearings. Jacobs (2001) highlights the need for supervision to feel safe enough to enable exploration of personal issues relating to work and feels that supervision should be therapeutic (whilst not offering actual therapy). One therapist commented: 'Sometimes I needed to be therapeutically held although I knew that it wasn't counselling.'

Since the practitioner is striving to be non-judgemental and to embody the core conditions in therapy, and indeed live them in life, it is important that supervision aims to provide the same conditions to the practitioner. This helps the practitioner to hold onto person-centred values and their own integrity in a process which may feel harsh and blaming. When the practitioner feels under emotional siege in this way, supervision and personal therapy may seem like a rare source of restoration. I believe that a supervisor can strive to accept a supervisee and provide potentially growthful conditions, even if the supervisor does not support or agree with the supervisee's actions—and that the supervisor can be honest about this.

The supervisor's authenticity

The supervisor being real, congruent or authentic in the supervisory relationship can be viewed as even more crucial throughout a complaint, where relationships can be tested. Supervisors' transparency in owning their own imperfections, fears, mistakes and their own feelings of powerlessness can promote relational depth in the supervisory relationship. Several therapists spoke of fears of judgement and rejection by their supervisor. One therapist explained how she felt empowered by her supervisor's disclosure of how she herself had survived a difficult complaint process. McNeill and Worthen (1996) reported supervisors' self-disclosure and relabelling of mistakes as sources of learning, reducing the need for self-protection in supervisees. One therapist explained to me how openness in the supervisory relationship enabled her to scrutinise her own practice in a climate of honesty and to explore the criticisms of her work. She said of her supervisor: 'I knew that she cared about me and respected me and trusted me—knew about my other mistakes and mess ups.'

Webb (2001) discusses the therapist's honesty in supervision in facing vulnerabilities and shortcomings and the barriers to this such as anxiety, shame, a poor supervision alliance, perceived unimportance, fear of negative evaluation or fear of negative repercussions. She feels that the irony is that 'those who are prepared to reflect upon their struggle to be open in supervision are likely to be the more mature, responsible and effective therapists amongst us' (pp. 24–25).

One therapist spoke of physically shaking in fear during a hearing. He held onto supportive cards which his supervisor had written and felt that he was part of a team. The supervisor had also previously disclosed some of her own mistakes, learning and fears in this area. She had also owned her own frustration with the process and the learning she experienced in supporting him through the procedure. This diminished the power differential in the relationship and enabled the therapist to take more risks and explore vulnerable areas of practice. They explored these areas, including ethical implications, in a safe space, in preparation for hearings and future practice.

THE SUPERVISOR BEING ACCEPTANT

Complaints are obviously a process of judgement. In contrast to this, unconditional positive regard in supervision can contribute to a climate where openness is possible, allowing the exploration of the issues raised. Kilborn (2000) carried out research which focused on how her clients and supervisees experienced her unconditional positive regard and whether it was beneficial to their work. Kilborn's research revealed a variety of expectations and experiences. One of her supervisees commented: 'I would not be able to bring all of my work with clients to the sessions if your acceptance was not there. I need to sense it in order for me to talk about the "less successful areas of my work"' (p. 161).

THE SUPERVISOR BEING EMPATHIC

Several supervisees who experienced a complaints procedure emphasised their ability to be open and non-defensive in the presence of what they perceived as empathic responses from their supervisor. Lambers (2000, p. 200) discusses empathy in the context of supervision: 'The supervisor's empathic presence can help the supervisee to settle and to focus on what she is bringing as she becomes aware of the complexity of what is going on for her.' Lambers emphasises how empathy in supervision needs to extend 'to the whole range of the supervisee's experience: feelings, thoughts, theoretical questions, moral and ethical concerns.' Worrall (2001, p. 208) discusses empathy in the context of supervising as helping to facilitate congruence. He feels that the more genuinely empathic he is, the greater the likelihood of his supervisees experiencing the relationship as accepting and non-judgemental and 'the greater the possibility that they will then bring themselves fully and authentically to their time with me.'

The person-centred therapist and the complaints *procedure*

Complaints procedures can be paradoxical in nature. Set up in good faith to protect and empower clients and to regulate practice, they can in actuality become an adversarial, trial-like process of judgement where, ironically, both practitioner and client feel a lack of power or justice, especially where an investigating party may have its own interests at heart. Bond (2006) highlights the situation where, for the person-centred counselling relationship, 'the client's subjective experience is positively valued independently of any moral considerations and how, by contrast, complaints focus on the judgment of behaviour' (p. 197). He goes on to say that: 'In effect the adjudicator's role could not be much further removed from that of the therapist as each requires constructing a relationship which is almost the antithesis of the other' (p. 197).

When supervising a practitioner through a complaints process I have found that both flexibility and accessibility are important. When appropriate, and by negotiation, I am open to telephone support and extra sessions as events unfold.

Attending to practical matters and other key areas

It is important to support the supervisee to gain access to, and make sense of, a range of resources, information, procedures and options, some of which are inevitably conflicting. Practitioners are often unprepared for the practical implications of a complaint, such as dealing with related correspondence which, in addition to requiring time, can also cause great anxiety. Supervision can be used to make sense of these practicalities, to look at options and to make decisions, whilst also offering a safe space to 'spill out' if necessary. For example, a supervisee might reflect on whether to obtain prompt legal advice and consult insurers, especially if the allegations are serious, in addition to exploring and possibly modifying practice. Issues relating to current practice and whether to take time out need immediate consideration.

Sources of consultation

The therapist may:

- Consult their insurer and gain their specific advice.
- Seek help from legal advisors and legal help lines.
- Consult their professional body for general advice.
- If he or she is a member of a trades union, seek its advice or representation in hearings.
- Be supported by organisational staff such as their manager.

- Have various sources of supervision.
- Consult practitioners with specific experience in the area of concern.
- Access relevant literature.

The therapist who is the subject of complaint will have to face and deal with the demands of the procedure, including:

- Drafting verbal and written responses to the complaint.
- Preparing for panels and hearings.
- Gathering and presenting relevant evidence, including a summary of what happened, when and, perhaps, why. He or she should do this in the context of relevant ethical frameworks, codes, policies and protocols.
- The outcome of the procedure, which they may find unfair and/or unreasonable.
- The publication of sanctions and, possibly, termination of membership of professional associations.
- Making specific changes in their practice in response to sanctions and outcomes as well as their own learning.
- Consulting a new approved supervisor if this is imposed by sanctions.

THINKING IN BOTH A LEGAL AND A PERSON-CENTRED FRAMEWORK

Since complaints procedures and processes are essentially adversarial in nature, the practitioner is thrust into a situation requiring him or her to think in a legalistic way. This can be difficult, if not impossible for someone whose everyday practice is predicated on being non-judgemental and empathic. The tension crystallises around two apparently competing sets of values: the legal and the personal, where the personal is represented by person-centred values of congruence and transparency, being non-judgemental, being empathic, and non-interference or non-directivity.

In addition, it is likely that the therapist will receive conflicting advice from his or her professional association/s, solicitor, and trades union. Practitioners need to consider the welfare of both the complainant and themselves. When much of the advice from such sources can be conflicting, prescriptive and conditional, supervision can be the place to disentangle the information and to arrive at self-directed decisions about how to proceed. In supervision, practitioners can feel less cluttered by apparently authoritative information and begin to think for themselves.

Possible conflicts can arise from different sources of information. Casemore (2001) recommends an immediate apology (p. 112). However, others with a more legal approach may advise the practitioner not to do anything that might be taken as an admission of liability and to disclose minimal information. The therapist may also struggle between legal advice relating to themselves and legal advice relating to the organisation for which they work. Tension arises when the person-centred practitioner's natural tendency towards transparent and open communication is set against legal advice not to reveal anything. Being honest might be seen by person-centred practitioners as holding integrity, but may be viewed by any legal team as naïve and as putting both the practitioner and the organisation at risk. This tension can be difficult to manage in supervision. The supervisee needs to find their own way of dealing with this tension, since some supervisees prefer to present and sort through the conflicting advice and information in a logical way in order to gain a sense of control; whilst others might pour out the intense feelings regarding the accusations and the procedure before moving on to look at an action plan.

A culture of litigation, such as ours, can sometimes demand that we gather evidence with which to defend ourselves. This is far removed from person-centred thinking and practice. Supervision can be a place where this jarring of values may be processed and the practitioner can be supported to find an acceptable compromise.

Focusing on the legal aspects can lose the 'essence' of the complaint. Emphasis is often placed on the verdict rather than what is most professionally useful, most therapeutic for both therapist and client, and offers the best chance of development, change and learning.

THE SUPERVISOR'S RESPONSIBILITY: SAFEGUARDING OR POLICING?

I believe that supervising a practitioner through a complaint ideally places less emphasis on judging (which is conducted by others) and focuses more on looking constructively and sensitively at what is needed and at ways of moving forward in a non-prescriptive way. However, complaints inevitably raise issues of the role and responsibility of the supervisor. Supervision does, in my view, involve the need to safeguard current and future clients. If the supervisor and supervisee are members of professional bodies, or working within organisational or professional frameworks and protocols, both have a responsibility to address ethical concerns. For example, the British Association for Counselling and Psychotherapy (BACP) states that supervision involves various foci, including ensuring that ethical standards are adhered to throughout the counselling process (BACP, 2005). Where there have clearly been transgressions, firm agreements and actions may be needed. There may be real issues of assessing practitioner competence and managing risks to clients, as well as supervisors, acting upon their own sense and understanding of ethical principles.

Carroll (1996) discusses supervision across modalities and states that supervisors see their task as reviewing the implementation of ethical codes rather than teaching them and taking steps to address issues of professional conduct. He suggests that a supervisor might recommend that a therapist ceases practice at least temporarily or, in rare situations, the supervisor might be unwilling to supervise the therapist. He also discusses supervisors' ethical responsibilities and the need to keep up to date, and recommends areas of practice which supervisors should discuss with supervisees. These include ethical codes, bad practice, critical evaluation, avoiding overworking, insurance, awareness of how therapists can abuse clients, and self-awareness. Feltham and Dryden (1994) discuss the importance of avoiding a possibly collusive supervisory relationship and of taking steps to minimise the risk of this.

Hackney and Goodyear (1984) interviewed Rogers who describes his own practice of offering the supervisee understanding to face anything that was 'bad' and of avoiding anything that seemed like criticism or instruction. Lambers (2000) discusses how, in a climate of fear of complaint and litigation, supervision could be seen as policing. She argues that supervisors who focus on ethics, contracts and boundaries may be less accepting: an attitude which can lead to supervisees becoming defensive or dependent. Worrall (2001) argues that, in this sense *person-centred* supervision as a contradiction in terms. He discusses protection, rather than sanction or surveillance, as a function of supervision. It therefore seems to be a challenge for the supervisor to strive to offer an accepting climate where practice can be discussed openly and non-defensively, balanced with an attention to moral and ethical obligations to ensure safe practice. Worrall points out that, as a supervisor, he might balance empathic understanding against moral, ethical, organisational or professional responsibilities, and his responsibilities to clients, as well as his own integrity. He also discusses the contextual, political and cultural influences which would be included in his focus. He says:

> I can therefore imagine occasions when I would deliberately and to some degree unwillingly step out of the exclusively empathic stance and choose either to stop working with a supervisee or to exercise some overt influence or authority over his or her practice. I might in Lambers terms 'become a policeman for a while'. (p. 214)

Mearns (2004) and Mearns and Cooper (2005) discuss the merits of the potentiality model over the deficiency model and feel that potentiality and policing are opposites that do not mix. They recommend explicitly naming an ongoing development agenda and see the supervisor as a confederate. They comment: 'The person-centred supervisor accepts the supervisee as a person in process and trusts the supervisee's potential for growth' (pp. 153–4). Mearns (2004) describes person-centred supervision as being based on a 'developmental model' and comments:

> In other words supervision is not about policing, where the emphasis is solely on 'checking up' on you. Instead the aim is to develop a relationship in which your supervisor is regarded as a trusted colleague who can help you to reflect on all dimensions of your practice and, through that process, to develop your counselling role. (p. 117)

False complaints, transgressions, mistakes and misunderstandings

Complaints can be formal or informal. They can be made to the practitioner themselves, to the organisation where the therapist practises, or to the professional organisations to whom the practitioner belongs. Complaints can highlight actual transgressions, but occasionally are false and sometimes arise out of misunderstandings. Regardless of the origin or nature of the complaint, or even the outcome, intensive complaint-driven supervision may reveal elements of practice which need to be reconsidered.

With an enormous variation in recommendations from well-respected figures, everyday practice regarding boundaries is extremely variable and can add to the complexity of a complaints procedure and the unravelling of what is ethical or unethical. Casemore (2001) is explicit in instructing practitioners to avoid touch. However, both Coffeng (2002) and Mearns (2003) see touch as sometimes appropriate, and discuss its potential merits and difficulties. Tudor and Worrall (2004, pp. 5–6) criticise Casemore's approach for being a non-negotiable prescription motivated exclusively by fear. Casemore's position is the extreme exemplar of practice determined by complaint avoidance rather than client benefit. Tudor and Worrall go on to discuss the critical balance between these two factors. Mearns and Thorne (2000) give an example of Dave 'loving' a client who can also scare him, and Dryden (1993) states that: 'It seems that any therapeutic approach that places emphasis on "loving" relationships with clients and trainees alike needs to place even more emphasis on the maintaining of therapeutic and training frames' (p. 22). Supporting a supervisee to unravel their practice in this climate is a complex process.

Carroll (1996) talks of supervisors managing their own anxieties, and how what one supervisor might consider beneficial another might see as malevolent. Wilkins (2003) also points out that, as well as actual transgressions, there are misunderstandings of person-centred practice and misuse of the actual term person-centred.

In addition to the above considerations, there are also confusing issues for the practitioner and supervisor such as numerous opinions and guidelines for specific interventions for specific conditions, which rarely name person-centred therapy as a 'treatment of choice'. Issues of clinical governance and evidence-based practice (Hurwitz, 2004) may be raised in complaints regarding limits of competency, especially when judged outside a person-centred framework. Person-centred therapy, after all, does not place any emphasis on expertise or specialisms. I am aware of several complaints against person-centred therapists which resulted in clinical judgements made from a theoretical framework or modality entirely different from that used by the practitioner, and in recommendations which fall outside of person-centred theory such as sanctions explicitly recommending that the therapist explore transference and counter-transference.

Mearns and Thorne (2000) discuss the issue of complaints arising from clients reviewing therapy 'from a different social perspective, perhaps aided by those who draw on a different construction of therapy' (pp. 31–2) and how unique responses in person-centred approaches rather than prescriptive policy-led responses might leave more room for this. Boundaries and dependency issues seem to be particularly difficult areas for both clients and therapists and so feature in many complaints. Mearns and Cooper (2005) comment that: 'Practitioners who experiment with boundaries can now be regarded as "not doing therapy" or even worse, doing therapy unethically' (p. 58).

POWER ISSUES IN COMPLAINTS AND SUPERVISION

Issues of power are often central to a complaints process. The complainant, the client (if different from the complainant), and the practitioner may each have their own sense of disempowerment at any stage of the process. There may be separate but parallel effects of what may feel like a very public enquiry, in which there may be surprisingly intrusive and seemingly irrelevant questions. The practitioner can feel protective of both him or herself and of the client. The complainant may see themselves as the victim of malpractice in which the therapist has misused his or her power. However, the therapist's power may be diminished when he or she becomes the person 'complained against'. Indeed, Fish (1999) asserts that complaints procedures are an important method of increasing client's *role power*.

Client, therapist and supervisor may all feel unheard and disempowered in the process of the complaint, depending on the specific circumstances, as institutional or other contextual issues can take priority for those in power. For example, an institution's priority might be to avoid damaging its reputation and legal liability. In contrast to this, supervision can offer a place for the practitioner to feel heard and empowered. Minimising the power differential in the supervision relationship, therefore, may become central to the supervision process. Supervision may be used as a process of supporting the therapist to hold onto their own sense of power, albeit diminished, in the face of challenge.

Complaints sometimes induce a strong sense of powerlessness as regards control and information. The therapist may feel at the mercy of an institutional system with rules which may have been created by non-practitioners, and judged by panels involving practitioners from a different modality. They may wait weeks or months for each stage in the procedure to be completed or for the information they need to take the next step forward. In the face of this, and by contrast, a supervisor can offer reliability, stability, openness and honesty.

The complaints process can catalyse an increased and explicit awareness of power issues in therapy, supervision, and organisations. This heightened sensitivity can have a significant impact on practice. Therapists with increased awareness might become more proactive in checking client satisfaction with therapy, as well as with regard to other areas such as the potential power of touch, boundary issues, contracting, and actively sharing decisions when a referral may be appropriate.

LEARNING AND MOVING ON

Surviving a complaints process can lead to therapists reporting an increased understanding of the meaning and application of the ethical framework to which they are committed. At best, there may be a deeper awareness of contextual issues and a more effective integration of theory and practice. The therapist may gain deeper insight into power dynamics, and the limits of his or her competence, and identify possible training needs. He or she may become more proactive in the introduction of changes such as more explicit contracting, revised boundaries and shared decision-making when deviating from usual practice. The process may influence changes in the workplace such as the development of revised protocols. However, some therapists have felt misunderstood and deeply damaged by the investigation process, and operate subsequently in a climate of fear. In supervision, the power dynamic may feel more equal as both the supervisor and therapist struggle through periods of difficulty to find ways forward.

CONCLUSIONS

Whatever appears to have 'gone wrong' in the therapeutic relationship, or the understanding of it which has led to a complaint, I believe that it is crucial for a therapist's supervisor to offer the conditions needed for open and non-defensive exploration of pertinent issues. This maximises the potential to maintain or develop safe, ethical practice. This can occur in a climate of warmth, support, honesty and understanding. As a supervisor it is also important to be able therapeutically (as discussed earlier in relation to containment) to hold the supervisee through periods of trauma and crisis.

Sometimes surviving the very formal process of a complaint and its practical demands overrides the therapist's opportunity to look at the issues in a deeper way until after the complaints process is complete. Therefore, as a supervisor supporting a practitioner through a complaints process, there are often two intertwined layers. Firstly, there is the issue of surviving the complaints procedure itself, its practical demands, and emotional effects. Secondly, it may be that, after the procedures are complete, there is an opportunity to facilitate an open exploration of difficult issues.

It is important for the supervisor to hold in his or her work an awareness of contemporary society and its demands. Nevertheless, I believe that a delicate balance can be achieved between avoiding naïvety and minimising policing. It is important to hold onto the essence of person-centred values, despite societal pressures. Certainly, I support Mearns and Thorne's (2000) stance in urging us not to capitulate to despair or 'to seek refuge in a sterilised and risk-free form of therapeutic activity which harms and benefits nobody' (p. 16). For the person-centred supervisor and the therapist I believe that this demands substantial courage.

REFERENCES

Bond, T. (2006) Responding to complaints. In C. Feltham and I. Horton (Eds.) *The Sage Handbook of Counselling and Psychotherapy* (2nd edn.) (pp. 197–8). London: Sage

Bozarth, J. (1998) *Person-Centered Therapy: A Revolutionary Paradigm*. Ross-on-Wye: PCCS Books

British Association for Counselling and Psychotherapy. (2005) *What is Supervision?* Information sheet S.2. Rugby: BACP

Carroll, M. (1996) *Counselling Supervision: Theory, Skills and Practice*. London: Cassell

Casemore, R. (2001) Managing boundaries: It's the little things that count. In R. Casemore (Ed.) *Surviving Complaints Against Therapists and Psychotherapists* (pp. 111–20). Ross-on-Wye: PCCS Books

Coffeng, T. (2002) Contact in the therapy of trauma and dissociation. In G. Wyatt and P. Sanders (Eds.) *Rogers' Therapeutic Condition: Evolution, Theory and Practice: Volume 4: Contact and Perception* (pp. 153–67). Ross-on-Wye: PCCS Books

Dryden, W. (1993) Person-centred therapy: A view from the outside. *Person-Centred Practice*, *1*(2), 22

Feltham, C. and Dryden, W. (1994) *Developing Counsellor Supervision*. London: Sage

Fish, V. (1999) Clematis's hat: Foucault and the politics of psychotherapy. In I. Parker

(Ed.) *Deconstructing Psychotherapy* (pp. 54–70). London: Sage

Hackney, H. and Goodyear, R. (1984) Carl Rogers's client-centered approach to supervision. In R.F. Levant and J.M. Shlien (Eds.) *Client-Centered Therapy and the Person-Centered Approach: New Directions in Theory, Research and Practice* (pp. 278–96). New York: Praeger

Hurwitz, B. S. (2004) The legal status of clinical practice guidelines. In P. Whitty and M. Eccles (Eds.) *Clinical Practice Guidelines in Mental Health* (pp. 37–8). Oxford: Radcliffe

Jacobs, M. (2001) Supervisors can change. *CPJ, 12*(1), 26–7

Kilborn, M. (2000) The quality of acceptance in person-centred practice. In T. Merry (Ed.) *The BAPCA Reader* (pp. 161–62). Ross-on-Wye: PCCS Books

Lambers, E. (2000) Supervision in person-centred therapy: Facilitating congruence. In D. Mearns and B. Thorne *Person-Centred Therapy Today* (pp. 196–211). London: Sage

McNeill, B.W. and Worthen, V. (1996) A phenomenological investigation of 'good' supervision events. *Journal of Counselling Psychology, 43*, 25–34

Mearns, D. (2003) *Developing Person-Centred Counselling* (2nd edn.). London: Sage

Mearns, D. (2004) How much supervision should you have? In BACP Information Services Editorial Board (Ed.) *Talking Therapies: An Essential Anthology* (pp. 117–19). Rugby: BACP

Mearns, D. and Cooper, M. (2005) *Working at Relational Depth in Counselling and Psychotherapy*. London: Sage

Mearns, D. and Thorne, B. (1999) *Person-Centred Counselling in Action* (2nd edn.). London: Sage

Mearns, D. and Thorne, B. (2000) *Person-Centred Therapy Today: New Frontiers in Theory and Practice*. London: Sage

Palmer Barnes, F. (1998) *Complaints and Grievances in Psychotherapy: A Handbook of Ethical Practice*. London: Routledge

Proctor, G. (2002) *The Dynamics of Power in Counselling and Psychotherapy: Ethics, Politics and Practice*. Ross-on-Wye: PCCS Books

Rogers, C. R. (1951) *Client-Centered Therapy*. London: Constable

Rogers, C. R. (1967) *On Becoming a Person: A Therapist's View of Psychotherapy*. London: Constable

Rogers, C. R. (1980) *A Way of Being*. Boston, MA: Houghton Mifflin

Rogers. C. R. (1990) The necessary and sufficient conditions of therapeutic personality change. In H. Kirschenbaum and V. L. Henderson (Eds.) *The Carl Rogers Reader* (pp. 219–36). London: Constable

Thorne, B. (2001) *Person-Centred Counselling: Therapeutic and Spiritual Dimensions*. London: Whurr

Tudor, K. and Worrall, M. (Eds.) (2004) *Freedom to Practice: Person-Centred Approaches To Supervision*. Ross-on-Wye: PCCS Books

Weaks, D. (2002) Unlocking the secrets of 'good supervision': A phenomenological exploration of experienced therapists' perceptions of good supervision. *Counselling and Psychotherapy Research, 2*(1), 33–9

Webb, A. (2001) Honesty in supervision. *CPJ, 12*(5), 24–5

Wilkins, P. (2003) *Person-Centred Therapy in Focus*. London: Sage

Worrall, M. (2001) Supervision and empathic understanding. In S. Haugh and T. Merry (Eds.) *Rogers' Therapeutic Conditions: Evolution, Theory and Practice. Volume 3: Empathy* (pp. 206–17). Ross-on-Wye: PCCS Books

CHAPTER TWELVE

SUPERVISION AS CONTINUING PERSONAL DEVELOPMENT

KEITH TUDOR AND MIKE WORRALL

Most professional organisations require their members to commit to continue their professional development. This usually refers to continuing professional development (CPD) post qualification. However, in its regulations about training, the United Kingdom Council for Psychotherapy (UKCP) (1990) states that: 'The Student must engage in a continuous process of analysis and self-examination, before, during and after training.' This tripartite time frame is significant in that it makes it clear:

1. That applicants for courses should demonstrate a commitment to some form of self-analysis, for example, through having experience of personal therapy—which, for some, stands as a prerequisite and even an entry requirement for undertaking training to be a therapist.
2. That all psychotherapists in training should engage in such analysis. This is a particularly important point in the context of moves towards statutory regulation of psychotherapy and of its training, whereby personal therapy hours are 'counted' as a part of an overall training requirement, rather than being something that a person wants to do. This is complicated by the fact that only two of the seven Sections of the UKCP require students training at its Member Organisations to be in therapy. For a history of this requirement see Tudor (2007, in press). Also, in recent years the British Association of Counselling and Psychotherapy (BACP) has moved away

from its previously held position on the importance of personal therapy by deregulating the requirement that its accredited counsellors have a minimum (of 40 hours) experience of personal therapy.

3. That all psychotherapists wishing to maintain their registered status should continue to undertake some form of self-analysis or reflective practice throughout their post-qualification career. This has led to an increasing interest in defining and promoting opportunities for CPD.

Interestingly, and we think significantly, the statement from the UKCP refers to 'a continuous process of analysis and self-examination'. It does not refer to *personal* therapy or, indeed, continuing *professional* development. The BACP's (2002, p. 3) *Ethical Framework* puts this in the following terms:

> The principle of self-respect means that the practitioner appropriately applies all the above [ethical] principles as entitlements for self. This includes seeking counselling or therapy and other opportunities for personal development as required. There is an ethical responsibility to use supervision for appropriate personal and professional support and development.

This wording suggests firstly, that personal and professional development are inseparable and, secondly, that supervision is an essential forum for such development. We discuss each of these implications.

THE PROFESSIONAL IS PERSONAL

Some in the field view professional development as concerned with knowledge and skills, and personal development either as everything else or, more specifically, concerned with ways of resourcing the self. However, we think that this distinction divorces knowledge and skills from the personal sphere or domain. Wilkins (1997) also takes this view and discusses the importance for therapists of rest, recreation, relaxation, reading, and writing—and having fun, holidays and adventure!

We see the distinction between the apparently personal and the apparently professional as arbitrary. There are, as far as we know, no commonly agreed or articulated guidelines as to what's appropriate to discuss in supervision, and what's better discussed in therapy. In effect, this gives individual supervisors freedom, opportunity and responsibility to decide for themselves what they will or won't work with in supervision. There may be little intrinsically wrong with this. Supervisor and supervisee may even on occasion agree explicitly that a particular issue falls outside their agreed focus and would be better addressed elsewhere. We have both, however, heard too many practitioners describe feeling unheard, unhelped and unsupported when their supervisor has decided, usually unilaterally, that they should stop talking about a particular concern on the grounds that it's a personal issue that has little to do with their work or with the task of supervision, and that they would therefore do better to deal with it in therapy.

This distinction between what's personal and what's professional is also *restrictive*, self-evidently, in that it limits discussion and examination; and *reductive*, in that it reduces its area of attention from the whole person of the therapist to one particular, professional persona. In our view, in so far as this circumscribes freedom of enquiry or expression, it compromises effective supervision.

The inseparability of the professional and the personal concerns the relationship between the two. Rogers (1959) sees outcome as simply a more or less differentiated aspect of process. In other words, process is continuous and fluid. Along the way, aspects of process sometimes cohere, constellate or crystallise together into something solid and stable enough to be called a provisional outcome. In a similar way, we see what is professional as simply a more or less sharply differentiated aspect of what is personal. Everything, that is, is personal. Some manifestations of the personal are boundaried, discernible and stable enough for us to differentiate them and call them professional. Just as outcomes emerge from and return to the flow of process, so the professional emerges from and returns to the personal. We can't sensibly talk about outcomes without recognising the processes of which they are a manifestation. Likewise, we can't talk intelligently about what's professional without recognising what's personal. We represent this in terms of domains of influence (Tudor and Worrall, 2004) in which the professional domain sits within the personal domain.

Personal development in supervision

There is in person-centred psychology a strong tradition of personal development. Merry (1999, p.130) asserts that 'effective person-centred counselling demands a great deal of commitment to an ongoing process of personal development.' However, such development is not necessarily equated with personal therapy and, Merry argues, does not necessarily have to be undertaken during training. Indeed, Mearns (1994, p. 35) is sceptical of the value of personal therapy and argues that 'Personal development for professional working is so crucial to the person-centered approach that it cannot be left to the vagaries of individual therapy.' In person-centred psychology and training, there is an emphasis on groups and on personal development in groups, as well as on a freedom of choice with regard to personal therapy.

Supervision and therapy are traditionally seen as different processes, with different agendas, different outcomes and different areas of enquiry and attention.

Many ethical codes and frameworks enshrine this difference, and further polarise the two activities by insisting that one practitioner cannot be both supervisor and therapist to the same person. Such thinking and practice sees supervision, broadly, as attending to a therapist's *professional* life, and therapy as attending more to his *personal* life. Supervision is, in this sense, a more specialised endeavour than therapy, with a particular and restricted focus.

One apparent difference between the two emerges when a supervisor identifies a supervisee's presenting or recurring experience as a 'therapy' issue, and suggests that a supervisee talk about this in therapy and not in supervision. This implies that the supervisor holds views about what is relevant in supervision, and therefore also about what a supervisee may and may not talk about, a perspective which is confirmed by Ladany's (2007) research, which reports on, and considers, the extent to which supervisees do not disclose matters to their supervisors. We're interested in a number of questions here:

- What are the criteria by which a supervisor decides what is and isn't relevant to the process of supervision?
- Are such criteria explicit or implicit?
- Are such decisions negotiated or imposed?
- What are the implications of such decisions for the process, outcomes and efficacy of supervision?

We take the view that there's no such thing as a 'therapy' issue. There are only issues which we work through—in therapy and in supervision, in love and in life, with family and with friends. Our own answers to the above questions look something like this:

- Our view about what's relevant in supervision follows a supervisee's self-assessment of what's most pressing or important to address in the moment of supervision. This is operational evidence of our trust in a supervisee's integrity, competence and self-awareness. We see such trust as a specific manifestation in a professional arena of a more general trust in a supervisee's tendency to actualise.
- As supervisors and trainers we make those criteria explicit.
- Given the above, we necessarily share any decisions about who discusses what, where.
- We think that our practice in this area emerges from, and is consistent with, person-centred principles. It seems to us an effective way to create an environment within which supervisees feel free enough to examine any

aspect of their work, however troubling. We think that this offers practitioners an opportunity to think rigorously, critically and fearlessly about their work. In our experience, most supervisees seize this opportunity, and in our view this offers a practitioner's clients as high a level of safety as any process of supervision can.

We therefore see supervision as an arena within which practitioners can grow both personally and professionally. We say this for two reasons, the first of which is to do with the nature of the human organism.

Rogers (1959) argues that the organism reacts *as an organised whole* to its experiential field. If we accept this proposition, two ideas follow:

i. Anything that affects us will affect us in all aspects of our being.
ii. Anything we learn or change in one aspect of our being will necessarily manifest as learning or change in other aspects.

If this is accurate, it doesn't much matter where we start or what we address in supervision. Issues and concerns that arise in the 'personal' areas of our lives will necessarily manifest in 'professional' areas too; and any discussion or resolution of personal issues will also necessarily manifest in the professional area.

The second reason concerns motivation and personal values. If we've chosen to train as therapists, to engage in this work and to take our work seriously, we have a significant and enduring personal investment in our professional practice. Henderson (2001) identifies reviewing the counsellor's motivation to be a counsellor as one of three possibilities of supervisory focus with regard to sustaining the mental health of the counsellor. (The other two are monitoring the counsellor's resilience and talking about self-care.) Our personal values will inform the professional work we undertake and the way in which we perform it. From a person-centred perspective, values are the expression of the tendency of any organism to show preference. In terms of professional values Boy and Pine (1982) identify a number of such values which they conceive as 'commitments', including:

- careful selection of the work setting;
- identification with colleagues who are, in turn, committed and concerned;
- organisational involvement; and
- ongoing self-assessment as well as periodic evaluation.

These lines of thought support our conviction that, given the nature of the human organism, it is impossible and, fortunately, unnecessary to make hard and fast distinctions between the personal and the professional. To do so, or to attempt to do so, shows atomistic rather than holistic thinking and runs counter to the organismic nature of person-centred thinking and practice.

We can say all of this more positively: supervision becomes more effective to the extent that it embraces and attends to the whole of the person of the therapist. In this sense, to paraphrase Thorne (2002), the supervisory relationship is an existential encounter at least as much as a professional contract. Spence (2006, p. 3) argues that this is primarily effected through love. He views supervision: 'as the offering of love in the form of a relationship in which the supervisee may openly and undefensively examine their experience of working with clients and to develop and grow as a person in their practice.' We agree with this view, especially in the context of codes which argue that supervisors are responsible for 'ensuring' a contract and a relationship in which supervisees can present their work as honestly as possible (see British Association for Counselling, 1996; British Association of Psychoanalytic and Psychodynamic Supervision, 2003). We see two ways in which this existential, holistic approach is true:

- Whatever a therapist chooses to talk about in supervision is current and available. Given that he's chosen to talk about it rather than about anything else, we can assume that it's pressing in some way, and also that it's open to attention and examination in dialogue. We think that it's worth following the energy and currency of this, even if he's talking about an apparently personal issue.
- The practice of therapy involves the whole person. Practitioners from some orientations may not agree, and the assertion may not hold true across the range of psychological therapies. It is, however, tenable within humanistic therapies in general and person-centred therapies in particular. It's consistent with this, therefore, and appropriate that a therapist should feel free to bring himself as fully to supervision as he does to his work as a therapist.

The implications of this argument blur, and may even dissolve, some of the distinctions many hold between supervision and therapy. As such, they constitute a challenge to received views and may sit uncomfortably with some practitioners. We believe, however, that the argument is sound, and that its implications offer possibilities of profound benefit to both practitioner and client.

References

Boy, A.V. and Pine, G.J. (1982) *Client-Centered Counseling: A Renewal.* Boston: Allyn and Bacon

British Association for Counselling. (1996) *Codes of Ethics and Practice for Supervisors of Counsellors.* Rugby: BAC

British Association for Counselling and Psychotherapy. (2002) *Ethical Framework for Good Practice in Counselling and Psychotherapy.* Rugby: BACP

British Association of Psychoanalytic and Psychodynamic Supervision. (2003) *Code of Ethics & Practice.* Redhill: BAPPS

Henderson, P. (2001) Supervision and the mental health of the counsellor. In M. Carroll and M. Tholstrup (Eds.) *Integrative Approaches to Supervision* (pp. 93–107). London: Jessica Kingsley

Ladany, N. (2007) *Supervision Secrets: Fibbing, Fighting, and Fornicating.* Paper presented at the Conference of the Society for Psychotherapy Research UK, Ravenscar

Mearns, D. (1994) *Developing Person-Centred Counselling.* London: Sage

Merry, T. (1999) *Learning and Being in Person-Centred Counselling.* Ross-on-Wye: PCCS Books

Rogers, C.R. (1959) A theory of therapy, personality and interpersonal relationships, as developed in the client-centered framework. In S. Koch (Ed.) *Psychology: A Study of a Science. Vol. 3: Formulations of the Person and the Social Context* (pp. 184–256). New York: McGraw-Hill

Spence, S. (2006, August) The amateur supervisor: Supervision as an offer of love. *Person-Centred Quarterly*, pp. 1–6

Thorne, B. (2002) *The Mystical Power of Person-Centred Therapy.* London: Whurr

Tudor, K. (2007, in press) To be or not to be—in personal therapy—that is the question. *Transactions*

Tudor, K. and Worrall, M. (2004) Issues, questions, dilemmas and domains in supervision. In K. Tudor and M. Worrall (Eds.) *Freedom to Practise: Person-Centred Approaches to Supervision* (pp. 79–96). Ross-on-Wye: PCCS Books

United Kingdom Council for Psychotherapy (1990, May) *Special General Meeting Resolution.* London: UKCP

Wilkins, P. (1997) *Personal and Professional Development for Counsellors.* London: Sage

CHAPTER THIRTEEN

SUPERVISORS IN THE DOCK? SUPERVISION AND THE LAW

PETER JENKINS

Supervisors are working in an increasingly wide range of therapeutic settings and are often involved in supervising new groups of professionals such as personal advisors, learning mentors or graduate mental health workers, with innovatory and perhaps unfamiliar roles. If supervisors play a key role in policing and sustaining standards of safe, competent and ethical practice on the part of therapists, then they are at the same time increasingly uncertain as to just how far their responsibilities extend. Are supervisors responsible for the mistakes, errors or malpractice of their supervisees? And is this responsibility a purely professional one, or does taking on the role of supervisor to another practitioner open the door to the supervisor becoming vulnerable to action in the courts by an aggrieved client or agency? The situation applying to supervision in the UK is perhaps made more complex and anxiety-provoking by the awareness that some supervisors in the US are, indeed, legally liable for the practice of their supervisees. The concern may well be that legal trends in the US offer supervisors in the UK a prospect of an uncertain and increasingly litigious future.

This chapter will set out a framework for understanding key principles of ethics and the law as it applies to the supervision of counsellors and psychotherapists. Some of the main concerns of supervisors, relating to defining differing forms of responsibility, managing risk, and the status of records, will be addressed. Concerns about heightened vulnerability to legal action against supervisors will be put in context.

Supervision and the law

Our starting point is that there is a tension between ethics and the law. If supervisors have a key role to play in supporting therapists to work to the appropriate ethical and professional standards, then it has to be acknowledged that what ethical practice necessarily consists of is not always straightforward or obvious. The British Association for Counselling and Psychotherapy's (BACP) *Ethical Framework* (2002) has moved away from a prescriptive code for counsellors and supervisors, towards an approach encouraging a more creative and autonomous reliance on ethical values, principles and personal qualities to underpin good practice with clients and supervisees. For example, a counsellor working in a secondary school setting provides counselling sessions for pupils. The school insists on gaining written evidence of parental consent before providing counselling. The counsellor is critical of this arrangement and raises this issue in supervision with her supervisor. The supervisor takes the view that it is preferable to have a service run on this basis within the school, as this reflects the school's values, i.e. a service based on close partnership with parents and families. From an ethical point of view, it may be that the service meets the needs of the majority of pupils. To challenge school policy might 'rock the boat' and lead to the counsellor being replaced by a volunteer counsellor or by a member of staff unqualified in counselling. Alternatively, an ethical argument might be that insisting on parental consent might exclude some pupils who either won't ask for permission to see the counsellor, or who are refused this by the parents.

Ethical dilemmas are, it seems, inescapably ingrained in therapeutic practice. A further complication is that ethics and the law do not always coincide. As Bond has suggested (2002, p. 124): 'What is ethical may not be legal. What is legal may not be ethical.'

Law and therapeutic practice

The relationship of the law to therapeutic practice and to its supervision is fairly complex. It is mediated by three main factors:

- by the *context or setting* in which the practitioner works, e.g. whether in a statutory agency, voluntary organisation or in private practice;
- by the nature of the specific *client group* the practitioner is working with, for example, children, or clients with significant and enduring mental health problems;
- by the practitioner's *employment status*, i.e. whether the therapist is employed or self-employed.

The latter point may strike some supervisors as odd. Surely responsibilities are defined primarily by the nature of the professional *relationships* between client, therapist and supervisor? In law, however, employment presents a key variable in defining patterns of legal liability, as will be outlined later in this chapter.

Finally, supervision within therapeutic work is emphatically separate from line-management responsibilities in a hierarchical sense. It is questionable whether supervision is the appropriate term for what is more accurately described as a form of professional consultation. The term 'supervision' implies a direct line of responsibility for the work of the supervisee, which may not apply in reality. The parallel term 'clinical responsibility' deriving from a medical model, is also imprecise, as it may elide the crucial distinction between *direct* responsibility for clinical or therapeutic work and responsibility for work *delegated* to another professional. Hence, a general practitioner may be seen, under this model, as retaining overall clinical responsibility for a patient referred to the practice counsellor in the same health centre. This model of delegated client or patient care is unlikely to apply in the case of therapeutic supervision, where the supervisor is a source of information, advice and support, but does not necessarily have a direct, legal responsibility for client welfare.

ETHICS AND THE LAW

The BACP's *Ethical Framework* (2002) sets out the principles, values and personal qualities which are required in order to undertake safe, competent and effective therapeutic work with clients. The ethical principles are derived from established models applying to medical ethics and other forms of ethical-professional discourse. Box 13.1 represents an attempt to translate the key ethical principles into a legal framework, in order to explore how therapeutic practice might be viewed from a legal perspective.

In terms of ethical responsibilities relating to supervision, practitioners are required to:

- have regular and ongoing formal supervision/consultative support for their work in accordance with professional requirements (BACP, 2002, p. 6);
- receive supervision/consultative support independently of any managerial relationships (ibid., p. 7);
- clarify who holds responsibility for the client (ibid., p. 7).

In addition (BACP, 2002, p. 7), 'Supervisors and managers have a responsibility to maintain and enhance good practice by practitioners, to protect clients from poor practice and to acquire the attitudes, skills and knowledge required by their

Ethical Principles (BACP)	Legal Concepts
Autonomy	Informed Consent Contract
Beneficence (Welfare)	Duty of care
Non-maleficence (Avoiding harm)	Duty to warn? Standard of care
Fidelity (Trust)	Duty of confidence Fiduciary duty
Justice	Non-discrimination
Self-respect	Pre-conditions necessary to fulfil duty to apply reasonable care and skill

Box 13.1 Ethical principles and legal framework

role.' The (now superseded) BAC *Code of Ethics and Practice for Supervisors of Counsellors* stressed the ethical duty of supervisors in slightly different terms, as being 'to ensure the safety of supervisees and their clients' (BAC, 1996, Paragraph A.3). This *ethical* duty, particularly towards clients, is quite distinct from any *legal* responsibility for the client's safety and welfare. While the supervisor retains an ethical duty towards the client's well-being, the form of the supervisor's and therapist's responsibility, in a narrowly legal sense, will vary according to the setting and context in which the overall work is carried out, as set out below. Interestingly, it should be noted that the current BACP *Ethical Framework* does *not* require practitioners to obey the law as such. Instead, there is a broader and looser requirement (2002, p. 6) that practitioners 'should be aware of and understand any legal requirements concerning their work, consider these conscientiously and be legally accountable for their practice'. This represents a distinct change from the earlier BAC *Code of Ethics and Practice for Counsellors*, which asserted unambiguously (1992, Para. B.2.6.1): 'Counsellors should work within the law.'

PROBLEM AREAS FOR SUPERVISION AND THE LAW

This discussion will focus on three main aspects of supervision and the law which can prove to be challenging for practitioners. These relate to:

- accountability and liability;
- confidentiality and risk; and
- access to records.

The chapter will attempt to separate the concept of accountability in an ethical, therapeutic and professional sense from a more restricted legal understanding of liability in law. It will also discuss the roles of both supervisor and therapist in managing varying levels of risk to the client and others. Finally, the problematic area of record keeping and managing access to information about the therapeutic process will be focused on. Some of these concerns will be relevant to the therapist working directly with the client. Others will relate more to the supervisor's specialist role, encompassing their activity in providing consultative support to the therapist.

ACCOUNTABILITY AND LIABILITY

The concept of accountability relates to the stakeholders who have a legitimate concern or interest in the work of the supervisor. Supervisors are accountable for their practice via a number of different routes; for example, through a complaint to their professional association(s), assuming that they are a member. Different associations have differing systems for complaints. Under the BACP complaints procedure, complaints can be brought under the headings of:

- professional misconduct;
- professional malpractice; and
- bringing the profession into disrepute.

If the supervisor is employed or works as a volunteer for an agency, then there may be an additional form of accountability via the organisation's system of line management, leading to disciplinary action. In statutory settings, supervision is seen as an integral part of the process of holding professionals to account for their practice and decision-making. This is particularly evident in settings such as social services departments where child abuse inquiries have commented adversely on the failure of supervisors to maintain required standards of work, as in the Jasmine Beckford and Victoria Climbie Inquiries (Blom-Cooper and Brent Council, 1985; Laming, 2003, respectively).

The separate concept of liability relates to the process of a legal challenge. This can take two main forms, depending on the supervisor's particular situation. The supervisor can be subject to a challenge in law for a breach of contract, if one exists, with the supervisee or the agency contracting for their services. The second route of legal challenge can be via action for breach of duty of care, again either to the supervisee or to the agency concerned. In plain terms, this is where the supervisor is being sued by the supervisee or by the agency to which they are providing a service. The concept of 'duty of care' is used much more widely in discussions about professional responsibilities, and is often used in an inaccurate way, as a kind of aspirational term. Hence, it might be claimed that therapists owe a duty of care to report child abuse, or to have regular supervision. In fact, these requirements might be *ethical* or *professional* ones, but they do not necessarily constitute *legal* requirements as such. The legal term 'duty of care' tends to be defined in narrow rather than broad terms by the courts. Existence of such a duty of care implies an actual liability in law, and therefore the potential for another party to sue for breach of that duty.

The supervisor retains a professional and ethical duty 'to protect clients from poor practice', as mentioned earlier (BACP, 2002, p. 7). This might involve the supervisor reporting a supervisee for engaging in a sexual relationship with the client, or for attempting to use techniques such as regression therapy, for example, which were particularly unsuitable or even risky for a highly vulnerable or suggestible client.

A final aspect of legal liability might concern action by a supervisee or agency for the provision of negligent advice. This is a fairly specialist aspect of law, mainly concerning financial or expert advice, where the professional concerned has a responsibility to ensure that the advice given as part of their services is accurate and well-informed. Of course, one argument could be that supervisors do not actually give advice but instead offer consultative support. The responsibility therefore lies squarely with the supervisee to decide whether or not to pursue a particular line of activity: to offer a client further sessions, for example, or to refer a client to another practitioner specialising in trauma work. It will be up to the courts to decide whether supervisors are potentially liable for negligent advice to a supervisee or agency, but the likelihood is that this remains a fairly remote possibility at present.

A key point of reference in any discussion about the supervisor's legal liability can be found in United States (US) case law. Under the US system, supervisors are seen to be much more closely aligned to a quasi-managerial role and therefore carry a significant level of legal liability for supervisee or malpractice. Falvey (2002) provides a useful summary of the developing case law for supervisor negligence in the US (see Box 13.2).

However, the UK legal system has yet to adopt the US stance with regard to supervisor liability. Under UK law, supervisor liability continues to be narrowly framed by contract and employment status, as discussed below.

> **Cases brought under US law on the grounds of negligence relating to supervision**
>
> Failure to *seek* supervision
> - on the part of an *individual therapist* (Gilmore, 1986)
> - due to lack of *agency policy re risk management* (Peck, 1985)
>
> Failure to exercise *control over* supervisee's client work (Steckler, 1992)
>
> Failure to act on perceived *risk to client*
> - by training agency (Almonte, 1994)
> - by supervisor (Tarasoff, 1976; Jablonski, 1983; Simmons, 1986; Pesce, 1987)
>
> *Box 13.2 Summary of US case law on supervisor liability (adapted from Falvey, 2002)*

FORMS OF ACCOUNTABILITY AND LIABILITY

The following table sets out the differing forms of accountability and liability. The employment context of the supervisor is a crucial variable here. If the supervisor is self-employed, then the supervisee carries personal liability for any breach of duty of care to the supervisee, or to an agency relying on their services. If, however, the supervisor is employed, then the employing agency carries vicarious liability for the actions of the supervisee as an employee. In practice, the divisions between self-employed status and employed status are not always clear. In the NHS, for example, it has been argued by therapists' organisations that counsellors who are on substantial self-employment contracts should be deemed to be employed and that 'self-employment' is a device used by NHS Trusts to escape their proper responsibilities as employers. Again, it may fall to the courts to determine whether a supervisor is self-employed or holds full status as an employee where this is contested, as this factor will decide whether the supervisor is individually liable or is protected by the employer's umbrella of vicarious liability. The table sets out the differing elements of the supervisory relationship as related to employment status and professional accountability (see Box 13.3).

FORMS OF DUTY OF CARE

The existence of a duty of care implies *liability* towards the person receiving the service. The duty of care is determined by the nature of the professional relationship, e.g. doctor and patient, or therapist and client, and also by the nature of the employment relationship of the professional concerned. Given that supervisors often work in a wide variety of contexts, this can make for a confusing

		Elements of the supervisory relationship	
		Professional responsibility	Legal liability
Employment context of professional practice	Individual e.g. self-employed	Personal accountability	Personal liability
	Organisational e.g. employee status	Personal and/or line management accountability	Vicarious liability

Box 13.3 Elements of the supervisory relationship (adapted from Jenkins, 2001)

range of differing forms of liability. This can shift almost daily, depending upon whether a supervisor is working on a contract with a fee-paying supervisee, on a freelance basis for an organisation, or is directly employed by an organisation to provide supervision to its staff. The three main types of employment pattern are set out below, indicating the ways in which the corresponding duty of care also may vary (see Boxes 13.4, 13.5 and 13.6).

In the first type, shown in Box 13.4, the supervisor is engaged in a classic private practice relationship with a supervisee, who pays a fee for their supervision, on the basis of a legal contract. Of course, many supervision arrangements tend to be fairly informal but the arrangement, even if only based on a verbal agreement, involves an exchange of supervision for payment. The supervisor owes a duty of care to the supervisee, namely to work to the appropriate professional standard

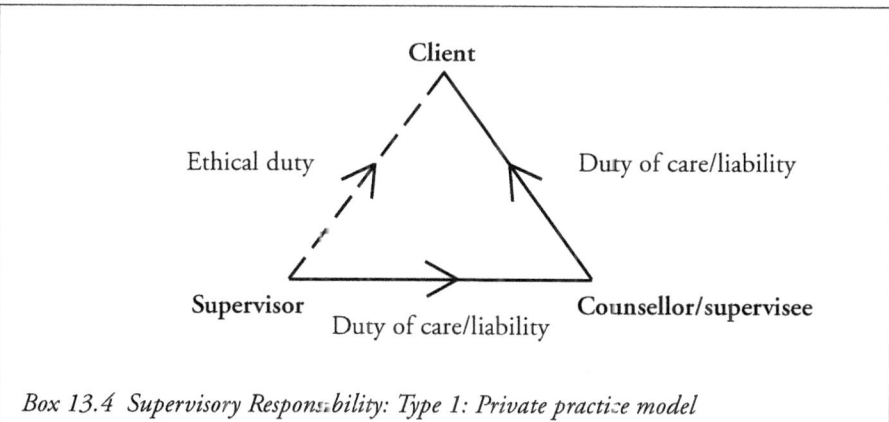

Box 13.4 Supervisory Responsibility: Type 1: Private practice model

for this kind of work. The supervisee, as therapist, in turn owes a duty of care to the client, to work according to the standard of care to be expected of a practitioner, according to 'competent, respected professional opinion' under what is termed the *Bolam* test. This is the standard test of competence, or 'good enough practice', derived from medical case law, which is applied to therapists in cases of alleged negligence. Perhaps controversially, the supervisor does not owe the client a duty of care. This is so for two main reasons. Firstly, the client is not a party to the original supervision contract. Secondly, the client is too remote (in a legal sense) from the activity of supervision to be considered as being owed a direct duty of care by the supervisor. Instead, the supervisor owes the client an *ethical* duty, under professional codes of practice, to safeguard them from harm.

In the second type of supervision arrangement, shown in Box 13.5, the supervisor is under contract to an organisation to provide supervision to its counsellor. The organisation pays the supervisor for his or her services. The supervisor owes a duty of care to *both* the counsellor *and* to the organisation to work to generally accepted professional standards. The organisation owes a duty of care to the client in providing the counselling service. Again, the supervisor, arguably, does *not* owe a direct duty of care to the client in legal terms, for the reasons outlined above. However, the supervisor has an *ethical* duty, as before, towards the client.

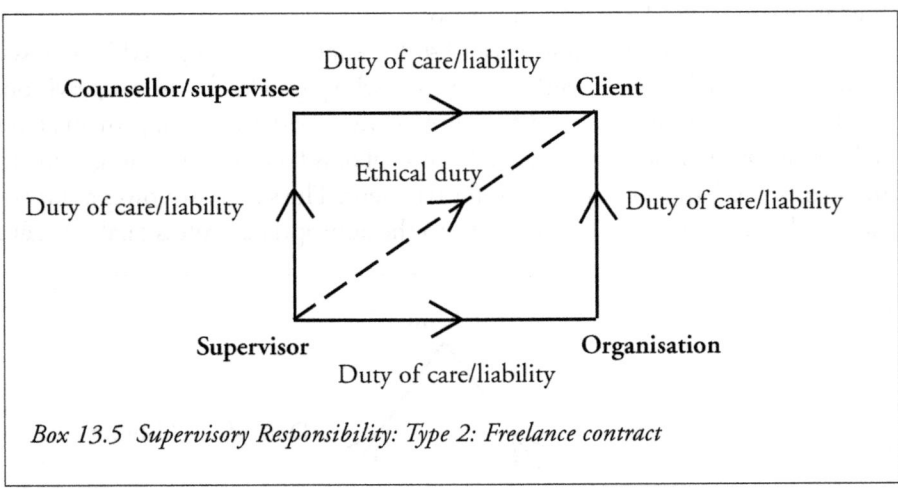

Box 13.5 *Supervisory Responsibility: Type 2: Freelance contract*

In the third type of arrangement shown in Box 13.6, the supervisor is *directly employed* by the organisation, which is providing counselling to the client. The organisation has a duty of care to the client and carries vicarious liability in this situation for the professional activity of *both* the counsellor *and* supervisor. If the client has a grievance against the counsellor or supervisor, essentially he or she will need to sue both organisation and supervisor. While protected to some extent by the vicarious liability of the organisation, the supervisor still continues to owe an *ethical* duty to the client.

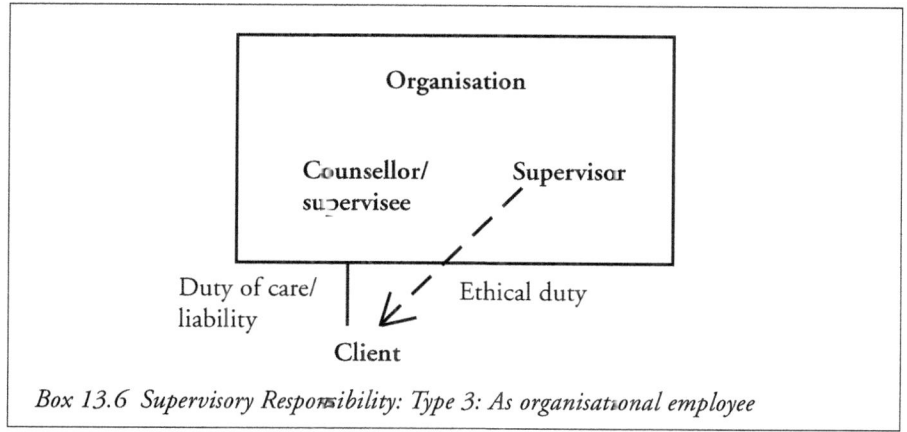

Box 13.6 Supervisory Responsibility: Type 3: As organisational employee

Managing confidentiality and risk

In the course of their work, the therapist and supervisor together come into contact with a large amount of highly sensitive personal information about clients. Therapy and its related supervision act as a *container* or a *custodian* for this material, which may also include information about unsafe or exploitative situations in a work setting, or abuse in domestic or residential settings. Part of the role of both therapist and supervisor when this information is shared in supervision, is to manage the level of perceived risk that this discussion might introduce. In exploring risky situations for the supervisee, for the client, for a third party, such as a child or partner, or an employer or the general public, the supervisor is engaged with the therapist in jointly managing levels of risk.

One way of responding to risk is to disclose information to individuals or agencies, who can then act upon it. For example, a supervisor might encourage a therapist working with a highly suicidal client to refer the client back to their GP. If the therapist refuses to do this, the supervisor might then be faced with the dilemma of whether or not to overrule the therapist and to contact the GP themselves, if he or she assessed the level of risk to be sufficiently severe. In this role, the supervisor is operating in a *proactive* capacity, with regard to confidential client material, in deciding whether or not to *initiate disclosure* to a third party or agency. Clearly, the supervisor owes a duty of confidence to the supervisee, under both civil law and statute. However, it is well established in law that a duty of confidentiality is rarely absolute. A therapist or supervisor could choose to breach confidentiality (i.e. disclose personal information without consent) if this is seen to be 'in the public interest' for example, in order to prevent a crime.

Supervisors have a key role to play in helping their supervisees and their agencies to work within the required boundaries of confidentiality. In order to do this effectively, they need to know what the law requires regarding breaching client or supervisee confidentiality. Legal requirements or possibilities for breaking confidentiality can be grouped in three main categories. Mandatory disclosure is when the law demands that certain types of information be passed on to the appropriate authorities, such as the police. Contractual obligations to disclose information may either arise from a contract of employment or form part of agency policy, without actually holding legal force as such.

Finally, there are some forms of disclosure which are discretionary, in that the supervisor may choose to disclose or not. These three levels of requirement to disclose are set out briefly in the table below. Of course, a supervisor working in private practice will not be bound by an agency contract of employment or protocol to report risk of suicide or employee fraud, and could choose whether or not to do this in the public interest. Alternatively, the supervisor could make it a term of their contract with a supervisee that any instances of a child being at risk of 'significant harm' will lead to the supervisor reserving the right to contact the relevant child protection team, if the supervisee has not already done so. The supervisor and therapist in private practice thus have a great deal of latitude to decide on their own framework for confidentiality, given that the legal compulsion to disclose is effectively limited to terrorism and drug money laundering (see Box 13.7).

Mandatory disclosure:
- Terrorism
- Drug money laundering

Contractually based disclosure (i.e. may be required under specific terms of a contract with an employer or with a supervisee):
- Child abuse
- Risk of harm to self /suicide
- Risk of harm to third party
- 'Whistleblowing' malpractice to an employer
- Reporting back to agency or training institution on supervisee competence or quality assurance issues

Discretionary disclosure (i.e. available as an option to a therapist or supervisor):
- Via qualified privilege (reporting malpractice to an appropriate authority)
- If a serious crime
- If in the public interest

Box 13.7 Disclosure of confidential information

Ethical issues in managing confidentiality and risk

For some therapists and supervisors, there is no problem at all in deciding on information which must be disclosed to a third party. It may seem unproblematic, and even self-evident, that *all* incidents of potential or actual child abuse *must* be reported to the authorities, even if it is not strictly a legal requirement as such. However, conflicts can arise, say for example, where the disclosure of abuse is made by the client, but the abuse happened some years ago, and there seems little risk of it recurring with that client. It may be that to report the abuse against the client's express wishes may lead to the client retracting their claim of abuse, or to undermining their trust in the therapist. Investigation and follow-up by the social services or by the police may, in some cases, be inconclusive or badly managed.

From an ethical point of view, there can be severe conflicts between different ethical principles in managing confidentiality and risk. These can be exacerbated by the contractual and reporting requirements which may apply to the supervisor. Agencies with statutory duties, such as health, education and social work, often frame their responses to risk largely in terms of the need to promote welfare and to avoid harm. This is clearly a necessary and legitimate stance, and reflects their specific role in society. However, for the individual supervisor or therapist, there may be a corresponding commitment to promote client autonomy and demonstrate fidelity to the therapeutic alliance, which may lead them to delay reporting risk on occasion, or even to choose to maintain confidentiality at all costs.

There may be a wider aspect to this conflict as well. Hawkins and Shohet have described the growing trend for supervisors to work with what they describe as 'complex organisational and interprofessional situations' (2000, p. 163). In many cases, this may involve supervisors working as members of complex multi-disciplinary teams, supervising therapists working with a high level of risk in child care, psychiatric or forensic services (Cordess, 2001). There may be danger in these situations that such teams adopt a lowest common denominator of risk to clients or to third parties. The supervisor working in this setting may find that the threshold for breaking confidentiality and reporting risk is set at a relatively low level, perhaps in part to reduce concerns of practitioners of facing criticism, or worse, should 'something go wrong'. Therapists and supervisors, conversely, may be accustomed to working with quite high levels of risk with clients, either through experience, or through a strong commitment to supporting a high level of client autonomy.

Clearly, managing risk in this way needs to be based on accurate assessment skills, sound professional practice and high levels of commitment to a common approach, rather than simply the expression of a cavalier disregard for the safety of clients or third parties. Supervisors need to maintain an independent, critical stance towards those agency reporting requirements which unduly constrain confidentiality. Similarly, the supervisor has a role to play in challenging provision for client entitlement, as an issue of ethical and professional concern. Counselling services which insist on evidence of parental consent for young people under sixteen, or which operate an unnecessary age restriction, should raise ethical issues for the supervisor connected with the practice. Again, agency policy may conflict with ethical principles, in introducing a blanket policy for reporting self-harm or illegal drug use, for example.

Supervisors are increasingly working as direct employees of organisations, whether the latter provide counselling directly to the public, or whether the service is provided in-house to their own staff (Copeland, 2005). However, there may be a substantial risk that in opting for enhanced status as direct employees of organisations, supervisors may become contractually locked into having to follow agency policies and reporting requirements which seriously constrain their professional autonomy and freedom of action (Morrison, 1993; Pritchard, 1997).

Managing access to records

The previous section looked at the processes involved in proactively managing confidential information and risk. This section explores the related process of managing access to records, whether of therapy or of supervision, in response to approaches or demands by external bodies for information. This distinction between the supervisor as *proactive* custodian of sensitive client information and in his latter role as responding in a more *reactive* way to demands for access to information is not a legal distinction, but simply a way of trying to structure the different aspects of the processes involved. In this second part of the process, supervisor and therapist are responding reactively to requests or demands made by external bodies for access to information about the therapeutic process. It is worth pointing out that there are two separate and distinct aspects of this access to client data, which are often confused or run together incorrectly. The first of these is via the courts and the legal system. The second is under the provisions of data protection law. While there is a small degree of overlap between the two routes, in that clients may seek access to their own records for use in legal proceedings, it is more helpful to try to keep these two routes fairly separate for discussion purposes.

Defining records
Managing access to records of therapy or supervision rather begs the question of what *form* these records actually take. What seems clear is that therapeutic record

keeping has been hugely influenced by the Data Protection Act 1998 (*DPA*). Previously largely unregulated, therapeutic recording has been brought within the remit of detailed, if somewhat complex, law and regulations. Therapy and supervision records, which were previously much more open to individual practitioner choice, have been opened up to scrutiny under the principles of transparency and accountability (see Jenkins and Potter, 2007). Under the Act, the nature of records are determined by two main factors. Record keeping requirements are determined in part by the *setting* in which they take place, so that records in health, education and social work contexts have particular provisions regarding qualified client access. The counselling records produced by a counsellor working in primary care would, arguably, constitute part of the overall patient's health record under data protection law; the counselling records of a child in school would similarly constitute part of their education record; a record of therapy carried out for a social services client could thus be considered to be part of their overall social-work file.

Outside of health, education and social work recording, records of therapy are determined primarily by their *structure and format*, namely whether they are electronic or manual in form. The *DPA* 1998 covers electronic and manual forms of recording. Electronic records can include those kept in computerised form, together with audio and video tapes. Manual records include those kept in 'relevant filing systems', i.e. in highly systematised forms capable of rapid information retrieval, and those which are 'unstructured', or kept in largely random or idiosyncratic order.

The technical definitions of recording set out by the *DPA* 1998 are at odds with the recording culture which has developed within many therapeutic circles over the past few decades. Within this culture, until recently, therapeutic records have been held to be defined by their *purpose*; namely whether they are designed for agency recording purposes, for personal reflection, for supervision purposes and so on. Allied to this, are the notions that records can also be classified according to the degree of personal *privacy* invoked by the therapist concerned. Some records are held to be highly subjective and personal and therefore not part of any more formal recording system and certainly not for managerial scrutiny or client access. Another approach has been to rate records as personal *possessions* of the therapist concerned, distinguishing between records 'owned' by the agency, and those 'owned' by the counsellor concerned. These distinctions between different sets of records, based on concepts of purpose, privacy and possession, do not figure highly in data protection regulations.

Client access
One of the main features of the *DPA* 1998 has been to introduce the principle of

client or 'data subject' access. However, there a number of limitations concerning certain types of therapeutic records. Client access is possible to health, education and social work files as described above, with limits on access where this might cause the client or a third party 'serious harm' or prejudice the confidentiality of a third party. Given that personal data within the definition of the Act refers to information about 'an identifiable living individual', it is unlikely that a client could access their supervision file where the latter was referred to, as is customary, simply by a first name or similarly disguised identity. Furthermore, supervisors and agencies keeping *only* manual records of client work do *not* have to notify under the Act nor make provision for client access.

Access to records via the legal system

The second route of access to records of therapy is via the courts and the legal system. This route can provide access to supervision records, assuming that the agency demanding access under a court order or similar authority is aware of their existence. Agents and agencies seeking access to records of therapy, including supervision notes, can include:

- an employing organisation, via the terms of a contract;
- police, via a warrant;
- courts, via a court order or witness summons;
- client, via a data subject request under ss 7-8, *DPA* 1998;
- solicitor as the client's legal representative, with appropriate client consent;
- agencies seeking a report on therapeutic work, i.e for criminal injury compensation or for social services in the case of pre-trial therapy for a child or vulnerable adult witness.

There seems to be evidence of substantial interest by the courts and the legal system in gaining access to records of therapy (and, to a lesser extent, of records of supervision) for use as evidence in criminal prosecution cases or for litigation. Research suggests that, in some cases, current or former clients will sign blanket consent forms for use by solicitors to gain access to therapy records for use in legal proceedings (Jenkins, 2003). Clients may not always be fully aware that the records thus gained may be of little value as evidence in support of their claim, for example, for workplace stress or whiplash injury. The records may even prove to be positively harmful to their case, if they reveal evidence of any prior psychological instability, drug or alcohol dependence or narrative inconsistency.

Conflicts over recording practice

There is a developing conflict here between the ostensibly primary role of therapy and supervision records as a 'container', or support for the working alliance, and their emerging role as a supplementary form of evidence in future legal proceedings. In the US, a strongly litigious culture has had a major impact on therapeutic practice. Professional opinion is divided, according to critic Bollas (2003), between those associations now recommending their members to write therapy notes with a view to their later use in court, and those associations recommending their members *not* to keep notes at all, for the very same reason. The interests of therapist, supervisor and agency may not coincide on this issue. From an agency and insurance perspective, full, detailed recording, kept on a long-term basis, provides a useful defensive 'shield' against future client complaint or legal action against the agency for alleged negligence. However, this assumes that the nature and content of the record will be effective in deterring or defending against future complaint or litigation, rather than simply becoming part of the evidence to be trawled through and used as evidence in an adversarial legal system.

Interestingly, data protection principles provide a contrary perspective on the growing pressure for defensive recording. Data protection principles simply require that records are kept 'no longer than is necessary', suggesting that practitioners and agencies could instead opt for leaner, 'fit for purpose' and strictly time-limited forms of recording, which are then routinely destroyed shortly after the end of client contact and after their use for agency audit purposes. The effect of the *DPA* 1998 has thrown therapy recording into some confusion. It has, at the same time, raised an important ethical and professional question regarding the *primary purpose* of recording and whether this should be driven by the needs of the agency, the therapist, the client or the therapeutic process, insofar as these can be separately defined. Rather than the oft-repeated question voiced by practitioners of 'how long should I keep my records for?' it might be more productive to ask 'what is the *purpose* of my recording?' Defensive, evidential records presumably accumulate added value in the long run to employers and agencies; in contrast, process records geared to underpinning therapeutic work or the process of supervision, arguably have little value beyond the date of their immediate use, and could, equally arguably, be destroyed when no longer current.

Records and potential harm to clients

From an ethical perspective, defensive recording may, in reality, do little to promote client autonomy or therapist fidelity. Disclosure of records and their use as evidence in court proceedings can have unintended adverse effects on the client and on the therapeutic work achieved in some cases. It may, therefore, actually *conflict* with the ethical principle of avoiding harm (Jenkins, 2003). Again, research suggests that therapists facing external demands for access to records in situations of 'contested disclosure' find the experience personally and professionally challenging. In looking firstly to their supervisor for support, many find that their supervisor, whilst offering valuable support at a personal level, is unable to provide the kind of accurate informed advice on legal procedure that they are seeking. Fortunately, professional protection societies and professional indemnity insurance societies have become aware of the need for a more proactive stance on this issue in offering legal advice to therapists facing this kind of demand for access to sensitive, confidential records, which should not be disclosed.

Conclusion

In terms of their role assisting supervisees to manage confidentiality and risk, supervisors need to be well informed about the legal limits to confidentiality and clear about their own ethical stance as a custodian of sensitive client and supervisee information. They need to be vigilant to ensure that their own professional autonomy is not unduly restricted by entering into agency contracts or protocols for reporting risk, which may have the effect of appreciably narrowing the space for undertaking effective therapeutic work with clients. Finally, supervisors may need to develop further their own knowledge and skills in the area of supporting their supervisees and themselves when facing external demands for access to sensitive client records for use as evidence in legal proceedings.

The image of 'supervisors in the dock' is a rather provocative and perhaps unhelpful one. Supervisors are much more likely to face a challenge to their work in the form of *a professional complaint* than in the form of legal action (though for an alternative argument, see Griffin, 2001; Leonard and Beazley Richards, 2001). Similarly, supervisors need to be prepared to support their own supervisees, who may well experience at least one serious complaint during their professional career. In terms of legal vulnerability, supervisors are probably more likely to face or initiate action over breach of contract than to be sued for breach of duty of care, despite the experience of their colleagues in the US. Opportunities for action by clients against supervisors for breach of duty of care are limited under the current legal boundaries, although these could change in the future. Supervisors are therefore unlikely to end up in the dock, in a strictly legal sense, at least for the time being.

Legal references (UK)

Bolam v. Friern HMC [1957] 2 All ER 118

Legal references (US)

Almonte v New York Medical College 851 F.Supp. 34 (D. Conn. 1994)
Gilmore v Board of Psychologist Examiners 725 P.2d 400 (Cr.Ct.App. 1986)
Jablonski v United States 712 F.2d 391 (9th Cir. 1983)
Peck v Counseling Service of Addison County, Inc. 499 A.2d 422 (Vt. 1985)
Pesce v Sterling Morton High School, District 201 830 F.2d 789 (7th Cir. 1987)
Simmons v United States 805 F.2d 1363 (9th Cir. 1986)
Steckler v Ohio State Board of Psychology 613 N.E.2d 1070 (Ohio App. 1992)
Tarasoff v Regents of the University of California 551 P.2d 334 (Cal. 1976)

References

Blom-Cooper, L. and Brent Council (1985) *A Child in Trust: The Report of the Panel of Inquiry into the Circumstances Surrounding the Death of Jasmine Beckford*. London Borough of Brent

Bollas, C. (2003) Confidentiality and professionalism. In C. Levin, A. Furlong and M.K. O'Neil (Eds.) *Confidentiality: Ethical Perspectives and Clinical Dilemmas* (pp. 202–10). Hillsdale, NJ: Analytic Press

Bond, T. (2002) The law of confidentiality—a solution or part of the problem? In P. Jenkins (Ed.) *Legal Issues in Counselling and Psychotherapy* (pp. 123–43). London: Sage

British Association for Counselling. (1992) *Code of Ethics and Practice for Counsellors*. Rugby: BAC

British Association for Counselling. (1996) *Code of Ethics and Practice for Supervisors of Counsellors*. Rugby: BAC

British Association for Counselling and Psychotherapy. (2002) *Ethical Framework for Good Practice in Counselling and Psychotherapy*. Rugby: BACP

Copeland, S. (2005) *Counselling Supervision in Organisations: Professional and Ethical Issues Explored*. London: Routledge

Cordess, C. (2001) *Confidentiality and Mental Health*. London: Jessica Kingsley

Falvey, J.E. (2002) *Managing Clinical Supervision: Ethical Practice and Legal Risk Management*. Pacific Grove, CA: Brooks/Cole

Griffin, G. (2001) Vicarious liability. *Counselling and Psychotherapy Journal*, 12(4), 8–9

Hawkins, P. and Shohet, R. (2000) *Supervision in the Helping Professions* (2nd edn.). Buckingham: Open University Press

Jenkins, P. (2001) Supervisory responsibility and the law. In S. Wheeler and D. King (Eds.) *Supervising Counsellors: Issues of Responsibility* (pp. 22–40). London: Sage

Jenkins, P. (2003) Therapist responses to requests for disclosure of therapeutic records: An introductory study. *Counselling and Psychotherapy Research*, 3(3), 232–38

Jenkins, P. and Potter, S. (2007) No more 'personal notes'? Data protection policy and practice in Higher Education counselling services in the UK. *British Journal of Guidance and Counselling*, 35(1), 131–46

Laming, H. (2003) *The Victoria Climbie Inquiry.* Cm 5730. London: The Stationery Office

Leonard, G. and Beazley Richards, J. (2001) How supervisors can protect themselves from complaints and litigation. In M. Carroll and M. Tholstrup (Eds.) *Integrative Approaches to Supervision* (pp. 192–97). London: Jessica Kingsley

Morrison, T. (1993) *Staff Supervision in Social Care.* Brighton: Pavilion Publishing

Pritchard, J. (Ed.) (1997) *Good Practice in Supervision: Statutory and Voluntary Organisations.* London: Jessica Kingsley

CHAPTER FOURTEEN

SUPERVISION OF SHORT-TERM THERAPY

KEITH TUDOR

This chapter discusses the implications of supervising therapists who are offering clients short-term therapy or working in contexts (such as the UK National Health Service) that frame therapy in terms of time limits. As there is nothing inherent in the nature of therapy that makes it short-term or long-term, placing and sometimes imposing a specific time-frame on therapy is more to do with particular economic and social concerns, which thus places this discussion in the context of the social domain of supervision. In the West we live in societies that value speed and quick solutions: 'short-termism' and short-term therapy is, as Thorne (1999) puts it, 'the *Zeitgeist*'. The first part of this chapter discusses common concerns of therapists working briefly and frames them in terms of time, limits and limitations. This stands as an introduction to the second part of the chapter, which reflects on certain considerations that supervisors have in supervising therapists offering short-term therapy.

TIME, LIMITS AND LIMITATIONS

The concepts of time, eternity and transience have preoccupied human beings since time began (see Hawking, 1988/1998; Davies, 1995). As Griffiths (2000) puts it: '"time" has, throughout history, been used like a mirror for human nature. It is a blank screen onto which societies have always projected images of themselves' (p. 32). Elsewhere (Tudor, 2002), I explore the meaning of time, limits and limitations, including the culture and politics of time. Here I identify three areas—with regard to structure and limits, contact and relationship, and expectations and responsibilities—which commonly present challenges for the therapist and are often present in, and the subject of, supervision of therapy in this context.

Structure and limits

As human beings we are time-limited. Just as life is time-limited, so all therapy—and supervision—is time-limited. When we talk about time, we talk, think about and resonate with the inevitable limits and limitations of life. As Taft (1933, p. 12) points out:

> time represents more vividly than any other category the necessity of accepting limitation as well as the inability to do so, and symbolizes therefore the whole problem of living. The reaction of each individual to limited or unlimited time betrays his deepest and fundamental life pattern, his relation to the growth process itself, to beginnings and endings, to being born and to dying.

In my view, it is better to be aware of this limit, and any other limitations, than not. There's a difference between the therapist who says to her client, simply: 'We've got six sessions', and one who says, almost apologetically: 'We've only got six sessions'. The second therapist may subtly be undermining his or her clients' ability to meet and deal with limits and limitations. Of course, there's a time and a place for challenging limits and for negotiating additional sessions, but, just as most therapists generally keep to the agreed or imposed time boundaries of a session and generally don't run over them, so there is a parallel and logic to working with and to limits. In this sense limits and limitations pose a challenge to the therapist and to a number of assumptions about:

- The nature of therapy—that it is, by definition, long-term.
- The nature of change—that it necessarily takes a long time.
- The nature of the client's problems and pathology—that they are not resolvable in a short time.
- The role of the therapist—that he or she is the sole assessor of the client; that he or she holds these assumptions; and that he or she is the gatekeeper to therapeutic services and is responsible for the client gaining or not gaining access to such services.

These assumptions are often, in my view, based on a lack of trust in the client and an inflated view of the role and responsibilities of the therapist. An alternative is for a therapist to deconstruct these assumptions by sharing with her clients her awareness of, and any concerns she has about, her clients and their problems, as well as those about the limits of the therapy. This perspective is supported by organismic and person-centred psychology, which views the individual human organism in an interdependent relationship with its environment, including environmental limitations. In *Time-Conscious Psychological Therapy*, Elton Wilson (1996) makes this point about consciousness and designs a way of working with it. She offers her model to practitioners (p. 7) and 'especially those critical of short-term work, as an invitation to use a range of considered options, to *design*, in consultation with their clients, an appropriate and practical package of focused psychological change'.

Contact and relationship: Brief encounter

When working with people in the short term or to a time limit, therapists, in effect, have a lot of brief encounters—and this affects us both as people and as therapists. Some therapists may adopt an attitude to 'short-term clients' that differs from the attitude they hold towards people they work with over a longer or open-ended term. For instance, as some clients are 'only' short term, some therapists, and especially those who favour long-term therapy, feel and think that the therapy is not as valuable, that the relationship is not as important and, subtly, that the client is not as deserving of his or her attention. In any case, for the therapist, short-term work may well raise issues of attachment, contact, engagement, and loss—and thus may appeal to some therapists and not to others. These issues or concepts may be a helpful framework for the therapist to explore for him or herself, and to understand the therapy and the client. Both in practice and in the literature, there is a view that the therapist shouldn't work too 'deeply' or 'go there' with the client in case there's something 'too big' or 'too difficult'. Elsewhere we (Tudor and Worrall, 2006) challenge the metaphor of 'depth' in psychotherapy and here, similarly, I think it is important to question what is too difficult and too big and for whom. I suggest that these concerns are quite often based on the assumptions identified above, and inform an over-concern with assessment with a view to screening out what are considered to be 'unsuitable' clients for brief therapy. I suggest that, whatever their presenting problems or their pathology, most clients would consider that some therapy, albeit time limited, is better than no therapy at all, or an assessment, followed by a referral on to a long waiting list. The challenges for person-centred therapists offering short-term therapy are:

1. To work with the limits and limitations of time and context.
2. To be in contact with clients, however briefly, and to work in that encounter,

meeting, or relationship. This includes acknowledging with the client the limits and limitations of the contact, contract, setting and therapy, as well as the client's feelings about these things. It seems to me much more respectful *and efficient* to spend the time we have with the client doing what can be done and acknowledging feelings of frustration and fear about limits, than to spend time assessing what can't be done and, in effect, closing down conversations. For most people, acknowledging these issues brings them into relationship.

3. To deal with their own issues about limits and limitations, attachment and loss, and brief encounters, including those with clients who are highly disturbed and distressed.

4. To focus more on *relating* than relationship. There is a danger of reifying *the* 'therapeutic relationship' or even therapeutic relationships (see, for example, Clarkson, 1995) which, amongst other things, lends weight to the argument that such relationships can only be developed over time to the detriment of therapeutic *relating* (see Summers and Tudor, 2000), a process which emphasises the active, present continuous form of meeting and encounter. Change can be effected in a short time precisely because of the nature of that meeting and of the therapist's contact, authenticity, acceptance and empathy and the client's experience of this. This statement is supported by generic research conducted by Rogers (1942, 1957), Barrett-Lennard (1978, 1986) and more recent studies such as those by Lambert (1992) and Hubble, Duncan and Miller (1999). All this research confirms the significance of the therapeutic relationship—or relating— with regard to therapy outcome.

Expectations and responsibilities
Writing about brief therapy in the context of a society that extols 'short-termism', Thorne (1999, p. 8) comments that 'the *Zeitgeist* exerts its own pervasive influence'. For many therapists working in services that offer short-term therapy, this influence impacts directly on their assessment of clients and the issue of selection; on the responsibility they feel for providing a service; and on the work itself with regard to the therapeutic contract, change and cure, the pace of therapy, and the ending of therapy.

A common argument in the literature on brief therapy focuses on the suitability of brief or short-term therapy for certain clients with particular issues and, therefore, for the necessity of an assessment which, in effect, screens people in or out of therapy (see, for example, Feltham, 1997). The logic of defining people by diagnosis or types of problem implies and, indeed, *requires* selection. Henderson (1999, p. 94), for example, is certain about the value of selection:

'Whatever the theoretical base, the counsellor needs tools and skills for agreeing a focus for brief work with a client … or their intervention may not fit what the setting (or the patient) requires of them.' The influence of the medical model on Henderson is apparent. She clearly prioritises the setting: the intervention may not fit what the *setting* requires of the counsellor. This argues that the counsellor in health care settings is an unquestioning agent of the medical system. This attitude, in effect, promotes a service-centred rather than a person-centred service. The counter argument, based on principles of equity and accessibility, is that services and, therefore, therapists should not select. Writing in the context of group therapy Berne (1966, p. 5) argues that: 'The real issue … is not the one commonly debated, "What are the criteria for the selection of patients?", but the underlying, usually unstated assumption "Criteria for selection are good."'

Of course, there is a real problem of the lack of resources and, for some therapists working in these settings, of being the only recipient of constant referrals. However, it is important in these situations that the therapist does not take on responsibility for the waiting list, and recognises that this belongs with the service, and the lack of resources with senior managers and policy makers. Therapists can—and should—take responsibility for being willing to be creative and to negotiate, for instance with general practitioners, about ways of working and structuring the service provided. The traditional argument from those responsible for resources suggests limiting or restricting numbers of session. Yet, quite often, when services don't restrict clients to a specific number of sessions, the average take-up appears to balance out. Wakefield (2005) gives an example of this in a primary health care setting in which she reports that, with no limits on the number of sessions, between sixty and seventy per cent of clients chose to use fewer than twelve sessions.

The influence of the external world inevitably impacts on the therapeutic work itself. In terms of the working agreement between the therapist and the client, it is important that any time limits are made explicit and that any extension to the contract is addressed and agreed in advance, not during what would have been the last session. This addresses the expectations of both parties about the outcome of the therapy and what can be achieved in a specific period of time. Therapists study ideas about change and cure. Therapists working in time-limited settings are often subject to external notions and definitions of change and cure. In a context in which limited resources are translated into limited time, these notions often exert a greater and undue influence on the therapist, creating a pressure on him or her to focus on outcomes and solutions, rather than process, and to adopt a pace different from one which is, or might have been, determined by the client. As one colleague put it:

> I've detected a worry and concern in myself, colleagues and supervisees which can be expressed as 'Not enough time to *do*', as distinct from the importance of the moment to *be*. The natural pace of the therapy can be contaminated, i.e. there's little or no time for reflection, and this is detrimental to engaging in the process.

Therapy may be brief or specifically limited in time, but such limitations should not be confused with definitions of therapy, its purpose or scope. Nevertheless, therapists working briefly do worry about effectiveness. Interestingly, Novey (1999), in his report on a US-based research study into the effectiveness of transactional analysis, strikes a note of caution about effectiveness, as, amongst other results, the research confirms that limits on therapy due to insurance requirements significantly decrease the effectiveness of therapy.

Finally, in terms of practice, there is the issue of ending. Therapists can be concerned that clients may feel abandoned and that this may echo or re-stimulate previous life events or previous experiences of therapy. Again, this is manageable if it is acknowledged and explored during the therapy.

These examples point to the importance of transparency and open communication in acknowledging the limits of short-term therapy, and discussing expectations, goals, the therapist's way of working, the ending and, when appropriate, referral. The person-centred approach is based on the view that the human organism tends to actualise, and on the importance of relationship in creating and mediating conditions which facilitate change. If one of the challenges of being a therapist is to be the best we can be, then that challenge in the context of short-term therapy is to be the best we can be in a shorter time.

Considerations for Supervision of Short-term Therapy

These preceding thoughts on what therapists who offer short-term therapy are dealing with, are presented as a background on brief therapy for the supervisor who is supervising therapists working in such settings. In many ways, supervisors simply need to listen and to be responsive to practitioners presenting with these issues and concerns, as well as to their feelings about them. Here, I discuss three considerations for the supervisor working with such therapists concerning their experience, the frequency of supervision, and the integrity of the person-centred approach.

Experience

Much literature on supervision emphasises the importance of the supervisor's experience. Feltham (1997) points out, and makes much of, what he sees as the lack of experience amongst supervisors of short-term work, and gets quite prescriptive about what trainee supervisors (p. 137) 'must be faced with' in order to supervise short-term work. This includes any reservations they may have! It seems that Feltham allows little room for honest doubt. He also suggests that a training course should require trainee supervisors to do short-term, time-limited work. This is a somewhat crude argument based on 'matching experience'—and, interestingly, not one he advances with regard to any other perceived lack of experience, such as working with clients of different cultures, races, sexualities and so on. Ultimately, this represents a hierarchical model of supervision, based on the view that the supervisor has to have more experience than the supervisee, and more experience that is relevant to what the supervisee/therapist is working with. This approach to supervision both mistrusts the therapist and misunderstands the facilitative, reflective and meta-role of the supervisor. I take a different view of experience (see Chapter 3) one which focuses on and values the experience of the supervisor *as a facilitator of the therapist's process*, and not necessarily as more knowledgeable in a particular field.

If person-centred supervisors working with therapists who are offering short-term therapy do require particular experience, it is perhaps experience of working with practitioners who work within particular contexts, and who retain their integrity in the face of the pressures and demands of those contexts and the complexity of their systems.

Frequency
The usual 'default setting' for supervision is once a month and, for therapy, once a week—though I know of one colleague who, post qualification, challenged this assumption in herself, and reported that her practice had improved exponentially as a result of regular, weekly supervision. One implication of this default setting for the supervision of short-term work is that a therapist may not get supervision for work with particular clients, whom she may have seen three or four times between supervision sessions. This then raises the issue of the frequency of supervision. Weekly supervision, however, has significant financial implications, whether for the private practitioner or the organisation funding supervision. Ryle (1990), a cognitive analytic therapist, offers the solution of weekly group supervision, and suggests that this is particularly important with regard to the first four sessions with the client. Clearly, more frequent supervision would generally be viewed as beneficial and, in the context of supervising brief therapy, both supervisor and therapist may consider this desirable and be creative about the frequency and form of supervision. However, I am cautious about the basis of this, as arguments about increased frequency may be based on a mistrust of the therapist and an undue sense of responsibility on the part of the supervisor. If

the argument is that the therapist should present every short-term client to his or her supervisor (and, therefore, to have more frequent supervision to accommodate this), then the question is whether this assumption also holds for the presentation of longer-term clients.

Integrity
Much of the literature on supervision in counselling and psychotherapy is presented as somehow free of theory or neutral as far as theoretical orientation is concerned, or, as in Henderson's (1999) case, positively dismissive of the impact and relevance of theory. In discussing group supervision, Feltham (1997) suggests dividing the time and responsibility with supervisees and says (p. 138) that 'these temporal aspects of supervision may be used to model ways in which time can be managed in time-limited counselling'. From a behavioural perspective, such modelling may be uncontentious but, from a person-centred perspective, it is. There is much more to be learned from the process of a supervision group if the supervisor facilitates rather than makes or 'models' a decision about the allocation of time. For a supervisor to say to a group of four meeting for three hours that they have three quarters of an hour each is time-limiting indeed! It is prescriptive, it invites scarcity and promotes individuality, and is certainly not based on any person-centred view of the human organism operating and cooperating with others in its environment. It is, in my view, better to work with the group about what individuals want from group supervision and how they can best achieve this, for instance, with regard to bids for and the allocation and monitoring of time (see also Chapter 7).

Again, in the generic literature on supervision, much is made of the supervisor's 'tasks' (see, for instance, Carroll, 1996). These tend to be about monitoring, evaluating, being responsible, and modelling and, as such, are more concerned with what Proctor (1988) calls the normative function of supervision. In general, I place more emphasis on the supportive (restorative) and formative (educative) functions of supervision and, therefore, see one of a supervisor's 'tasks' as helping therapists to maintain and enhance their integrity as a practitioner. This includes the congruence or fit between a therapist's own personal philosophy, professional practice, and the philosophical principles of the theoretical model he or she espouses. So, rather than the supervisor's role being one of gatekeeping and social control to enforce conformity as Feltham (1997) would wish (see above), I view the supervisor's role as one of supporting—and challenging—the therapist to think for himself and, where necessary, to question practice and policies. This reflects, as Villas-Boas Bowen (1986) describes it, a philosophy-oriented rather than form-oriented supervision. In my experience as a supervisor, this is the best approach and the best I can do with, and for, the person in front of me, i.e. the therapist. If supervisors take a person-centred approach with their supervisees (as distinct from a client-centred approach in which the primary focus is on their clients) and the supervisees experience this, then they are free to practise and to work more effectively with their clients from whatever perspective and in whatever form and setting.

REFERENCES

Barrett-Lennard, G.T. (1978) The Relationship Inventory: Later development and adaptations. *JSAS Catalog of Selected Documents in Psychology*, 8(68). (MS 1732)

Barrett-Lennard, G.T. (1986) The Relationship Inventory now: Issues and advances in theory, method and use. In L.S. Greenberg and W.M. Pinsof (Eds.) *The Psychotherapeutic Process: A Research Handbook* (pp. 439–76). New York: Guilford Press

Berne, E. (1966) *Principles of Group Treatment*. New York: Grove Press

Carroll, M. (1996) *Counselling Supervision: Theory, Skills and Practice*. London: Cassell

Clarkson, P. (1995) *The Therapeutic Relationship*. London: Whurr

Davies, P. (1995) *About Time: Einstein's Unfinished Revolution*. Harmondsworth: Penguin

Elton Wilson, J. (1996) *Time-Conscious Psychological Therapy*. London: Routledge

Feltham, C. (1997) *Time-Limited Counselling*. London: Sage

Griffiths, J. (2000, March/April). Local time. *Resurgence*. No. 199, pp. 32–34

Hawking, S. (1998) *A Brief History of Time*. London: Bantam Press. (Original work published 1988)

Henderson, P. (1999) Supervision in medical settings. In M. Carroll and E. Holloway (Eds.) *Counselling Supervision in Context* (pp. 88–103). London: Sage

Hubble, M.A., Duncan, B.L. and Miller, S.D. (Eds.) (1999) *The Heart and Soul of Change: What Works in Therapy*. Washington, DC: American Psychological Association

Lambert, M.J. (1992) Implications of outcome research for psychotherapy integration. In J.C. Norcross and M.R. Goldstein (Eds.) *Handbook of Psychotherapy Integration* (pp. 94–129). New York: Basic Books

Novey, T. (1999) The effectiveness of transactional analysis. *Transactional Analysis Journal*, 29(1), 18–30

Proctor, B. (1988) Supervision: A co-operative exercise in accountability. In M. Marken and M. Payne (Eds.) *Enabling and Ensuring*. Leicester: Leicester National Youth Bureau/Council for Education and Training in Youth and Community Work

Rogers, C.R. (1942) The use of electronically recorded interviews in improving psychotherapeutic techniques. *American Journal of Orthopsychiatry*, 12, 429–34

Rogers, C.R. (1957) The necessary and sufficient conditions of therapeutic personality change. *Journal of Consulting Psychology*, 21, 95–103

Ryle, A. (1990) *CAT: Active Participation in Change*. Chichester: Wiley

Summers, G. and Tudor, K. (2000) Cocreative transactional analysis. *Transactional Analysis Journal*, 30(1), 23–40

Taft, J. (1933) *The Dynamics of Therapy in a Controlled Relationship*. New York: Macmillan

Thorne, B. (1999) The move towards brief therapy: Its dangers and challenges. *Counselling, 10*(1), 7–11

Tudor, K. (2002) Introduction. In K. Tudor (Ed.) *Transactional Approaches to Brief Therapy or What Do You Say between Saying Hello and Goodbye?* (pp.1–18). London: Sage

Tudor, K. and Worrall, M. (2004) Person-centred philosophy and theory in the practice of supervision. In K. Tudor and M. Worrall (Eds.) *Freedom to Practise: Person-Centred Approaches to Supervision* (pp. 11–30). Ross-on-Wye: PCCS Books

Tudor, K. and Worrall, M. (2006) *Person-Centred Therapy: A Clinical Philosophy*. London: Routledge

Villas-Boas Bowen, M. (1986) Personality differences and person-centered supervision. *Person-Centered Review, 1*(3), 291–309

Wakefield, M. (2005, August) Person-centred practice in primary health care: Evidence that without time limits the majority of clients opt for short-term therapy. *Person-Centred Quarterly*, pp. 1–5

Chapter Fifteen

Person-Centred Supervision Across Theoretical Orientations

Mike Worrall

In the first volume of *Freedom To Practise* Hitchings (2004) raised two questions about cross-theoretical supervision and addressed one of them specifically. He looked at some of the issues involved when practitioners from other orientations supervise the work of person-centred therapists. This chapter complements and completes that one and addresses his second question: what are the issues involved when person-centred practitioners supervise the work of therapists from other theoretical orientations? Do person-centred practitioners need to understand, say, psychodynamic or gestalt theory in order to supervise psychodynamic or gestalt practice? Our answers to this question both manifest and help clarify our philosophy of supervision.

If we see ourselves as responsible for helping a therapist practise in a particular way then it follows that we need to know the form of that practice. We can't facilitate effective psychodynamic or person-centred practice unless we can recognise such practice, notice deviations from it, and help a practitioner find a way back to it if necessary. This kind of supervision resembles mentoring, in which a practitioner experienced in the field helps induct a less experienced one into the ways of the profession. Beginning practitioners who are less secure in their work may need or benefit from such mentoring. It also resembles what Villas Boas-Bowen (1986) calls 'form-oriented' supervision. Strictly speaking, form-oriented supervision is where (p. 293) 'the supervisor seems to have a preconceived idea of how supervisees should behave in order to preserve the forms the supervisor is committed to'. In the supervision I'm describing here, the supervisor is helping the practitioner to stay within the boundaries of a form to which the *practitioner* is committed. The substantive point remains: that supervision of this sort is about helping the practitioner work in a particular way.

If we see ourselves as responsible for helping a therapist to articulate the relationships he sees between his practice and whatever theory he believes himself to be working to, and for helping him to explore his experience of his work in the light of that articulation, we do not *need* to be familiar with the detail of whatever theory he works to. It's probably helpful to share a conceptual vocabulary; so it may be important for a supervisor to be familiar with the basic ideas of a supervisee's approach to therapy. It may not, however, be necessary to be familiar with the fine detail. That remains the responsibility of the supervisee. This kind of supervision more closely resembles classical person-centred therapy, where the therapist's first task is simply to understand his client's experience empathically. In supervision of this sort, the supervisor works towards an empathic and accepting understanding of his supervisee's work. He is neither attached to nor working towards particular outcomes, and doesn't feel responsible for the form of his supervisee's practice.

Villas Boas-Bowen (1986) calls this 'philosophy-of-life oriented supervision' and suggests (p. 294) that it is characterised by, amongst other things, 'an emphasis on the internal locus of evaluation of the supervisee'. Person-centred supervisors are perhaps especially well placed to offer this kind of supervision. As therapists, they are interested in understanding the lives and worlds of their clients empathically. As supervisors, they bring a similar level of empathic attention to their relationship with their supervisees. Supervisees who are relatively experienced practitioners, well-versed in the philosophy and theory of their own discipline and who prize freedom of thought, expression and practice, are especially likely to thrive in such supervision. This leaves the question of whether beginning practitioners might also benefit from supervision such as this. There seems, in principle, no reason not to trust even inexperienced therapists to thrive under such conditions and to find their own way to practise effectively. In practice, my experience is that many beginning therapists benefit from a form-oriented focus, especially if their supervisor holds that focus lightly and relinquishes it as early as possible.

There are, of course, supervisors and person-centred supervisors who enjoy the authority and expertise that can come with the title of supervisor and the practice of supervision. The supervision I'm describing in this chapter, though, demands supervisors who are comfortable in their own ignorance; who don't need to impress, control, or teach; and who are genuinely willing for their supervisees to be accountable and responsible for their own work, even and perhaps especially when they think and practice differently. Again, such radical non-attachment and non-possessiveness is consistent with person-centred philosophy and may come more easily to person-centred practitioners than to some others.

There are positive benefits as well for supervisors secure enough in their own work to let themselves understand and be changed by the work and thinking of another. If we supervise practitioners from other disciplines we necessarily learn something of their philosophy, practice and theory. We may question our own cherished beliefs and adapt our own practice in the light of evidence from other orientations. This encourages critical thinking and inclusive practice, and guards against unhelpfully tribal or parochial attitudes towards our work.

This line of thinking suggests that supervision is a meta-activity that stands apart from the various theoretical orientations to therapy and, as an activity in its own right, can apply to or be in relationship with any of those orientations. The values of the person-centred approach may make it a particularly appropriate model on which to base a meta-theory of supervision. Its insistence, for instance, on the centrality of empathic understanding and unconditional acceptance of another's experience means that person-centred supervisors are in a position to witness and value the work of other practitioners in their own right: they do not have to attract other practitioners towards their own way of working. This allows them also to supervise the work of practitioners who are not, themselves, counsellors or therapists (see, for example, Freeth, 2004). In this sense, supervision resembles coaching rather than mentoring: it works towards supporting practitioners to be the most effective they can be within their own discipline, whatever their area of practice, and however remote it may be from the supervisor's own orientation or discipline.

One final implication of seeing supervision as a meta-activity concerns the assumption that supervisors need to be practitioners as well as supervisors. The British Association of Psychoanalytic and Psychodynamic Supervision (BAPPS) takes the contrary view, asserting (BAPPS, 2003, B1 iii) that: 'It is normally unethical for members to offer supervision if they are not also currently practising as therapists appropriate to their training and experience.' I disagree. If supervision is an activity in its own right, and especially if it is an activity that stands in its own right in relation to other activities, there seems less need for supervisors to be practitioners in the same field as those whose work they supervise. Their function is to facilitate practitioners in their relationship with their work and that is a task in itself for which supervisors do not need to be, and may not even be qualified to be, in the same line of practice.

REFERENCES

British Association of Psychoanalytic and Psychodynamic Supervision. (2003) *Code of Ethics & Practice*. Redhill: BAPPS

Freeth, R. (2004) A psychiatrist's experience of person-centred supervision. In K. Tudor and M. Worrall (Eds.) *Freedom to Practise: Person-Centred Approaches to Supervision* (pp. 247–66). Ross-on-Wye: PCCS Books

Hitchings, P. (2004) On supervision across theoretical orientations. In K. Tudor and M. Worrall (Eds.) *Freedom to Practise: Person-Centred Approaches to Supervision* (pp. 203–24). Ross-on-Wye: PCCS Books

Villas-Boas Bowen, M. (1986) Personality differences and person-centered supervision. *Person-Centered Review, 1*(3), 291–309

PART FIVE

TRAINING

CHAPTER SIXTEEN

TRAINING SUPERVISORS

KEITH TUDOR AND MIKE WORRALL

This chapter reflects our experiences of, and thinking about, training supervisors, and our collaboration as facilitators of person-centred supervision courses over ten years. During this time, one of the authors (KT) has also designed and run several generic supervision courses. The participants in these courses have, predominantly, been counsellors and psychotherapists supervising the work of other counsellors and psychotherapists. Other participants have included coaches, healers, homoeopaths, managers, mentors, nurses, occupational therapists, and organisational consultants.

With regard to the practice of therapy and the training of therapists, we think in terms of a tripartite model which encompasses practice, philosophy and theory, usually in that order. We take our cue for this from Rogers, who argues (1957/1990, p. 402) that when we practise as therapists we necessarily give 'operational evidence of an underlying value orientation and view of human nature', and that it is, in his view, preferable 'that such underlying views be open and explicit rather than covert and implicit'. We find this useful also when working with practitioners who are already qualified and experienced, and who are now thinking about becoming supervisors, (see Tudor and Worrall, 2004d). We suggest that our practice as supervisors evolves out of our practice as therapists and gives similar evidence of our own values and philosophy.

In this chapter we reflect on the training of supervisors, with reference firstly to a person-centred philosophy of education and training and, secondly, to the practice of training supervisors, with examples drawn from courses as well as some responses to a questionnaire completed by a number of participants. In the third part of the chapter we identify and refer to some theory which we find useful in training supervisors.

A PERSON-CENTRED PHILOSOPHY OF EDUCATION AND TRAINING

Rogers sums up his philosophy of education in the title of his (1969) book *Freedom to Learn* in which he outlines an approach to education and *learning*, as distinct from *teaching*, characterised by a number of features:

- It assumes an unconditional trust in the organism, manifested in a non-directive attitude and facilitated by certain conditions.
- It is, therefore, responsive in the first instance always to the needs of individual learners and groups of learners.
- It focuses primarily on individual and group processes.
- It resists external control in the form of prescribed curricula and assessment criteria.
- It recognises that systems of professional accreditation or academic validation are primarily ways of legitimising what students learn, or of giving it currency in the outside world, rather than about learning itself.

Drawing on Angyal's (1941) model, we may say also that what Rogers called freedom to learn includes, at its best, the freedom to reflect and think for oneself as an expression of *autonomy*, in the presence of a learning community which represents *homonomy*, and which necessarily brings us up against the difference, or *heteronomy*, of others. One of the virtues of Angyal's thinking is that it recognises the inevitable presence of the heteronomous other in the processes of life and learning. We agree with Rogers about the need for effective learning environments to resist unnecessary *controls* from the outside. Such controls are often the result of political or professional agendas and serve those agendas rather than the learning needs of the group or individual students. We recognise, however, that *within* the learning environment, simply by virtue of being external to one another and in relationship with one another, we necessarily *influence* and therefore learn from one another.

It follows from this organismic perspective that experience is primary. Rogers (1969, p. 4) was clear that he valued 'significant, meaningful, experiential learning' and always prioritised experience over theory. A number of implications follow from this:

- That students are encouraged to access, learn from and share their own experience.
- That this allows students access to what Rogers (1951, p. 437) calls 'a broad experiential knowledge of the human being in his cultural setting'. The wider the range of cultural diversity within the group, of course, the more broad this knowledge can become.
- That students are active participants in their own learning rather than passive recipients of another's. This challenges the view of education as the transfer of knowledge from one 'bank' to another (see Freire, 1967/1976, 1972; and also Embleton Tudor et al., 2004).
- That trainers are there to facilitate this process, and therefore that training is better conceived of, and practised, as the facilitation of learning.
- That it's important for students to have an *experience* of learning that mirrors *what* they are learning.
- That as we are recognising and valuing individual experiences we are necessarily valuing difference and diversity.

As both students and facilitators experience freedom and acknowledge experience, this tends to release a range of experience: thinking and feeling as well as behaviour. Rogers' interest in the whole and holistic organism predates current interests in:

- The theory of multiple intelligences (Gardner, 1983/1993). This acknowledges that, in addition to linguistic and logical–mathematical intelligences—the development of which are prioritised and favoured in contemporary Western schooling—human beings have musical, spatial, bodily kinesthetic, intrapersonal, interpersonal, and naturalistic intelligences. Appreciating that people have different interests and strengths can, and perhaps should, have an impact on the facilitation of learning.
- The creation of a 'thinking environment' (Kline, 1999). This work suggests that certain behaviours or environmental components encourage thinking. These include: attention, equality, ease, appreciation, encouragement, the expression of feeling, diversity and the importance of place or space. As qualities or attitudes, many of these are familiar to person-centred facilitators. In terms of promoting independent thought, we would add the importance of facilitating divergent, as distinct from convergent, thinking. Tudor (2007) views this as a necessity in promoting anti-dogmatic practice.

In all of this the role of the trainer is threefold:

- To co-create environmental conditions conducive to learning.
- To facilitate group and individual learning.
- To manifest the attitudes of the person-centred approach, not so as to model them—since the notion of modelling derives from a learning theory that is antithetical to the person-centred approach (see Wood, 1995)—but in a spirit of congruence, and so as to offer students an experience of receiving what they might be aspiring to offer.

Consistent with what we've argued above, our own beliefs inevitably manifest in how we facilitate learning. We believe that students want to learn, that they learn most effectively from their own experiencing, and that we can trust them to direct their own learning. Our work is to facilitate their own innate curiosity. To this end, we aim to create a culture that:

- values curiosity over certainty;
- values questions over answers;
- allows for diverse experience and divergent opinion;
- encourages playful experiment;
- challenges dogma and orthodoxy; and
- deconstructs received or introjected wisdom.

In all of this, we recognise our own experiences and expertise and are willing to share what we have learned from our own experience, reflection and reading.

We agree with Rogers that it is, ultimately, not possible to train person-centred therapists. We think the same about training person-centred supervisors. Our work is to offer a learning environment informed by person-centred principles, within which we support therapists to become the best supervisors they can become.

THE PRACTICE OF LEARNING

When we reflect on our work as teachers and facilitators, we are especially interested in the congruence between our philosophy of education and our practice as educators. Some of the feedback we have received about the courses we facilitate—that they offer a space to explore ideas, a supportive and non-judgemental environment and dedicated time to reflect at the participants' own pace—indicates that we are broadly effective in practising what we espouse.

We generally begin both the training as a whole, and each day within it, with some open time in which participants can identify, articulate and reflect upon their own personal process and practice, share whatever they want of that with the training group, and reflect on any group process. This process usually evolves into discussion, negotiation and agreement about a subsequent agenda which might include any, or all, of the following:

- practice in small groups;
- a demonstration and discussion in the whole training group;
- specific teaching input and
- discussion of clinical, professional, ethical, personal, social or cultural issues (see Tudor and Worrall, 2004b).

When we facilitate groups in this way, we find that participants tend to report their experiences of, and concerns about, supervision. We've written separately in this volume about two of those concerns: issues of responsibility (Chapter 3), and the relationship between supervision and personal therapy (Chapter 12). These are some of the other concerns that emerge consistently:

- Previous experiences of supervision and training
  A person-centred approach to training and learning often challenges students used to more traditional forms of learning. As a result, practitioners may and do question the training and the approach, as well as their previous experiences of training and of supervision. Some people have been oppressed by didactic and dogmatic supervision and training. One effect of this is that some practitioners have construed the tasks and processes of supervision and the responsibilities of supervisors in somewhat rigid ways. We notice and often challenge explicit statements of belief about how to do supervision and how to be a supervisor. This helps create an environment in which participants articulate and question their implicit beliefs and assumptions, and begin to deconstruct whatever they may have received and accepted over the years as 'wisdom'. One supervisee reported that, over the course of a year, she had questioned and deconstructed certain rules about being a practitioner, including, significantly, rules she hadn't even known she'd been holding.

- Current experiences of supervision
  Any training based on reflective process invites participants to reflect on their own experiences. When training to supervise, participants tend to reflect on their own experiences of receiving supervision. For some, this course confirms their choice of supervisor. Others question their current experiences of supervision and either 'supervise up', by which we mean

that they teach their supervisors, implicitly or explicitly, how best to supervise them; or 'actualise out', by which we mean that they find another supervisor. Our response is to help participants to define the criteria by which they chose their professional support and to make their own decisions about this. For more on this, see Chapter 1 in this volume.

- Supervising trainees
  Beginning supervisors are often especially anxious about supervising trainees, whom they may see as needing more guidance, teaching, and support than qualified or more experienced practitioners. In such circumstances, supervisors seem often to be falling back on implicitly held developmental models of growth and education. In our experience, such models invite supervisors to see therapists in training as less experienced and therefore as also less competent and less trustworthy than other supervisees. In our view, less experienced does not necessarily mean less competent or trustworthy.

- Supervising trainees on placements
  Some placements and training organisations expect supervisors to take 'clinical responsibility' for the work of their supervisees (see Chapter 3). Others don't allow volunteer therapists to take information out of the placement, even for the purposes of supervision. Placements and training organisations may also expect supervisors to be part of a regular assessment process, an expectation which, if met, we think risks the safety and integrity of the supervisory space. All of these issues require a process of careful and comprehensive contracting that includes all of the involved parties: therapist, supervisor, placement, training organisation and, in some circumstances, client.

THEORY

As Lewin (1951/1964, p. 169) observes: 'there is nothing so practical as a good theory'. We think that, following clarification of a practitioner's philosophy and the elaboration of his or her experience, theory is useful in order to support his or her practice. Carroll (1996, p. 4) argues that individuals should move away from 'counselling-bound models of supervision (i.e. in which supervision is closely allied to the counselling orientation of the supervisor) to developmental and social role models of supervision (which start with the learning situation of the supervisee)'. He bases this argument on a view that supervision is more akin to a formative or educational process than to therapy. We have some sympathy with this perspective in that we too think that supervision is a meta-activity and, as such, can be applied across approaches and disciplines (see Freeth, 2004; Hitchings, 2004; Townsend, 2004 and Chapter 15). However, we think also that supervisors have inevitably a more or less explicitly articulated philosophy of practice. For therapists who supervise, we believe that this will be based on their personal philosophy and the underlying assumptions of the theoretical orientation to therapy they espouse, both of which are likely to be congruent one with the other. Rather than thinking or feeling that their model of supervision is 'bound' by their model of therapy, supervisors might be interested to examine what happens if they apply the principles of their therapy to their practice of supervision. In this sense, we think that Carroll proposes a development which polarises education and training from therapy, and divorces the supervision of therapy from the supervisor's approach to therapy. Of course, we acknowledge that the person-centred approach as an *approach* does emphasise the application of its principles to all aspects of life.

In our previous book on person-centred supervision, we elaborated person-centred theory and its applications to supervision with reference to:

- Personality theory.
- The necessary and sufficient conditions of therapy—and other conditions of knowledge, experience, currency and generosity.
- The process and outcomes of therapy (see Tudor and Worrall, 2004d).

We then elaborated person-centred perspectives on generic theories of supervision with regard to:

- Definitions of supervision.
- Functions of supervision.
- The roles of supervisor and supervisee.
- Developmental models of supervision.
- The organisation and tasks of supervision.
- The context of supervision.
- Process models of supervision (see Tudor and Worrall, 2004c, 2004e).

For us these three chapters reflected two necessary tasks in developing theory: firstly, to apply the theory of the particular approach to the practice of supervision (and, for that matter, to the practice of teaching); and, secondly, to take a view from the particular approach, in this case, person-centred approaches, of other theories and models, whether these are generic, claimed to be generic, or explicitly written from another theoretical orientation. This is supported by the feedback from course participants.

From this, the most important theoretical feature of the courses appears to be the application of person-centred theories to the practice and process of supervision, including an expressive approach (see Chapter 5). Participants also appreciated Warner's (2000) levels of interventiveness, which offers a meta-theoretical model of practitioners' 'interventions' or responses (see Tudor and Worrall, 2004e).

Of other theories and models of supervision which trainee supervisors appear to find helpful, Hawkins and Shohet's (1989, 2000, 2006) process model appears to be the most popular. In our previous book we comment on their (2000) process model.

However, the most important theoretical aspect of the courses, in our view, is that participants articulate, examine and develop their own theory. One respondent captures this well: 'I am beginning to realise that I have my own theory, now ... my next stage is being able to express it without feeling inadequate or shy ... I need to very finely analyse ... what I do and how it fits with other models.'

REFERENCES

Angyal, A. (1941) *Foundations for a Science of Personality*. New York: Commonwealth Fund

Carroll, M. (1996) *Counselling Supervision: Theory, Skills and Practice*. London: Cassell

Embleton Tudor, L., Keemar, K., Tudor, K., Valentine, J. and Worrall, M. (2004) *The Person-Centred Approach: A Contemporary Introduction*. Basingstoke: Palgrave

Freeth, R. (2004) A psychiatrist's experience of person-centred supervision. In K. Tudor and M. Worrall (Eds.) *Freedom to Practise: Person-Centred Approaches to Supervision* (pp. 247–66). Ross-on-Wye: PCCS Books

Freire, P. (1972) *Pedagogy of the Oppressed*. Harmondsworth: Penguin

Freire, P. (1976) *Education: The Practice of Freedom*. London: Writers and Readers Publishing Cooperative. (Original work published 1967)

Gardner, H. (1993) *Frames of Mind: The Theory of Multiple Intelligences* (2nd edn.). London: Fontana Press. (Original work published 1983)

Hawkins, P. and Shohet, R. (1989) *Supervision in the Helping Professions*. Milton Keynes: Open University Press

Hawkins, P. and Shohet, R. (2000) *Supervision in the Helping Professions* (2nd edn.). Buckingham: Open University Press

Hawkins, P. and Shohet, R. (2006) *Supervision in the Helping Professions* (3rd edn.). Buckingham: Open University Press

Hitchings, P. (2004) On supervision across theoretical orientations. In K. Tudor and M. Worrall (Eds.) *Freedom to Practise: Person-Centred Approaches to Supervision* (pp. 203–24). Ross-on-Wye: PCCS Books

Kline, N. (1999) *Time to Think: Listening to Ignite the Human Mind*. London: Cassell

Lewin, K. (1964) *Field Theory in Social Science*. New York: Harper and Row. (Original work published 1951)

Rogers, C.R. (1951) *Client-Centered Therapy*. London: Constable

Rogers, C.R. (1969) *Freedom to Learn*. Columbus, OH: Charles E. Merrill

Rogers, C.R. (1990) A note on 'the nature of man'. In H. Kirschenbaum and V.L. Henderson (Eds.) *The Carl Rogers Reader* (pp. 401–8). London: Constable (Original work published 1957)

Townsend, I. (2004) Almost nothing to do: Supervision and the person-centred approach in homeopathy. In K. Tudor and M. Worrall (Eds.) *Freedom to Practise: Person-Centred Approaches to Supervision* (pp. 225–45). Ross-on-Wye: PCCS Books

Tudor, K. (1998) Value for money? Issues of fees in counselling and psychotherapy. *British Journal of Guidance and Counselling, 25*(4), 447–53

Tudor, K. (2007) *On Dogma*. Paper presented at the Institute of Transactional Analysis Annual Conference, York

Tudor, K. and Worrall, M. (Eds.) (2004a) *Freedom to Practise: Person-Centred Approaches to Supervision*. Ross-on-Wye: PCCS Books

Tudor, K. and Worrall, M. (2004b) Issues, questions, dilemmas and domains in supervision. In K. Tudor and M. Worrall (Eds.) *Freedom to Practise: Person-Centred Approaches to Supervision* (pp. 79–96). Ross-on-Wye: PCCS Books

Tudor, K. and Worrall, M. (2004c) Person-centred perspectives on supervision. In K. Tudor & M. Worrall (Eds.) *Freedom to Practise: Person-Centred Approaches to Supervision* (pp. 43–64). Ross-on-Wye: PCCS Books

Tudor, K. and Worrall, M. (2004d) Person-centred philosophy and theory in the practice of supervision. In K. Tudor and M. Worrall (Eds.) *Freedom to Practise: Person-Centred Approaches to Supervision* (pp. 11–30). Ross-on-Wye: PCCS Books

Tudor, K. and Worrall, M. (2004e) Process in supervision: A person-centred critique. In K. Tudor and M. Worrall (Eds.) *Freedom to Practise: Person-Centred Approaches to Supervision* (pp. 65–77). Ross-on-Wye: PCCS Books

Warner, M.S. (2000) Person-centered psychotherapy: One nation, many tribes. *The Person-Centered Journal, 7*(1), 28–39

Wood, J.K. (1995) *The Person-Centered Approach to Small Groups: More than psychotherapy*. Unpublished manuscript

ABOUT THE EDITORS AND CONTRIBUTORS

KEITH TUDOR and MIKE WORRALL have worked and written together for over thirteen years. They have designed and facilitated courses, including a person-centred supervision course which they have run for the past ten years (for current details of which see www.temenos.ac.uk). In that time they have co-written and co-edited a quartet of books on the person-centred approach, including this one, all of which emphasise the organismic and relational basis of person-centred psychology: (with others) *The Person-Centred Approach: A Contemporary Introduction* (Palgrave, 2004), *Freedom to Practice: Person-Centred Approaches to Supervision* (PCCS Books, 2004), and *Person-Centred Therapy: A Clinical Philosophy* (Routledge, 2006).

JULIE BARNES works independently as a counsellor, supervisor and organisational consultant, using person-centred principles and Appreciative Inquiry. Graduating in social sciences, she has worked in social care research, inspection and policy development for local and national government. She has been developing her private counselling and supervision practice since 1996 and working with Appreciative Inquiry since 2002. She loves working with individuals and groups in creative ways and would like more opportunities to apply this empowering approach in different settings. Julie lives in Nottingham and works across the UK. E-mail: julie.barnes@yahoo.co.uk.

JENNY BELL has been a person-centred therapist for over 30 years. She graduated in psychology from Manchester University and became Management Development Counsellor at Rolls Royce Aero-engines. She went on to establish the Counselling Services at the Universities of Sussex and Sheffield and is currently Head of Service at Loughborough University. She has a deep interest in creativity and therapy and is inspired by the work of Natalie Rogers. Other inspirational women include her brilliant expressive trainer Tess Sturrock, her friend Lucila Machado Assumpçao (Brazilian artist and philosopher), her supervisor Ivis Kennington and her colleague Fiona Strodder (expressive therapist).

LOUISE EMBLETON TUDOR is in independent practice offering psychotherapy, supervision and training in Sheffield where she is also a Director of Temenos and a facilitator on both its BSc and MSc courses in person-centred psychotherapy and counselling. She is the author of a number of publications in the field of mental health and psychotherapy. Her particular interest is in human development and, pertinent to her contribution to this book, she recently attended her niece at the birth of her great-nephew.

MARVIN FRANKEL, PhD (University of Chicago) had a clinical internship in client-centered therapy at the Counseling Center, University of Chicago. He is the author and co-author of chapters on Skinner's approach to personality, on morality and psychotherapy, on Socratic self-examination by means of empathy, and on the demise of empathic, non-directive counseling. Since 1972 he has been a member of the Sarah Lawrence College faculty, Westchester, New York where he teaches courses on 'The Final Solution', 'The Empathic Attitude', 'Deception', and 'Self-deception and the Place of Fact in a World of Propaganda.'

CAROLIN FRIEDERIKE HERWIG was born near Munich in Germany and has been living in the UK for over twenty years. She trained and worked as a car mechanic and lecturer in car mechanics before training as a person-centred therapist. Her experiences of working in a male-dominated trade, and living in the UK having come from Germany, have taught her about oppression based on gender as well as origin. This area is of particular interest to her in her work as a counsellor and lecturer in Further Education. She likes to mountain bike and hike when she is not working.

PETER JENKINS is Co-Director of Counselling and Psychotherapy at the University of Salford, a member of the UKCP Ethics Committee and a BACP Accredited Counsellor Trainer. In addition to his teaching and research work at Salford University, he works part-time as an honorary counsellor at Manchester University. He has published widely on legal and ethical aspects of counselling and psychotherapy, including (with Debbie Daniels) *Therapy With Children* (Sage, 2000), as editor of *Legal Issues in Counselling and Psychotherapy* (Sage, 2002), (with Vincent Keter and Julie Stone) *Psychotherapy and the Law* (Whurr, 2004), and *Counselling, Psychotherapy and the Law* (2nd edn) (Sage, 2007).

COLIN LAGO was Director of the Counselling Service at the University of Sheffield from 1987 to 2003. He now works as an independent counsellor, trainer, supervisor and consultant. Trained initially as an engineer, Colin went on to become a full-time youth worker in London and then a teacher in Jamaica. He is an accredited counsellor and trainer and Fellow of the British Association for Counselling and Psychotherapy. He is currently a visiting lecturer to the Universities of East Anglia and Strathclyde. Deeply committed to transcultural concerns, he has had articles, videos and books published on the subject, which include: (edited with Barbara Smith) *Anti-Discriminatory Counselling Practice* (Sage, 2003), (edited with Roy Moodley and Anissa Talahite) *Carl Rogers Counsels a Black Client* (PCCS Books, 2005), and *Race, Culture and Counselling* (2nd edn) (Sage, 2006).

DR. GARRY PROUTY was trained in person-centered/experiential psychotherapy by Eugene Gendlin at the University of Chicago. He developed his own therapeutic approach at clinics and hospitals dealing with psychotic and retarded clients. Dr. Prouty was a Fellow of the Chicago Counseling, Psychotherapy and Research Center, and is a member of the Chicago Psychological Association. He has served as an editorial consultant to *Psychotherapy: Theory, Research and Practice* as well as the *International Journal of Mental Imagery* and is currently a consultant to the American, English, Austrian and Italian client-centered journals. He is the author and co-author of a number of books, and of numerous professional papers. In 2004 he was awarded a Lifetime Achievement Award for Pre-Therapy by the Chicago Psychological Association and was elected President of the Chicago International Society for the Psychological Study of Schizophrenia. He is currently elected as a scientific associate for the American Academy of Psychoanalysis and Dynamic Psychiatry.

LISBETH SOMMERBECK, MSc (University of Copenhagen) is a clinical psychologist. She is certified as a psychotherapist and supervisor of psychotherapy by the Danish Psychological Association. Lisbeth has been a practising psychotherapist, teacher and supervisor of psychotherapy for thirty years at a psychiatric hospital. She is the author of several articles and book chapters on non-directivity and on client-centered therapy with people with psychosis as well as of a book *Client-Centred Therapy in Psychiatric Contexts* (PCCS Books, 2003). In 2002 she initiated the foundation of the Danish Carl Rogers Forum.

GERALDINE THOMSON works as a therapist and supervisor in Cornwall. She is a tutor and recognised supervisor at The Metanoia Institute in London and is interested in the challenges written work presents to trainees and the supports they need as they develop an authorial person-centred voice. In partnership with Mike Worrall she offers facilitation and consultancy in higher education, building more effective relationships between managers, tutors and students. She is also a trainer for The Child Bereavement Trust and has developed training for them and Cruse Bereavement Care, Scotland, for which she is a course consultant for its validated training 'Supporting Bereaved Children and Young People'.

WENDY TRAYNOR has worked in the field of mental health for eighteen years. She currently practises as a therapist and supervisor in the voluntary sector and in private practice. She is involved in a project offering groups for children and young people who self-injure. She is currently a doctoral research student at the University of Strathclyde studying the effectiveness of person-centred practice with clients who experience 'psychotic process'. She is interested in person-centred practice as a positive support option for clients who experience complex process.

DION VAN WERDE studied at the Catholic University of Leuven, and is a clinical psychologist and person-centered psychotherapist at Psychiatrisch Ziekenhuis Sint-Camillus, Sint-Denijs Westrem in Gent, Belgium. He is ward psychologist on a person-centered ward which treats people suffering psychotic functioning by means of a multidisciplinary contact milieu, and is run along the lines of Prouty's Pre-Therapy. With Garry Prouty and Marlis Pörtner, he is the co-author of *Pre-Therapie* which has been translated into four languages. Dion is the coordinator and trainer of the Pre-Therapy International Network, and serves on the editorial advisory board of the journal *Person-Centered and Experiential Psychotherapies*. E-mail: dion.vanwerde@sint-camillus.be.

JEANNIE WRIGHT is Associate Professor in Counselling at Massey University, New Zealand. She moved from the UK to Palmerston North in August 2006 and teaches undergraduate and postgraduate courses in counselling, and supervises postgraduate research. She is interested in innovative approaches, such as writing therapy and online/e-mail counselling. Her research and recent publications have tended to focus on the therapeutic potential of expressive and creative writing, and writing as a vehicle for reflective practice. Jeannie is also interested in diversity and especially gender, culture and class in counselling. She is the co-editor of *The Writing Cure: An Introductory Handbook of Writing in Counselling and Therapy* (Brunner-Routledge, 2004).

Author Index

American Counseling Association, 104
Amini, F., 35
Anderson, H., 45–6, 48
Annis Hammond, S., 44
Angyal, A., 24, 35, 86, 212
Anthony, K., 107
Atwood, G., 87

Bachelor, A., 123
Balint, M., 92
Barlow, D., 137
Barnes, J., 44
Barrett-Lennard, G., 88, 89, 198
Beazley Richards, J., 192
Bergin, A., 133, 134
Berne, E., 199
Bion, W., 89, 93
Blom-Cooper, L., 180
Bochner, A., 107
Bohart, A.C., 17
Bollas, C., 191
Bolton, G., 102, 105, 106, 107, 108
Bond, T., 159, 177
Boss, M., 73
Bozarth, J.D., 89, 126, 127, 155
Bramley, W., 93
Brent Council, 180
Brice, A., 105
British Association for Counselling, 27, 29, 33, 174, 179
British Association for Counselling and Psychotherapy, 27, 29, 30, 31, 32, 33, 34, 161, 170, 177, 178–9, 181

British Association of Psychoanalytic and Psychodynamic Supervision, 3, 28, 29, 30, 174, 207
Boy, A.V., 173
Brockleman, P. 74
Buber, M., 73, 88
Burton, A., 73

Carroll, M., 30, 32, 85, 95, 162, 163, 202, 216
Casement, P., 1, 95
Casemore, R., 154, 160, 163
Clarkson, P., 198
Coffeng, T., 163
Cooper, M., 162–3, 164
Cooperrider, D.L., 38, 39, 40, 41, 44, 46
Coghlan, D., 90
Copeland, S., 188
Cordess, C., 187
Cronwall, M., 72

Davies, P., 195
Department of Health, 31
Dick-Read, G., 18, 21
Dodds, P., 77
Douglas, M., 31
Dryden, W., 162, 163
Duncan, B.L., 198

Edwards, B., 60
Ellis, C., 107
Elton Wilson, J., 197
Embleton Tudor, L., 5, 89, 213

Falvey, J.E., 181, 182
Feltham, C., 12, 162, 198, 200–1, 202
Fenichel, M., 102
Fish, V., 164
Foulkes, S.H., 93
Francis, M.E., 104
Frankel, M., 121, 122, 123, 125
Freeth, R., 207, 217
Freire, P., 213
Fromm, E., 28

Gardner, H., 213
Gaskin, I.M., 20, 22, 23
Gazzola, N., 5
Gendlin, E.T., 76
Giesekus, U., 87
Gittings, R., 143
Goodyear, R., 12, 162
Goss, S., 107
Greenberg, L.S., 17
Griffin, G., 192
Griffiths, J., 195
Grohol, J., 107, 115

Hackney, H., 12, 162
Haigh, R., 83
Hawking, S., 195
Hawkins, P., 1, 61, 68, 69, 95, 97, 187, 218
Henderson, P., 173, 198–9, 202
Hitchings, P., 6, 205, 217
Horvath, A., 123
House, R., 27
Houston, G., 88, 97
Hubble, M.A., 198
Hurwitz, B.S., 164

International Society for Mental Health Online, 107

Jacobs, M., 157
Jenkins, P., 27, 183, 189, 190, 191
Joubert, N., 6, 86

Kellner-Rogers, M., 89
Kelm, J., 46
Keen, S., 17
Keyes, C.L.M., 87
Keys, S., 32

Kilborn, M., 158
King, D., 29
Kline, N., 213
Koenig, T.R., 73
Kreeger, L., 91
Krietemeyer, B., 72
Kubiak, M., 72, 73

Ladany, N., 2, 172
Lago, C., 103, 104, 107, 108, 111
Lambers, E., 95, 158, 162
Lambert, M.J., 133, 134, 198
Laming, H., 180
Lammers, W., 95
Langer, S.K., 16
Lannon, R., 35
Layard, R., 87
Leonard, G., 192
Lepore, S.J., 105, 107
Lewin, K., 216
Lewis, K., 103, 104
Lewis, T., 35
Lietaer, G., 3, 129–30
Lockett, M., 26, 30, 95

McGaw, W., 89
McIlduff, E., 90
McNeill, B.W., 157
McWilliams, K., 72
Mearns, D., 12, 30, 114, 124, 129, 154, 162– 3, 164, 166, 171
Mente, A., 87
Merry, T., 44–5, 171
Miller, C.J., 47
Miller, S.D., 198
Monte, C., 131
Morrison, T., 188
Morton, I., 72, 77
Mowbray, R., 27

Natiello, P., 31, 89
New, B., 38
Novey, T., 200

Odell, M., 40
Orton, J.W., 90

Palmer Barnes, F., 154, 155–6

Parker, I., 27
Patterson, C.H., 61, 112
Pennebaker, J.W., 104, 106, 107
Perls, F.S., 72
Peters, H., 72
Pietrzak, S., 72
Pine, G.J., 173
Pörtner, M., 72, 77
Potter, S., 189
Proctor, B., 32, 68, 73, 94, 95, 96, 97, 202
Proctor, G., 167
Proctor, K., 96
Prouty, G., 72, 73, 75, 77, 78
Pritchard, J., 188

Raeburn, J., 6, 86
Rapoport, A., 124
Raskin, N., 127–8
Richards, K., 2
Rich-New, K., 38
Roberts J.P., 92
Rogers, C.R., 4, 17, 26, 31, 47, 61, 72, 75, 76, 88, 89, 90, 122, 125, 126, 129, 131–2, 134, 135, 141, 142, 143, 144, 145, 146, 147, 148, 149, 150, 151, 152, 155, 156, 171, 173, 198, 211, 212
Rogers, N., 59
Rowan, J., 85
Roy, B., 73
Ryle, A., 105, 201

Sanders, P., 3, 18
Schmid, P., 88
Schore, A.N., 22
Seagal, J.D., 107
Shohet, R., 1, 61, 68, 69, 95, 97, 187, 218
Shostrom, E., 122
Smyth, J.M., 105, 107
Sommerbeck, E., 73, 121, 122, 123, 125, 134
Speedy, J., 105
Spence, S., 28, 29, 174
Stark, M., 87
Stolorow, R., 87
Sturdevant, K., 90
Summers, G., 198

Taft, J., 17, 196
Theriault, A., 5
Thorne, B., 12, 114, 124, 154, 163, 164, 166, 174, 195, 198
Torres, C.B., 37
Totton, N., 27
Townsend, I., 217
Trosten-Bloom, A., 40
Tudor, K., 1, 5, 31, 33, 34, 61–2, 68, 88, 94, 95, 140–1, 152, 163, 169, 171, 195, 197, 198, 211, 213, 215, 217, 218

United Kingdom Council for Psychotherapy, 169
United Nations, 32

Van Werde, D., 72, 77
Villas-Boas Bowen, M., 21, 112, 202, 205, 206

Wakefield, M., 199
Warner, M.S., 3, 218
Weaks, D., 156
Webb, A., 29, 31, 157, 158
Wheatley, M.J., 89
Wheeler, S., 2, 26, 29, 30
Whitney, D., 33, 39, 40, 41, 44, 46, 54
Wibberley, M., 89
Wilkins, P., 97, 154, 163, 170
Wood, J.K., 89, 214
Worrall, M., 1, 11, 34, 61–2, 68, 88, 94, 140–1, 152, 158, 162, 163, 171, 197, 211, 215, 217, 218
Worthen, V., 157
Wright, J.K., 104, 107, 108, 110

Yalom, I.D., 86, 87

Zinschitz, E., 72

SUBJECT INDEX

acceptance, 14, 34, 53, 67, 87, 123, 146, 149, 151, 152, 158, 198, 207
access to records, 180, 188–92
accountability, 26, 34–5, 155, 156, 180–2, 183, 189
and liability, 180–2
actualising tendency (*see* organism's tendency to actualise)
American Counseling Association, 104
analogy, 17, 18, 19–23
appreciative inquiry (AI), 37–56
applications of, 40
assumptions of, 39
definitions of, 38
model, 41–3
and the person-centred approach, 46–7
principles of, 39, 40
questions, 47–8
stages of, 41–3
and supervision, 37–56
assessment, 30, 135, 137, 141, 172, 197, 198, 212, 216
risk, 31, 187
self-, 30, 173
Association for University and College Counselling, 104
authenticity, 131, 137, 155, 157–8, 198
autonomy, 27, 86, 114, 179, 187, 188, 191, 192, 212

being received, 34
birth, 17–24, 65
stages of, 19–23
birthing, 16–24
brain, 20, 60, 98
British Association for Counselling, 104
British Association for Counselling and Psychotherapy, 5, 68
British Association of Psychoanalytic and Psychodynamic Supervision, 3
British Association for Supervision Practice and Research, 6

case examples, 49–52, 62–4, 64–5, 65–6, 67, 73, 113–4, 122–5, 126–9
case law, 181, 182, 184
challenge, 11, 14, 22, 31, 42, 45, 51, 86, 88, 98, 105, 111, 123, 132, 135, 137, 155, 162, 177, 192, 196, 197–8, 200, 213, 214, 215
legal, 180–1
change, 38, 39, 40, 41, 43, 44, 53, 76, 88, 89, 105, 143, 152, 160, 173, 196, 197, 198, 199, 200 (*see also* conditions)
facilitation of, 142–4
and learning, 142, 143, 161
personality, 134
therapeutic, 122, 156 (*see also* conditions)
childbirth, 18
natural, 18
client, rights of, 26, 30, 32
clinical responsibility 29–30, 178, 216
code of ethics, 27, 28, 29, 33, 96, 179

Subject Index

communication, 33, 73, 79, 89, 92, 103, 111, 112, 116, 122, 125, 161, 200
  electronic, 103, 106, 115
  e-mail, 103, 110, 113, 115
  and meaning, 115
  and technology, 108–9
  text-based, 105
complaint/s, 154–68, 180
  and person-centred therapists, 154–66
  and power, 164–5
  procedures, 154, 159–60
conditions, 13, 14, 44, 45, 47, 53, 105, 122, 127, 155, 156, 157, 165, 200, 212, 214
  necessary and sufficient, 16, 134, 154, 217
  of worth, 123, 124, 125, 125, 131, 142
confidentiality, 13, 34, 180, 190, 192
  and risk, 185–8
congruence, 53, 55, 89, 111, 125, 158, 160, 202, 214
contact, 13, 14, 34, 72, 77, 78, 79, 198
  behaviours, 72
  functions, 72, 79
  reflections, 72, 73, 74–5
  and relationship, 197–8
creative connection, 60
creativity, 85, 95, 97, 139, 141, 142, 146–51
  conditions of, 148, 150, 152
  Rogers on, 146–51
curiosity, 113, 143, 145, 146, 214

data protection, 32, 288–9, 191
development
  personal, 32, 39, 89, 156, 169–75
  professional, 30, 49, 89, 91, 106, 154, 169, 170–1
  in supervision, 171–5
disclosure, 185, 186, 187, 191
  contested, 192
  mandatory, 186
  of records, 191
diversity, 26, 27, 33, 88, 113, 135, 213
domains of influence, 4, 171
duty of care, 26, 29, 95, 179, 181, 182–5, 192 (*see also* liability)
  forms of, 182–5

education, 27, 60, 61, 130, 135, 189, 216, 217
  person-centred, 142–6, 211, 212–4
e-mail supervision, 102–18
empathic
  following, 73, 115
  reflections, 122, 123, 137
  resonance, 73
  understanding, 14, 17, 55, 87, 114, 135, 146, 150, 151, 162, 207
empathy, 17, 19, 53, 62, 65, 97, 111, 122, 123, 124, 128, 133, 134, 135, 137, 149, 158, 198
  existential, 79
encounter, 20, 76, 87, 130, 131, 132, 144, 155
  brief, 197–8
  existential, 174
  groups, 88, 89
ethical
  duty, 179, 181, 183, 184, 185
  framework, 11, 27, 28, 152–3, 160, 162, 165, 170, 172, 177, 178
  guidelines, 104
  issues, 187–8
  practice, 13, 43, 102, 158, 161, 166, 176
  principles, 30–3, 161, 170, 178, 179, 188, 191
  responsibilities, 26–36, 162, 170, 178
ethics
  code/s of, 27, 28, 29, 33, 96, 179
  and the law, 176, 177, 178–9
evaluation, locus of, 12, 113–5, 148, 151, 152, 206
experience, hierarchy of, 23
expressive therapy supervision, 59–71

facilitation, 85, 88–90, 92, 96, 114, 142, 143, 213
frame of reference, 73, 78, 122, 123, 124, 125, 127, 129, 130, 131, 133, 134, 135, 137

group
  facilitator, 91, 92, 93
  as organism, 88, 90
  supervision (*see* supervision, group)

229

heteronomy, 212
homonomy, 86, 212
humility, 18, 24, 133, 136

Independent Complaints Organisation, 5
insight, 16–25
integrity, 12, 13, 14, 21, 49, 155, 157, 161, 172, 200, 201, 202–3, 216
intelligence, multiple, 213
interdependence, 86, 88
Declaration of, 86
International Society for Mental Health Online (ISMHO), 102, 104, 107
intersubjectivity, 87, 88

justice, 33, 159, 179

law, 12, 13, 27, 28
    supervision and the, 176–94
    and therapeutic practice, 177–8
learning, 33, 40, 42, 44, 46, 48, 54, 85, 87, 116, 139, 140, 141, 142, 147, 148, 149, 150, 151, 153, 157, 158, 160, 161, 165, 173, 212, 213, 214
    environment, 212, 214
    experiential, 146, 212
    integrated, 142, 145, 151
    practice of, 214–6
    Rogers on, 142–6
legal
    context, 32
    liability, 26, 164, 178, 183
    references, 193
liability, 33, 161, 182, 183, 184, 185
    and accountability, 180–2
    legal, 26, 164, 178, 183
    vicarious, 182, 183, 184, 185
love, 22, 28, 66, 122, 174

maieusis, 17, 18–19
metaphor, 16, 17, 60, 89, 197
midwife/ves, 17, 18, 19, 20, 21, 23
midwifery, 17, 18
mutuality, 70, 140, 144

narrative, 105, 106, 122, 123, 124, 127, 132, 136, 190
non-maleficence, 30, 31, 179

organism, 20, 26, 73, 88, 89, 90, 124, 126, 127, 128, 140, 141, 142, 145, 147, 173, 174, 197, 200, 202, 212, 213
    and its tendency to actualise, 140–1, 172
    trust in the, 212

personal
    development, 32, 39, 89, 156, 169–75
    power, 31, 34
    therapy, 156, 157, 169–70, 171
person-centred approach/es
    to expressive therapy, 59–60
    values of, 16, 21, 160, 207, 214
pre-expressive functioning, 77, 78
Pre-Therapy, 72–9, 134
    historical introduction to, 75–6
    method and supervision, 76–9
    principles of, 73–4
    supervision, 76–9
professional development, 30, 49, 89, 91, 106, 154, 169, 170–1
psychological contact, 72, 73 (*see also* contact)

reflective practice, 106–7, 115, 170
regulation, 22, 27, 169, 189
research, 1, 2, 5, 22, 34, 38, 40, 87, 102, 104, 105, 106, 107, 108, 125, 126, 133, 134, 135, 136, 158, 172, 190, 191–2, 198, 200
responsibility/ies, 26–36 (*see also* supervision, responsibilities in, and supervisor/s responsibility/ies)
    clinical, 29–30, 178, 216
    ethical, 28, 29, 30–1, 32, 35, 162, 170, 178
    of group supervisor, 95, 96
    legal, 28, 35, 178, 179
    professional, 32, 162, 181, 183

safety, 31, 150, 151, 156, 173, 179, 187, 216
self-respect, 170, 179
Socrates, 17
supervisee/s, 16, 17, 19, 20, 21, 22, 23, 24, 28, 29, 30, 34, 35, 42–3, 45, 46, 47, 48, 54, 55, 59, 61, 62, 64, 70, 92, 93, 94, 97, 98, 105, 106, 108,

Subject Index

109, 110, 111, 112, 113 115, 125,
126–30, 139–53, 157, 158, 159,
161, 162, 163, 166, 170 172, 173,
174, 179, 181, 182, 183 185, 186,
192, 201, 203, 206, 214
-centred, 1, 12, 21, 45, 92, 203, 206,
207
responsibilities of, 28, 30, 34, 206
supervision
client-centred, 1, 92, 93
as collaborative inquiry, 44–6
as continuing personal development,
169–75
e-mail, 102–18
advantages of, 115–16
and ethical responsibilities, 26–36,
162, 170, 178
experience of, 12, 13–14, 22, 28
expressive, 59–71
form-oriented, 21, 202, 205 206
frequency of, 94, 109–10, 201–2
functional model of, 32, 68, 202
group, 85–101
approaches to, 92–3
creative possibilities of, 97–8
types of, 91–2
and the law, 176–94
and love, 22, 28, 66, 122, 174
as maieutic process, 16–25
as meta-activity, 207, 216
and personal development, 169–75
and personal therapy, 32, 155, 215
philosophy(-of-life)-oriented, 21, 202,
206
and power, 164–5
and Pre-Therapy, 72–81
and reflective practice, 106–7 115, 170
research in, 1–2, 5, 102, 107 158, 172
responsibilities in, 26–36
of short-term therapy, 195–204
student-centred, 72–81
of students/trainees, 139–53
and teaching, 32, 162, 216
of therapists through a complaint,
154–68
and training, 23, 26, 32, 93, 106, 133–
7, 139–53, 165, 182, 186, 201,
207, 211–18

supervisor/s
acceptance of, 14, 152, 158
authenticity of, 13, 155, 157–8
choosing a, 11–15
empathy of, 55, 97, 111, 135, 137,
158
experience of, 200–1
as midwife, 17
qualities of, 24
requirements of, 28–34
responsibility/ies of, 21, 26, 27, 28–34,
94, 95, 96, 155, 161–3, 170, 176,
178, 179, 181, 183–5, 201, 215,
216 (*see also* supervision, responsibilities in and supervisory
responsibilities)
self-employed 177, 182
tasks of, 30, 32
training of, 211–19
supervisory
relationship, 26, 27, 61, 69, 102, 139,
142, 150, 153, 156, 157,
162, 174, 182, 183
elements of, 183
as existential encounter, 174
responsibilities, types of 183–5
supportive environment, 6, 43, 50, 51, 54,
86
symbol, 16, 17, 41, 43, 111

Temenos, 6
theoretical
models, 68–70, 202
orientation, 6, 30, 94, 96, 205–8
therapist/s
as midwife, 17
'Rogers-1', 121–38
'Rogers-2', 121–38
time, 53, 77, 91, 92, 93, 94, 98, 105, 109–
10, 116, 117, 191, 195–200, 201–2,
214
limits, 191, 195–200, 201, 202
training, 76, 90 97, 98, 106, 133–7, 139–
53 (*see also* supervision and training)
of supervisors, 211–19
trust/ing, 13, 14, 18, 19, 20, 21, 23, 31,
34, 42, 48, 50, 51, 65, 89, 112,
140, 141, 143, 144, 145, 147, 148,

231

150, 151, 152, 153, 156, 157, 163, 172, 179, 187, 206, 212, 214

unconditional positive regard, 53, 55, 111, 114, 122, 124, 125, 131, 133, 135, 137, 158
United Kingdom Council for Psychotherapy, 5, 28
University of Chicago's Counseling Center, 75, 132

values, 16, 21, 160, 207, 214

Women's Empowerment Project, 40
writing, 102, 103, 104, 105, 106, 107, 108, 109, 115, 116, 170
   electronic, values of, 107–8
   paradigm, 104, 105, 108